NEW CATHOLIC WOMEN

A Contemporary Challenge to Traditional Religious Authority

Mary Jo Weaver

1817

Harper & Row, Publishers, San Francisco

Cambridge, Hagerstown, New York, Philadelphia
London, Mexico City, São Paulo, Singapore, Sydney

FIRST EDITION

Library of Congress Cataloging-in-Publication Data

Weaver, Mary Jo.
    New Catholic women.

    Bibliography: p.
    1. Women in the Catholic Church — History — 20th century.   2. Feminism — Religious aspects — Catholic Church.   3. Catholic Church — Doctrines.   I. Title.
BX2347.8.W6W42   1985   282'.088042   85-45371
ISBN 0-06-069287-1

85 86 87 88 89 RRD 10 9 8 7 6 5 4 3 2 1

Contents

This book is dedicated to my friend and Jewish muse,
    Susan David Gubar
and to the three women who gave me body, mind, and spirit:
    Gertrude Divan McDowell, my grandmother,
    Ann McDowell Weaver, my mother,
    Joan Huber, my first mentor.

Introduction

This book has taken shape over the last few years and so might begin with its own story were there not more pressing items in the news. I have in mind the shocking murder of Father Daniel Rossiter (age 64) in Onalaska, Wisconsin, in February 1985. According to stories in the *New York Times* and the *National Catholic Reporter,* "A man upset because girls were reading from the Bible at a special children's mass . . . opened fire with a shotgun . . . and killed a praying priest, a janitor and a parishioner."[1] The school principal, Sister Rose Frances Phalin, later told police that "a man entered the sacristy and was upset because Rossiter was allowing two sixth-grade girls to give scripture readings. The man questioned the pastor's authority to allow girl readers, . . . apparently returned to the church after mass and shot the three men."[2] The man in question was twenty-nine years old, which is disturbing in that it indicates that he was reared in a church supposedly open to change and new direction.

The killing of Father Rossiter has a terrifying insistence about it, and shows the possibilities for violence in the hostility against women in the church. At a less dramatic, but no less costly, level, the continual repetition of the church's ban against artificial birth control can also be assessed in terms of its life-threatening consequences for women and its attempt to keep women "in their place," confined to nurturing roles and secondary status. The investigative committees set up by the Vatican to review and "offer pastoral help" to congregations of American sisters pose significant threats to their religious lives. Finally, the abrogation of due process by the Vatican in cases of individuals and of religious orders also brings with it the fear of death. This book is about women's attempts to create life for themselves in an environment that is often harmful to them.

Although this book focuses on some women in the American Catholic church and sets the issues within the context of the women's movement, I recognize that repressive moves against women are part of a wider spectrum of official reactions within the last few years: the campaign against nuns and priests in political office who hold left-wing views; the attempted discrediting of Leonardo Boff and others who espouse liberation theology; repressive moves against *Concilium* theologians, especially those who have articulated alternatives to papalism, for instance, against Hans Küng, who questions infallibility, or Edward Schillebeeckx, who offers daring new concepts of ministry within the Catholic church; threatening moves against various congregations of American sisters, active and contemplative, usually accompanied by directives that tell them to conform or resign; the attempted suppression of gay ministry, with decided strategies against New Ways Ministry in general and its founders in particular; directives to remove women from seminaries as teachers, students, or spiritual directors; and patriarchal directives to congregations of American sisters that require a return to wearing the religious habit, to a preconciliar concept of authority, and to an antiquated model of Christian life. All these actions and words are meant to support papalism and are usually held together by an appeal to "the church's teaching" or to "the official position of the church," when that position is no more than papal opinion as supported by reactionary political and social groups.

The issues raised by feminists in the church—new ecclesiological models, questions of authority, nontraditional understandings of "women's place"—come at a time of peril in the life of American Catholicism.[3] Women's concerns, whether they are large, general questions of "rights" or specific-issue controversies like the "pluralism in abortion" statement in the *New York Times*,[4] occur within the context of a battle over authority. At the present time there is a concerted effort on the part of the pope and the Curia to halt the progress of the Second Vatican Council. Historical precedent exists for this action, full of telling symbols carefully chosen by past pontiffs to reclaim their absolute power.

Perhaps an earlier historical conflict can help to illuminate our own. Conciliarism, a fifteenth-century reformist movement that claimed that councils are superior to popes in matters of ecclesiastical authority, provides an illustrative footnote. In 1516, the pope issued a decree which condemned conciliarism. The first words of that decree—words that should have set it apart from all other documents past and future, since no two decrees ever begin with the same words—were *Pastor aeternus.* Yet in 1871, when papal infallibility was declared by the First Vatican Council, the opening words of that decree were *Pastor aeternus.* Was this a coincidence, or a symbol of a return to papal absolutism? Further, the Council of Constance, which met in 1415 to mandate frequent conciliar meetings and assert the superiority of councils over popes, was called by Pope John XXIII. Since he was later deposed, his name and number were forgotten until 1958 when Angelo Roncalli chose to call himself Pope John XXIII. Coincidence, or symbol of a return to conciliarism?

It may be impossible to raise issues within the institutional church without seeing them collapse into questions of authority and infallibility. If that is the case, then we might expect to see more repressive moves enacted all over the world, especially in the institutions of the Roman Catholic Church. We can also expect those out of sympathy with both women and postconciliar Roman Catholics to exacerbate divisions and to fuel horizontal confrontations. If forewarned is forearmed, then we need to think of solidarity as the strategy for survival, not simply as an emotional bond holding women together.

The present confrontation between the pope and confirmed postconciliar Catholics is part of an old battle within the church. Women are now caught up in that battle, but not necessarily as victims: at this point they present a contemporary challenge to traditional religious authority and so have become targets in a more generalized struggle for control within the church.

This book has been organized around the need to change structures and to reconceptualize old patterns of authority within the Catholic church. In some ways it is about women's work, reflecting some of the things American Catholic women are doing with their lives; but it is more properly concerned with the kinds of questions raised by women's frustration as they attempt to attain full status in an institution dedicated to thwarting that attempt.

I have taken some of the major theoretical issues and tenets of the women's movement and shown how they intersect with some tortured questions within the contemporary American Catholic church. Though the book reflects my own background—Catholic, Irish, middle-aged, and midwestern—its examples are, I hope, generalizable and useful in interpreting conflicts within other religious traditions. My intended audience includes three disparate groups: religious studies professionals who may have little understanding of the women's movement; feminist scholars who may have little sympathy for religion; and women in the Christian tradition whose rooted religious convictions and budding feminist concerns urge them to attempt some sort of reconciliation.

This book explores fundamental changes in the lives and influence of women in the American Catholic church. On almost all levels—parish, ritual, and vowed "religious life," as well as that of theological reflection and protest, and social and political activism—Roman Catholic women are redefining themselves and their roles and are challenging the American Catholic church to move in radically different directions. Since their challenge to the church is extensive and reflects a conflict of attitudes within the church, it is currently part of a deep and widening division among Catholics. Roman Catholic women are questioning basic notions about religious authority, divinity, and liturgy. Their questions, impinging as they do on the social, psychological, and political nature of spirituality, elicit revisionist, revolutionary, or reactionary responses from all concerned.

In the last one hundred years there have been three major attempts to open the Roman Catholic church to its critical responsibilities in the modern world: the "liberal Catholicism" of the 1840s, associated with Lord Acton, among others; the "modernist controversy" at the turn of the century, centering on questions of biblical criticism; and the new wave Catholicism in France in the 1930s associated with Pierre Teilhard de Chardin, among others. All these movements—small, European, and intellectual—were either crushed by clear inquisitorial strategies from church authorities or defeated by retreats into prudential silence on the part of those who worked for change. The women's movement is yet another challenge to the Catholic church, one made particularly serious by virtue of its international character, its ubiquitous activism, and its numerical strength. Although this book is confined to the American Catholic sector of the women's movement, the movement's implications may go beyond its geographical boundaries. The women's movement, as it is reverberating throughout the Catholic church, is speaking its mind honestly and, so far at least, has resisted the appeals to silence suggested by those who misconceive loyalty as docility.

The first three chapters set the Catholic feminist movement within the larger context of feminist questions: women's invisibility in history, their frustration in traditional roles, and their essentially powerless position within the institution show us where women have been and might still be stuck. The last three chapters attempt to show what is possible when we reimagine the world in our own terms: the collective energy of the Womanchurch movement, the revisionary work of Catholic feminist theologians, and new, though tradition-based, currents in feminist spirituality open the questions up to the future. Though many see feminist challenges to traditional Catholicism in terms of a "fall" (as in the "fall of Rome"), I think we could just as well perceive them as legitimate calls to new life. In assessing the changes in Roman Catholicism in the postconciliar church, Langdon Gilkey suggested that Catholics might justifiably see themselves as a covenant people forced by the prophets and by the changes of their history to look for and acknowledge a *new* form of the covenant because the old one has been destroyed and made useless.[5] If this book is predicated on the demise of old Catholicism, it also sees in that death the seeds of new life and takes joy in the prophetic role women play as we search for a new form of covenant.

EXPLANATORY NOTES

I have written this book from a clearly interested perspective. It will be evident to readers that I am a convinced feminist who is decidedly Catholic. Though I could make the argument that Irish Catholicism is an ethnic identification from which one cannot escape, I claim my Roman Catholicism as more than an interesting default and am not chagrined to find a strong passion for the tradition deep within myself and occasionally present in this book. At the same time, I am a feminist and find that I am diametrically opposed to Roman patriarchal structures and methodologies: my critique of

Catholicism as a "land of the fathers" is also a clear part of this work.

I have tried to make a case for the Catholic context as a legitimate one for realistic feminist concern and, at the same time, have argued that women's needs and frustrations constitute an important dimension in the continuing life of the Roman Catholic church. In moving around in each of these arenas, I switch between "we" and "they" language. Where I can identify wholeheartedly with a position, or where I feel that the conflict I am describing is also my own, I use we-language. In defining an alien ideology or writing in a historical mode, I tend to use they-language. I hope that these switches are illuminative rather than confusing and that they make my own ideas clear.

I have dared to call this book *New Catholic Women* and thus to give rhetorical suggestion to the idea that I have been all-inclusive. Sad to say, that is not the case. In confining myself to Roman Catholicism I have omitted any consideration of Greek Orthodox women and must content myself to salute the ground-breaking work of Eva Catafygiotou-Topping.[6] Although my debts to Protestant feminism will be clear, and although I discuss some of the important work of Goddess feminists, I make no extended forays into this territory. Roman Catholicism offered me more than enough problems for one book. I have recorded the experience of mostly white, middle-class, American Catholic women who are unhappy in a patriarchal church but unwilling to leave it. In this respect, I suppose, it could be argued that I have written about a slim minority. Black and Hispanic feminists can legitimately criticize me for not including their experiences, and I can only agree and apologize; I was continually aware of my present inability to include some of these rich veins of women's experience in the present volume. Also I am using the term *American* to refer to the experiences of women in the United States: Canadians and Latin American women who feel that I have betrayed the extensiveness of the adjective are right: I hope to evidence broader knowledge in the future. My limitations as an author have accompanied me throughout the writing process as both friends and enemies: they have kept me within the boundaries of my present abilities as they nagged me to learn more. Lastly, I have written this book for women and realize that male readers may take me to task for that choice. I hope that those men who share my ecclesiological concerns and feminist ideas will like the book—I have not necessarily tried to exclude them—but I recall Teresa of Avila's disclaimer in the introduction to the *Interior Castle*: women, she said, will "better understand the language used between women . . . so, I shall be speaking to them while I write; it's nonsense to think that what I say could matter to other persons."[7] Whether it matters to others or not, I speak mostly to women here.

The plural noun is an important part of my title. Over these past few years of writing, some of my colleagues referred to the book as *The New Catholic Woman,* casting it in the masculinist ideal of individuality. It is important to me that this book is about *women*, even though I cannot and do not include all the women who ought to be here. Even though women constitute a majority of the world's population and a majority of Catholics, their "movement" points to the sad reality that they experience much of their life within the church from the perspective of a tolerated, sometimes despised, minority. In that regard Catholic feminists have real links to any liberation movement in a struggle for existence: oppressed groups have a sense of themselves as a *people* (rather than a collection of individuals) in the process of liberation. The Hispanic church in the United States, for example, contains in its history many of the experiences now shared by Catholic feminists trying to develop their own style of Catholicism: both groups begin with consciousness raising, flow into liturgical expressions of their beliefs, extend themselves to other forms of oppression by way of social justice ministries, and insist on redefining the "problem" in their own terms.[8]

Let me explain the underlying presuppositions and limitations of my research. Because this book has been written in the 1980s, when so many things are happening, it has been difficult to end my research. For the most part, I have not included events occurring after January 1985 even though some of them might give me more material. The Vatican action against the twenty-four sisters who signed the *New York Times* statement, for example, has been omitted from the book because it is an ongoing conflict not resolved by the time this book went into production.

It is virtually impossible to describe the collective rage of women who feel themselves excluded from the Catholic church: their pain has sustained much of my work, but has not emerged as forcefully as I have found it articulated in conversations with these women. This book is not based on sociological data, but is a synthesis of interpretations and opinions on the lives and work of women. Where data has been available, I have used it—especially in chapter two—but my purpose has not been to offer a statistical analysis. I have tried to be faithful to the hopes and dreams of American Catholic women as I found them articulated in conferences, movements, and feminist celebrations.

Underlying my interpretation is a reaction against complementarity. I interpret "complementary" as "completing" or "mirroring," which suggests a nature not complete in its own right. It would follow, therefore, that complementarity and inferiority are at least subliminally linked. If women are not inferior to men, then why does complementarity function to treat them as if they are? Official Catholic teaching about women is a religious form of sex-role stereotyping which Catholic feminists oppose.

Complementarity has affected clerical perceptions about women, and explains why women have been invisible in American Catholic history. It also explains why their present struggles are often resisted by way of trivialization. Complementarity also involves the institutional church in a form of hypocrisy: women's roles are defined as complementary, but assigned as if they were inferior. Women are seldom called upon to initiate, create, or give dynamism to projects within the institutional church.

This book describes the anguish of women who feel rejected by the institutional church. At the same time, it celebrates the seeds of new life that are present in the women's movement within the American Catholic church.

Two last notes are needed, one about style and the other explaining an important omission in my dedication. I have, throughout this book, used the words *nun* and *sister* interchangeably. I know the difference between them: those in active orders are, technically speaking, sisters, whereas those in contemplative communities, perpetually enclosed, are nuns. For stylistic reasons I have used the terms as if they were equivalent and hope that I have offended neither sisters nor nuns by doing so. In my dedication I have omitted my father, not because he is not also responsible for my body, mind, and spirit, but because I wanted to draw exclusive attention to the women in my formative life. My father's blend of support and neglect, permissiveness and rigidity, sent me out into the world with a determined independence and also served to immunize me from some forms of patriarchy. For these things and more, and despite his absence from the dedication page, I thank my father.

ACKNOWLEDGMENTS

The debts of gratitude I have accumulated throughout the writing of this book are enormous, and I can only begin to discharge them here. My colleagues in the Department of Religious Studies at Indiana University have read parts of the book and been both generous with their comments and patient with my occasional distractions from the "real life" of the department. I am particularly indebted to Patrick Olivelle for providing departmental support, to James G. Hart for his encouragement and his careful reading of chapter five, and to my friend Judith Berling for her moral and intellectual support. Tim Mitchell and Lauren Bryant worked as graduate assistants and editors for me with great energy and accuracy. Erin Cornish was a thorough and accurate proofreader. Finally, I'd like to thank John Loudon, Dorian Gossy, and Virginia Rich of Harper & Row for their clear direction and encouragement.

Colleagues from other places read parts of the manuscript and made suggestions for its improvement: David O'Brien, Philip Gleason, Patricia McNeill Dolan, Mary Cove, James Kenneally, Barbara Misner, Donna Quinn, and Joann Wolski Conn all read chapters and returned them with constructive criticism and dispatch. I thank them all for their time and energy in my behalf. Grant support from the National Endowment for the Humanities (1982–1983) gave me a full year to work, travel, and think in relative peace and quiet, and it is fair to say that I would not have been able to finish this book without their help.

I have also received generous support from the Lilly Endowment, and with it an opportunity to experience the joys of collective process. Because of a grant from the Lilly Endowment to the Department of Religious Studies, I was able to design and participate in more than half a dozen seminars with religious leaders in the state of Indiana. All of the seminars were geared toward writing this book. The grant allowed me to gather twenty (mostly Catholic) women from Indiana, Kentucky, and Ohio in order to spend time together thinking about the many dimensions of the women's movement and the Roman Catholic church. We were able to bring in a variety of resource people, all of whom spent two or three days with us and so insured that the process was more of an ongoing conversation than the simple delivery of a paper. We met at retreat centers around the state, usually at the Beech Grove Benedictine Center in Indianapolis. In the course of three years I got to know some exceptional women: we read, fought, played, compiled bibliographies, and in many ways learned more than we ever would have in a traditional setting. Most of all, we came to understand ourselves as "new Catholic women." When the book was finally finished, many of the seminar members returned for a "group reading." In a marathon weekend we went over the ideas, argued over the phrasing, and celebrated the conclusions. I have, therefore, received enormous amounts of help with this book and have profited from the creativity and dedication of these women. I am pleased to express my deep appreciation to: Mary Bohlen, Terese Boersig, Katherine Dilcher, Valerie Dillon, Cathy Doherty, Pat McNeill Dolan, Marianne Doran, Mary Margaret Funk, Janet Gottshalk, Chris Gudorf, Helen John, Jeanne Knoerle, Bernice Kuper, Jean Alice McGoff, Mary Mahowald, Elizabeth McGee, Pamela Montagno, Teresa Mount, Pat O'Connell, Madeline Reno, Gerianne Savage, Judith Shannahan, Nancy Tarbox, and Kathy Tillman. In the setting of the seminars I would also like to thank Mary Burke, Mechthild Hart, Dianna Trebbi, and Joan Williams. A special debt of gratitude goes to Judith Davis who not only brought a special kind of grace to every seminar but who read through the entire manuscript with a creative editorial flair.

I am grateful to Indiana University: its support systems, libraries, and means of encouragement are wonderful, and a grant-in-aid-of-research from the university helped me to complete the book.

In the course of my research I have worked in many places, imposed on the goodwill of many people, and found myself overwhelmed with kindness. I thank Annette Kane at the National Council of Catholic Women and Delores Lecky, Executive Director of the Bishops' Committee on the Laity, both of whom were generous with time and materials, patient with my questions, and gracious in helping me track down important documents.

The Sisters of Charity of the Blessed Virgin Mary (Chicago Region), the Maryknoll Sisters in New York, and Carmelite nuns in Vermont, Maryland, and Indiana were all generous with their constitutions, conversations, and support: I am grateful to them for their hospitality and indebted to them for new insights and refinements in my thinking. Lora Ann Quiñonez and Rita Hofbauer at the Leadership Council for Women Religious were helpful as I tried to sort out the story of American sisters; Lora Ann read my chapter on sisters and saved me from more than one mistake. Margaret Ellen Traxler, Donna Quinn, Marjorie Tuite, and Maureen Reiff, who bring much energy and dedication to problems confronting women in the church, shared their expertise with me and made my life a good deal more complicated: their passionate involvement and activism made it impossible for me to tie everything up in neat ribbons.

We all know that the world runs on the collective skill and goodwill of secretaries. Our department secretary, Elizabeth Mitchell, has been a marvelous help on this project. I am indebted to our new secretary, Jill Webb: she has learned the technicalities of computer transcription, suffered through what must have seemed endless revisions, and done a superb job while keeping both of us cheerful. I would have gone under without her.

This project has taken longer than anticipated, and I have counted on the indulgence of my friends more heavily than I ever imagined I would. Jean Alice McGoff, the most genuinely optimistic person I know, has always been there to absorb my frustrations and recommend that I "do something nice" for myself. Gena DiLabio, whose friendship has sustained me for more than twenty years, has been especially supportive over these last few years as I wrote and suffered through the vicissitudes of my own personal life. Sarah Marks, my oldest friend, continues to say exactly the right thing at the right time. Anne Carr has been a great help as a friend and colleague. Edward, Molly, and Simone Gubar have become a surrogate family: I have learned to count on them for affection and support over the years. Some friends in the university have been steady companions as well. Finally, Marianna Bridge, though a new friend, is perhaps my most important reader.

I have dedicated this book at one level to three women who shaped me: my feisty grandmother, Gertie McDowell, gave me a strong sense of independence and determination; Ann McDowell Weaver, my mother, gave me a love for Catholicism and a blend of Irish wit and melancholy; and Joan Huber, now the Dean of Social and Behavioral Sciences at Ohio State University, but in my youth the marvelous woman next door, gave me a hunger for the academic life and an early introduction to feminism. I am what I am because of these women and because of what I have done or not done with what they have so generously given me.

Most of all, however, I present this book to my friend and muse, Susan Gubar, neither new nor Catholic. We thought of this book one day in the Indiana University cafeteria and have very much suffered through its birth together. Limitations aside, I hope this book pleases her enough to be some small measure of my gratitude for her friendship and nurturance over the last several years.

Mary Jo Weaver
St. Patrick's Day, 1985

1. Who *Can* Find A Valiant Woman? American Catholic Women in Historical Perspective

My heart is moved by all I cannot save:
So much has been destroyed.

ADRIENNE RICH

Woman suffrage is an unjust, unreasonable, unspiritual abnormality. It is a hard, undigested, tasteless, devitalized proposition. It is a half-fledged, unmusical, Promethian abomination. . . . It is the anti-thesis of that highest and sweetest mystery — conviction by submission and conquest by sacrifice.

JOHN BOYLE O'REILLY

The militant, not the meek, will inherit the earth.

MOTHER JONES

When we look at the history of American Catholicism it is easy to miss the women: they seldom appear in the books, and most American Catholics can name no more than four important women in the history of their church.[1] One could point out that American Catholic history has been written with a clerical bias that misses laypeople in general, but a careful counting of men and women will show that whereas lay*men* are few and far between, women are invisible. It might be argued that most of the histories I am referring to were written before the current wave of the women's movement and ought to be judged mercifully: their omissions result from invincible ignorance rather than from willful neglect. Yet, look at James Hennesey's 1981 book *American Catholics*[2] and see that fewer than 50 of the nearly 1,300 index items refer to women in any way, and that in 331 pages of text, the material about women adds up to approximately 10 pages. Though it must be admitted that Hennesey, by just mentioning 50 or 60 different women, did something no other historian of American Catholicism has done, the point remains: women are invisible in American Catholic history.

Historians usually fail to include something because it is not interesting to them, not relevant to their field, or judged to be not historically important. Americanists might legitimately ignore Medieval history because it is not interesting *to them*; labor historians might neglect the development of the Metropolitan Opera because it does not relate to their investigations; but how does one know whether or not something is historically important? How do historians decide what belongs to history and what does not? One answer to that question turns upon the relationship of any material to what we might call the landscape of a particular field.

The shape of any discipline is limited by its investigative categories: those who control the categories set the limits of inclusion and exclusion by telling practitioners what is and what is not significant. For example, until very recent times the organizing principles of American Catholic history have been controlled by those with a definite clerical bias. Our understanding of the American Catholic narrative, therefore, has been confined to the organized institutional operation of the church, and our presuppositions about success, failure, progress, retrogression, and renewal have been shaped by an ecclesiastical mentality. An inclusive and more clearly representative understanding of American Catholicism—a task well outside the intentions and limitations of this book—will require many new perceptions, new definitions of Catholicity, sharp challenges to dearly held assumptions, and the opening of new historical categories that will include women's experience.

Female invisibility in history is not accidental. The landscape of history, as of every other discipline, has been defined by men so as to exclude women. Women, says Edwin Ardener, are "mere black holes in someone else's universe."[3] The careful work of feminist scholars in all fields has shown that women's ideas, work, texts, rituals, and lives have a non-real status. As Gerda Lerner puts it: "Men have defined *their* experience as history and have left women out."[4] The first jolt for a feminist historian, therefore, is the realization that women have been denied their history. Male historians describe the field in a way that legitimizes the omission of women.

How might the discipline change? Nonfeminist historians might say that they could be persuaded to change the parameters of the field *if* it could be shown that women make a difference to the landscape. In American Catholic history, therefore, we would have to take the main lines of the story and show how the lack of women impinges upon the story: the field cannot be redefined, some say, unless and until historians see how the omissions affect the field as it is presently conceived. But if the categories of historical investigation have been drawn so that the omission of women makes no difference, it is impossible to show how the omission of women makes a difference — catch-22.

In order to show that women are historically important, therefore, we must ultimately insist on structural change within the field. The central argument of this book focuses on the fact that women's experience has been omitted from every conceivable arena of religious identity: women's history, roles within the church, the very structures of the church — its language, ministry, theology — have been defined by men for men, with women as eavesdroppers. The feminist task within the church, whether it is theological, ministerial, structural, or historical, demands that we begin to devise strategies for changing the landscape.

The women's movement is necessary within the church precisely because women have not been recorded or acknowledged, have had no ways to shape the church's ideology, participate in its ministry, or locate themselves in its history. More importantly, perhaps, the omission of women's accomplishments from American Catholic history presents us with a distorted picture: American Catholic history as we have it today is the history of a clerical minority, not the history of the American Catholic people. In fact, the way American Catholic history has been conceptualized, buildings are more concrete manifestations of Catholic life than people. In the bicentennial volume edited by Robert Trisco, *Catholics in America 1776–1976*,[5] one picture is worth a thousand words: of the sixty photographs included in this handsome, celebratory volume, half are of men, seven are of women, and the rest are of buildings or are political cartoons. Significantly, buildings outnumber women by a margin of two to one.

In order to uncover the abyss in our knowledge of American Catholic history that results from the omission of women's words and deeds from the generally accepted recitation and that distorts our understanding of the present crisis, it will first be necessary to discuss women's invisibility in general and to sketch out the main lines of the arguments of some feminist historians. We can then look at the invisibility of women in American Catholic history vis-à-vis some of their real accomplishments and suggest that the contributions of women need, first of all, to be included in traditional categories of American Catholic history, in order that we might begin to have a fairer understanding of our past. I am not making an argument for "women's history" as a subfield of American Catholic history but as an integral part of the story, one that will eventually, one hopes, lead to changing the parameters of the discipline to give us a more honest picture whence to interpret the future.

WOMEN IN HISTORY IN GENERAL: SOME THEORETICAL ISSUES

Any attempt to deal with women in history (or in any discipline) inevitably leads one to confront the issue of invisibility. If women and "women's issues" seem to be particularly visible today, it is partly because women have been virtually invisible in every aspect of life for as long as we can remember. Feminist anthropologists, psychologists, historians, theologians, and literary critics all argue that women have been ignored, discounted, marginalized, and rendered invisible. Women's psyches, cultures, viewpoints, and experiences have been determined by men; women's own contributions to human understanding have had no place. Up until ten years ago in American history, for example, a student using any one of the twenty-seven leading textbooks in that field would learn virtually nothing about women. A study of those textbooks conducted by Delores Barracano and Earl Robert Schmidt showed that they "devote from a high of 2 percent . . . to an infinitesimal .05 percent . . . of the textual material to American women."[6] Furthermore, what *is* presented about women in these textbooks is often denigrating or offensive. History books today include many more women, but "those notable women who matter most to women are [still] not included in the majority of texts."[7] Women fare no better in other disciplines. Elaine Showalter, examining the effects of the literary curriculum on female students, concluded that by "the end of her freshman year, a woman student would have learned something about intellectual neutrality; she would be learning, in fact, how to think like a man." Women are hopelessly outnumbered by men in literary anthologies (the *Norton Anthology* includes 169 men and 6 women), and "figure much more prominently in literary history in their relation to male artists, as martyred mothers, pathetic sisters and difficult wives."[8]

These observations about the exclusionary proclivities of the dominant male perspective confirm what everything else in our society tells us: the masculine viewpoint, or what Anne Wilson Schaef calls the "White Male System"[9] is considered to be normative and all others divergent. Despite the fact that women are the majority of humanity, they seldom appear on the tapestry of history. It is not surprising, therefore, that women feel marginal and unimportant, but that feeling must be resisted. In literature, for example, Judith Fetterley urges women to be "resisting readers." American literature confuses women, she argues, by claiming to be universal and comprehensive when, in fact, it is overwhelmingly male. As resisting readers, women refuse to assent to a lopsided version of reality.[10]

But, what *is* reality where women are concerned? Have women made important and significant contributions to history, or have they been totally subjugated? Did the masculine viewpoint assert itself as normative by dominating women, or by ignoring them? One of the important questions about women's place in history centers on these issues and involves the writings of two of this century's most famous interpreters of women's experience, Mary Ritter Beard (1876–1958) and Simone de Beauvoir (b. 1908). In 1946, Beard published her most famous book, *Woman as Force in History,* to argue that the "false and tyrannical idea that women have always been a subject and oppressed sex was manufactured by the American feminist movement in the middle of the nineteenth century."[11] In 1949, de Beauvoir's *The Second Sex* stated flatly that "throughout history [women] have always been subordinated to men . . . have gained only what men have been willing to grant. . . . [Woman has] always been man's dependent, if not his slave."[12]

Beard and de Beauvoir were not engaged in a head-on debate on this issue, nor is there any evidence that they read each other's work; but their different perceptions of women's reality help to frame some contemporary questions about women's history.

The women's movement had its political origins in the abolitionist campaigns of the 1830s. Female abolitionists had to fight to participate in the antislavery movement on an equal footing with males: they were not permitted to be members of some groups, not permitted to vote or to speak in public. When they finally did win the right to speak out in public against slavery, they were often ridiculed or denounced from pulpits for ungodly and unnatural behavior.[13] Among the first to demand their rights as women were the Grimké sisters, Sarah (1792–1873) and Angelina (1805–1879). In 1837 Sarah Grimké articulated one of the major themes of the women's movement, one that Mary Beard later objected to. Challenging male superiority and women's status, Grimké said:

> All history attests that man has subjugated woman to his will, used her as a means to promote his selfish gratification, to minister to his sensual pleasures, to be instrumental in promoting his comfort; but never has he desired to elevate her to that rank she was created to fill. He has done all he could to debase and enslave her mind; and now he looks triumphantly on the ruin he has wrought, and says the being he has thus deeply injured is his inferior. . . . But I ask no favors for my sex . . . all I ask of our brethren is that they will take their feet from off our necks and permit us to stand upright on that ground which God designed us to occupy.[14]

Not believing that men had subjugated women, Beard wrote *Woman as Force in History* as a polemic against the "myth" of women's subjugation and "against feminists who adopted and propagated the myth."[15] De Beauvoir, on the other hand, would have agreed with Sarah Grimké and other feminists who declared at Seneca Falls: "The history of mankind is a history of repeated injuries and usurpations on the part of man toward woman, having the direct object of the establishment of an absolute tyranny over her."[16]

Both Beard and de Beauvoir fought for the rights of women, and both wrote with rhetorical flourish and some inconsistency. As they interpreted history, both pointed to some major achievements of women, but came to different conclusions about them. Beard's thesis, that "women have always been a very real, although unrecognized, force in society,"[17] was formulated in direct contradiction to those nineteenth-century feminists who argued that women had always been a subjugated group. If women think they have always been oppressed and helpless, then they will internalize that image and be crippled by it; the only way for women to be free, she argued, lies in the discovery of their own splendid history. Beard's argument, reduced to its briefest form, is that since women have made such major contributions to human history, they cannot have been subjugated; their very contributions show that they have had power and influence. While Beard's argument is not without problems,[18] it is extremely useful to contemporary feminist historians because Beard shows how the invisibility of women is directly related to the *categories* of historical interpretation: women are invisible, she argued, not because they have not accomplished anything, but because history has been focused on *male* issues. Beard's work, therefore, provides us with one side of the feminist argument, namely, that to have an authentic history, we must change our historical categories so that historians focus on female as well as on male issues.

De Beauvoir's perspective is philosophical, not historical: her arguments are decidedly more complex and subtle. As an existentialist, she believes that human beings are totally free and responsible for what they make of themselves; she defines individual fortune "not in terms of happiness, but in terms of liberty." Building on some of the early work of Jean Paul Sartre and her own belief in the power and inevitability of transcendence, she analyzed the history of women in terms of "otherness." "Humanity is male," she said, "man defined woman not in herself but as relative to him; she is not regarded as an autonomous being. . . . He is the Subject, he is the Absolute—she is the Other."[19] To put it more bluntly, when de Beauvoir analyzed history she saw the male regarding the female as virtually nonexistent, as an entity that is simply there, having no significance for his own existence. Transcendence, for de Beauvoir, is not so much an urge to get beyond oneself as it is a refusal to be nailed down to any category. To her way of thinking, if women can define themselves existentially, they will refuse to be "the Other" and can then begin to take responsibility for their own freedom and existence. De Beauvoir shows philosophically what Beard argued historically: men define existence (or history) androcentrically, so that women have no significance. By identifying the philosophical roots of oppression, de Beauvoir's argument is rhetorically useful to feminist historians. Whether or not woman is "Other" in existentialist terms, Joan Kelly–Gadol has argued that the "sense of 'otherness' . . . is essential to our historical awareness of women as an oppressed social group."[20]

In some ways, Beard and de Beauvoir stand at, not only opposite, but extreme, ends of the argument. In explaining the roots of oppression, de Beauvoir painted perhaps too bleak a picture, but Beard overstated the case by virtually ignoring the fact that women *have* been oppressed thoughout history.[21] Whether or not women have been a powerful force in history is not an issue that can be solved in the present conceptual framework, because when we ask questions about subservience or significance we are really asking questions about the landscape. The present historical framework forces us to ask the question this way: Were women invisible to historians *(a)* because what women did was not usually valued by historians (Beard's position)? or *(b)* because untypical women's contributions — the works of "Shakespeare's sisters," for example[22] — were not thought to be as good or as important as what untypical men did (de Beauvoir's argument about women being perceived as "Other")? Neither side of the question leads us to a place in which we can solve the problem. What we need, therefore, is a new way to frame the question, one that includes both perspectives, admitting that women *have* accomplished much *and* that they have been oppressed.

The most articulate arguments for a new approach to women's history have come from Gerda Lerner.[23] Women themselves, she says, are part of this enormous problem: they constitute a majority, yet have the status of an oppressed minority; they have been excluded from political and economic power, yet as wives and mothers have often been closer to that power than many men; they have been exploited and exploiters, have been dissatisfied with their options, yet have usually adjusted to those options and resisted change; they have been basically conservative, yet their organizations often have been radical and supportive of revolutionary causes. If women themselves present huge problems to the historian, so does society and its values: motherhood is said to be essential, yet mothers are not rewarded, and the fact that wives and mothers are unpaid workers affects our attitude toward the kind of work that they do; service work and nurturance are held in low esteem by a society that claims to value them.

Echoing Mary Ritter Beard, Lerner argues that women are invisible in history because history has been male-defined as great events, wars, and politics. Women's history, therefore, will offer a whole new way of interpreting historical data, and it is clear that no single method will fit the complexities involved. Lerner suggests three steps toward a new history: first, one adds new historical categories — sexuality, reproduction, role indoctrination, female consciousness — to traditional ones and analyzes them with a wider focus; then, one explores the possibility that women's history might just be the study of separate womens' cultures with separate occupations, status, experiences, rituals, and consciousness; finally, one aims at a dialectical synthesis of the tension between the two cultures, a tension based on comparative studies. We have been denied our history, Lerner says, yet have been essential to its making: "All history as we know it is merely pre-history. Only a new history firmly based on this recognition and equally concerned with men, women, the establishment and the passing of patriarchy can lay claim to being a truly universal history."[24]

The interpretive problems are obviously not simple. Finding lost women and publicizing their contributions are important steps in the process, and though it is clear that compensatory history is not enough, it *is* crucial to a reconceptualization of the field. Only by filling in the blanks can a real redefinition begin to occur. Furthermore, the new history must be relational. As Joan Kelly-Gadol has written, the "activity, power and cultural evaluation of women simply cannot be assessed except in relational terms: by comparison and contrast with the activity, power and cultural evaluation of men, and in relation to the institutions and social developments that shape the sexual order."[25] And furthermore, a redefined field must take pains to include the majority of women. Rescuing some notable women from historical oblivion is only a first step, one that gives us heroes but tells us little about most women. Focusing on "women's contributions" is also problematic. " 'Contribution' history is an important stage in the creation of a true history of women," Gerda Lerner has noticed, "but it mostly describes what men in the past told women to do and what men in the past thought women should be." History, like everything else, has to be reinvented. The notion that women's history might be allowed within the general framework of history as a "subfield" misses the point of the feminist argument. As Lerner has argued:

> At this time, as during earlier periods of feminist activity, women are urged to fit into the empty spaces, assuming their traditional marginal "sub-group" status. But the truth is that history, as written and perceived up to now, is the history of a minority, who may well turn out to be the "sub-group."[26]

As we turn to the historical problems of American Catholic women, it is important to keep these arguments in mind. Though my own examples are efforts at contribution history rather than data for new interpretive categories, I hope that they are useful as consciousness raisers and that they will help to stimulate a revision of American Catholic historiography. When we consider women in American Catholic history we will see (with Beard) that women are invisible because what they typically did was not valued by historians; yet we will be able to say (again, with Beard) that women even in traditionally defined categories *have* been an amazing and powerful force in the history of the church in the United States. We will also see (with de Beauvoir) that women have been consistently marginalized and oppressed within the church, as within the general society, and that our freedom lies in our ability to define ourselves and to make our perceptions of reality count. Finally, we will be drawn to conclude (with Lerner and other feminist historians) that finding some "lost women" and extolling their contributions is only a first step, but an important one on the way to creating a more truly representative and universal history.

WOMEN'S INVISIBILITY IN AMERICAN CATHOLIC HISTORY: HOW AND WHY

Catholic women are in a peculiar position vis-à-vis their own history. On the one hand, they have constant liturgical reminders of women saints and heroes, and on the other, they, themselves, have little power. On the one hand, they can look to Mary, the "mother of God," to be reminded of the church's elevation of womanhood, and on the other, they can, with Mary Daly, trace devastating misogynism throughout the history of the church and in the teachings of its major theologians, canonists, and popes.[27] When it comes to history, American Catholic women suffer from the same problems of invisibility that other women experience: There is virtually no mention of women in the standard texts of American Catholic history. Even sisters, who were important figures in the existing categories, crucial to the founding of schools and hospitals, and who have documentary evidence of their work, are almost totally absent when it comes to historical recognition.

American Catholic historians have had an uphill battle to get their own work recognized as legitimate. In their efforts to change a landscape that ignored *them*, they have had to show that "Catholic history" was not a parochial subfield of American religious history, and that religious history was not a subfield of general American history. The tendency of historians to ignore religion in general and Catholicism in particular framed the territory in which the pioneers of American Catholic history had to explore. In some ways, therefore, it is not surprising that American Catholic historians did not find "women's history" important: their attempt to break into the androcentrically defined field of American history without rocking the boat and their devotion to their own clerical biases led them to play by those rules that relegated "women's contributions" to peripheral status. Interestingly, American Catholic women were ignored both by Catholic historians and by early feminist historians: religious historians (mostly male) ignored them because they were women, and feminist historians ignored them because they were Catholics.[28]

In moving American Catholic history into the landscape, Catholic historians defined categories that marginalized or ignored women because those categories were developed by men, for men, in pursuit of a clerical ideal. Influenced partly by a pre-Vatican II ecclesiology that separated the secular from the sacred and tended to identify the clergy as the church, early Catholic historians identified American

Catholic history as the collected stories of episcopal success. John Gilmary Shea's magisterial but outdated *The History of the Catholic Church in the United States*[29] is almost entirely focused on bishops and diocesan development. His two most prolific and important successors, John Tracy Ellis and the late Thomas McAvoy, both priests, wrote important textbooks on the history of the American church which ignored women almost completely: to read their work one would think that women played no role at all in the history of Catholicism in the United States.[30] Still, though a clerical focus accounts for some of the benign neglect of women, it is not a sufficient explanation. In John Tracy Ellis's *Documents of American Catholic History* (1956) only 11 of the 163 primary documents are about women, whereas three times that many appear for nonclerical men.[31] Women fare no better in popular or scholarly histories written by laymen rather than priests,[32] nor do they make any real, significant progress in histories written well after the second wave of the women's movement.[33]

In addition to shaping their story around a clerical ideal, American Catholic historians were also inclined to focus on the amazing successes of the immigrants and to identify success with property development. A tendency to talk about building programs reinforced the stereotype of American "brick-and-mortar" bishops and gave outsiders a clear norm for evaluating Roman Catholic progress in America. A secondary, but not unimportant, way of measuring Catholic success was a tendency to feature (even to count) converts. Catholic success could then be measured, not just by what structures were built, but by the kinds of people who were attracted to use them. Sometimes a person's conversion was considered more important than other aspects of character or accomplishment. In Ellis's *Documents of American Catholic History*, for example, four pages are devoted to the conversion of Eliza Allen Starr (1824–1901) without mentioning that she was the vice-president of the Isabella Association, the suffragist wing of the Columbian Exposition (1893).[34] That she was a pioneer teacher of art, a writer, lecturer, and poet, the first to make extensive use of photographs and slides in public lectures, and an active suffrage worker are as nothing compared to the fact that she converted from Unitarianism to Catholicism in 1854.

Another possible reason for women's invisibility in American Catholic history may be that it was dictated by the parameters of mainline American history. When historians *did* talk about women, they tended to discuss their role in the suffrage movement.[35] Since early suffrage struggles were an upper middle class phenomenon, due in part to the relationship between voting rights and property ownership, one would not expect to find many Catholic women active in the movement. Suffrage was not a class-appropriate struggle for immigrant women. Since male historians defined suffrage as the only historically interesting woman's issue, and since most Catholic women were not involved in it, historians of American Catholicism had yet another reason to ignore women.

Finally, when asking about women's invisibility in American Catholic history, we must inquire about the availability of documents. It may appear as if the only sources for the study of American Catholic history were to be found in chanceries rather than convents, that is, that the clerical focus was dictated by circumstances of available evidence. It cannot be successfully argued that material about women in American Catholicism has just recently turned up: the work of Barbara Misner and Elizabeth Kolmer demonstrates that primary and secondary sources have been available all along for those who were interested in them. The monumental work of Evangeline Thomas is a testament to the richness of the congregational archives of American Catholic and Protestant sisterhoods.[36] The fact is, historians have not bothered to look for materials on women.

Defined as generally uninteresting, women's work, even when performed admirably in traditional "male" categories (building, for example), and their fabulous collections of primary documents were not attractive to historians of American Catholicism. John Paul Cadden's *Historiography of the American Catholic Church 1785–1943*[37] leads one to believe that no one, not even female historians, was interested in female contributions to the American Catholic church. Cadden's work gives, he hopes, a complete historiography up to 1943; it shows that all the great historians were male and that historians of American Catholicism focused on four areas: bishops, priests, buildings, and missionary activity. Even the buildings exclude female contributions: hospitals and schools are ignored in favor of churches, parishes, and dioceses, and notable building-oriented women like Mother Joseph of the Sacred Heart (1823–1902), acclaimed by the American Institute of Architects as "the Pacific Northwest's first architect," are not mentioned at all.[38] Since fifty-four women are mentioned in the text as authors or subjects, but only seven works are *about* women, can we conclude that in the 158 years covered by the Cadden historiography no historian—male or female—was moved to write about women?[39] Barbara Misner's bibliography for her "Historiography of Women's Religious Communities in the Nineteenth Century"[40] lists 118 sources for or about women published before 1918. One has to conclude, therefore, that Cadden—no different from other male historians—was not interested in women's history and did not count women's contribution to American Catholicism as noteworthy or as part of the historiography of the American Catholic church.

· Things have changed somewhat in the last forty years, but not dramatically. In *A Guide to American Catholic History* (1982), edited by John Tracy Ellis and Robert Trisco, the editors say, "We have aimed at complete coverage up to the end of 1979."[41] Of the approximately 1,400 index items, 310 refer to women: 65 are about individual women, 70 are about orders of sisters, and 175 are women authors. In the section "Religious Communities," women do better than men; Ellis and Trisco can list 62 items pertaining to women's communities and only 57 about male religious communities. As James Hennesey says, "Religious communities, especially those of men, have a long way to go in writing their histories."[42] In the section "Biographies, Correspondence and Memoirs," however, only 47 refer to women out of a total of 447.

Clearly the task at this point is twofold: more effort has to be made to locate and publicize already published sources, and historians must begin to find American Catholic women historically interesting. In James Hennesey's "American Catholic Bibliography 1970–1982," only 24 of the 497 items are about women and two thirds of those about religious communities of women. As the author says, "Increased attention is being paid to archival holdings, particularly by religious women."[43]

As historians, including those whose area is American Catholicism, begin to find women "historically interesting," they may find themselves immersed in some of the issues raised by feminists. They will recognize the need to begin filling in the gaps, yet knowing (with Joan Kelly-Gadol) that compensatory history is not enough.[44] They may be drawn to what Gerda Lerner calls "contribution history" but, with her, will recognize it to be inadequate. Perhaps some will be attracted to investigate those places that represent some form of a "separate woman's culture" that Lerner speaks about.[45] Finally, however, the task involves thinking about American Catholic history in such a way that it opens new categories to include and value women's experiences. Standard textbooks and bibliographic guides do not include such categories and, furthermore, have led us to believe that women have played no significant role in the history of the church in the United States as it is traditionally defined. Women were, however, crucial to the growth of American Catholicism. As we start to fill in the blanks in our own story, perhaps we will begin to understand the need for structural change in the field so that we can move toward a time when the history of American Catholicism is truly representative of the wealth of Catholic experience.

SOME NOTABLE AMERICAN CATHOLIC WOMEN: FILLING IN THE BLANKS

In American Catholic history even relatively famous women have been none too visible and have usually functioned as tokens. The four most publicized women are Catherine Tekakwitha (1656–1680), Elizabeth Bayley Seton (1774–1821), Frances Xavier Cabrini (1850–1917), and Dorothy Day (1897–1980). Seton and Tekakwitha are the two most likely to turn up in textbooks and bibliographies and the average Catholic could probably remember that Tekakwitha was an Indian convert sometimes called the "Lily of the Mohawks" and Seton the first American-born citizen to be canonized as a saint, though they would probably not know that she was the founder of the American Sisters of Charity. Cabrini and Day both worked with the very poor and are sometimes wrapped up in sanctity and summarized without being taken seriously; average Catholics might know that Cabrini was the first United States citizen to be canonized and that Day founded the Catholic Worker movement in the 1930s, but they would have no idea that Day's movement marked the real beginning of Catholic radicalism in the United States. They would not remember that Day was not allowed to speak on Catholic college campuses in the 1930s and might be surprised to learn that she was highly influential and crucially important in such contemporary issues as nuclear disarmament.[46] In confining Day to her soup kitchens, historians have missed an opportunity to query their own assumptions about Catholicism and Catholic "progress."

The inadequacy of the American memory where women are concerned reflects the kinds of biases we have already examined and leads to the conclusion that our present version of American Catholic history is a false one.[47] A work like the present one can only *begin* to redress the balance by filling in some of the blanks and pointing to some lost women. As I did the research for this chapter, I discovered many more women than I can possibly mention in this book and was left with intriguing theoretical questions I cannot begin to resolve. Can we assume commonality for women? Did they have similar problems despite differences in social class or education? Can we suppose that they shared certain situational perspectives either with respect to America or with respect to Catholicism? Since many of the women I will mention did the kinds of things men did, do they offer us avenues of comparison that take us beyond compensatory history?

My purpose in this chapter is twofold, and my theoretical questions and arguments outdistance my ability to address them. I have raised some of the methodological questions posed by feminist historians in order to challenge American Catholic history, but I believe that the new historiographical assumptions needed for a more accurate picture of American Catholicism can only be developed after years of painstaking work by historians alive to feminist questions. As will be increasingly evident in this book, I also believe that new conceptions of "church" as adumbrated in the documents of the Second Vatican Council and articulated in the experience of American Catholic women will lead to a radically new understanding of Catholicity, one that will, by definition, be generally unable to exclude women. On a practical level, I have chosen four areas in which women played an important role—women's rights, the labor movement, the frontier, and the missionary movement—and have tried to show that women as well as men are important contributors in our traditional understanding of American Catholic "success." Though these categories are different from the four major areas of interest reflected in the Cadden historiography—bishops, priests, buildings, and missionary activity—they do, with the exception of the women's rights question, reflect some of the main lines of American Catholic history. I have concentrated on "lost" or invisible women and so have not included more notable figures, even though women like Dorothy Day can help to challenge our unquestioned assumptions about progress and success. My purpose is modest: I hope to suggest a broad, general distortion in each category and then begin to correct it by showing that women's contributions, even to history as we presently conceptualize it, were important to the development of American Catholicism.

SUFFRAGE: CATHOLIC WOMEN AND WOMEN'S RIGHTS

It has already been observed that suffrage was not a class-appropriate struggle for Catholic women. Because most immigrant Catholic women were poor and did not own property, the right to vote was not high on their agenda, and we ought not to expect to find them anywhere in the movement, let alone in its forefront. We must remember, however, that the suffrage movement took a long time, and that by the turn of the century immigrant women were beginning to claim voices for themselves and to get involved in a variety of movements that would make women's lives substantially better. In the first decades of the twentieth century, therefore, we do find some Catholic women active in women's rights questions, though their role in the suffrage movement, reflective of newly acquired social status, tended to be fairly conservative. An article by Helen Haines in *The Catholic World*, 1915, is not untypical of upper middle class Catholic interest in the suffrage issue. Catholic women ought to vote to protect Catholic ideals, she says, and to ensure fairness and decency for working women and children. Although devout religious women have always arisen to "protect the home" by way of institutional supports (orphanages, convents, schools, etc.), now women can offer their moral strength to the world through the vote: "Votes for women injects into this situation [national decadence] the most moral element in our nation," she says; "woman's insight, comparable only to man's breadth of vision, will be an asset to our great democracy in our troubled times."[48] Just as we might expect upper middle-class women to take a conservative, "cult-of-true-womanhood"[49] approach to women's rights, we might predict that more radical women would choose the suffrage movement over the church as an object of their loyalty and concern. As James Kenneally suggested in 1976, at "this juncture in American Church history there is need for an analysis of feminism's apparent erosion of the faith of Catholic women."[50]

Yet, there was one notable exception to these generalizations: Lucy Burns (1879–1966) was a nationally prominent radical suffrage leader, able somehow to balance her Roman Catholic faith with the most daring demands of the movement. Burns, an Irish-American Catholic, not only supported suffrage, she was militant in her tactics and spent "more time in jail than any other American suffragist."[51] When the suffrage campaign was floundering in the early years of this century, women were divided about tactics and strategies; some wanted a national suffrage campaign, and others thought it more prudent to work for suffrage in each state; some believed that persuasion and politeness were the keys to victory, others were convinced that radical militancy was the only answer to what then seemed to be an impasse. In 1913, when Carrie Chapman Catt (1859–1947) was president of the National American Woman Suffrage Association (NAWSA), it was a large and ungainly organization that had made no significant progress on the issue for some time: no state had granted suffrage since 1896, though there were twelve (mostly western) states that did grant suffrage to women within their borders. In April of 1913, Alice Paul (1885–1977), a member of NAWSA, convinced of the value of militant tactics and radical publicity and equally convinced that women ought to be seeking a national suffrage, founded a small group known as the Congressional Union, later reorganized as the Woman's Party. "If Paul was the chief strategist, Burns was the major organizer."[52]

Born in Brooklyn, Burns earned a degree from Vassar (1902) and appeared to be headed toward an academic life. For the next seven years she did some graduate work (at Yale and in Germany) in languages and taught high school for two years (1904–1906). During this time she became increasingly interested in the suffrage question, and by 1909, when she went to study in Oxford, it had become a burning issue for her. In England she met Emmeline Pankhurst (1858–1928) and her two daughters, Christabel (1880–1958) and Sylvia (1882–1960), who, with others, had founded the Women's Social and Political Union (WSPU) in 1903 to work for suffrage in England. The Pankhursts, tired of using polite means toward their goal, began to use militant tactics in 1905: they gave public speeches, disrupted meetings, resisted arrest, were imprisoned, went on hunger strikes, were beaten and force-fed.[53] They attracted attention and support, even though the media coined the term *suffragettes* (not to be confused with suffragists) to describe them, as if the diminutive could somehow diminish their cause. Burns joined their efforts, was arrested with them, and joined in their hunger strikes; she ceased working toward her doctorate and became a paid staff member of the WSPU from 1910–1912.

More importantly, while in England Burns met and became good friends with Alice Paul, another young American woman attracted to the work and strategies of the Pankhursts. When Paul founded the Congressional Union in 1913, she and Burns were close friends and eager collaborators; when NAWSA removed Alice Paul from its Congressional Committee, Burns resigned from it so the two of them could put their energies into Paul's organization and into a series of militant, dramatic actions in support of national suffrage. As in England, both were arrested, beaten, force-fed, but not broken: they organized parades, took trainloads of women to campaign against Wilson in western states,[54] gave speeches, lobbied, educated other women, and published a newspaper. "Lucy Burns brought a fierceness and resoluteness to the American woman suffrage movement that was rarely equalled."[55] When suffrage passed in 1919, Paul and Burns were largely credited for it.

Burns retired from active work after suffrage passed, "exhausted from the long campaign."[56] From 1923 to 1944 she reared an infant niece and refused to join in working for additional causes for women. Lucy Burns was the only Catholic woman in the radical wing of the suffragist campaign. "Over one third of the women identified as feminists by the editors of [*Notable American Women*] left the church in which they were born for a more liberally structured one, or abandoned religion altogether, a trend not noticeable in analyzing leading anti-suffragists."[57] Burns, a devout Catholic, "remained close to the church"[58] until she died.

While it is true that not many Roman Catholic women were active in the suffrage movement, the presence of Lucy Burns helps us to ask some pertinent questions. How did Burns reconcile her Catholic faith and her non-lower-class status with her role in the radical wing of the suffrage movement? The official Catholic position toward suffrage was negative, and many Catholic bishops, led by Cardinal Gibbons, attacked the movement and made no secret of their hostility toward women's rights issues.[59] Is there any historical connection between hierarchical opposition to suffrage and contemporary episcopal discomfort with the Equal Rights Amendment? Is there a clear connection between class and conviction on this issue, that is, is Phyllis Schlafly historically predictable? If Burns *did* know how strongly the American hierarchy opposed suffrage and yet did not waver in her views or tone down her radical behavior, does this tell us something about her, or, more generally, about determined women? In a time when many American feminists feel constrained to choose between their church and their commitment to the women's movement, can Burns and/or the hierarchical position on suffrage offer us any interpretive help?

THE LABOR MOVEMENT: IMMIGRANT WOMEN FIND A VOICE

In the old slogan that spelled out women's options in life — *aut maritus, aut murus* — women were told to choose between a husband and the convent.[60] "Women's work," a euphemism for unpaid labor, could be done in either place. Since women were not supposed to work outside the home (or convent), it may be surprising to see how many women were involved in the American labor movement. There is no question that the labor movement is one of the most important and exciting chapters in the history of American Catholicism. Millions of immigrants made a good life for themselves and a better one for their children because of the movement and because the American bishops identified the needs of the laborer as pastoral ones: some interpreters conclude that the American church did not lose its working classes precisely because of the energetic support the bishops gave to the labor movement.[61]

As we read American Catholic history, we see that the development of the Knights of Labor is an important question, yet the role of Catholic women within the fledgling organization is ignored while the leadership of a Catholic male, Terrence Powderly, appears with favorable comment in every textbook about American Catholicism. Similarly, the Women's Trade Union League, the most effective source of labor support for women in the early twentieth century and an organization dominated by Catholic women by the turn of the century, is not considered to be historically important. Reading the history of American Catholicism, one would have to conclude that women played no role in an important movement encountered by millions of immigrant Catholics. The omission of women can even appear logical if one assumes that the labor movement did not really solidify until the American Federation of Labor was founded in 1886. Since the AFL was markedly hostile to women and their needs, one could conclude that women played no major role in the labor movement in this country. Still, the work of Philip Foner[62] and others points to the clear and significant contribution of women to the labor movement, a story that needs to be part of the history of American Catholicism. The two most notable arenas of women's activity were the idealistic Knights of Labor, founded in 1869 as a secret society, and the Women's Trade Union League, an organization of union women and middle-class reformers.

In the early part of the nineteenth century virtually everyone believed that "woman's work was in the home." Trade unionists, novelists, religious leaders, doctors, and most women apparently believed that "employment [of women] especially wives, violated natural law and endangered the nation."[63] Paid working women, hoping that their wretched factory lives were only temporary, were not much interested in unions, and middle-class women were not interested in the dismal working condition of their unladylike sisters; suffragists, drawn largely from the middle classes, were not of one mind on the issues of paid working women and unions.[64] Occasionally women banded together to form a protective union, as in the Workingwomen's Protective Union (formed in 1863 by New York seamstresses);[65] but union reformers and suffragists — both logical sources of help for them — were ambivalent about women in unions: male union organizers thought women belonged at home, and female suffragists, hoping to form a strong coalition of women in support of the ballot, were more interested in suffrage than in the condition of working women and thus often alienated union-oriented women.

The first real chance women had to participate in a nationally prominent union came when the Knights of Labor held its first national convention in 1878. The Knights of Labor sought "equal pay for equal work" as early as 1878, but not because the organization had any commitment to women: "Fearing the effects of new machinery . . . and the increasing use of lower paid unskilled females . . . delegates sought to protect themselves."[66] Still, because of that position and other factors, the Knights did permit women to join the union, and that opened up avenues of participation for them.

One of the most significant women in the Knights of Labor was Leonora M. Barry (1849–1930), an Irish Catholic immigrant who became their first General Investigator of "Women's Work" in 1886.[67] Barry immigrated to this country as a child and by the time she was thirty-two was the widowed mother of two small children. Unable to see well enough to take on the traditional women's work — sewing — she went to work in a hosiery mill and learned quickly enough what life held in store for her: her first week's wages were sixty-five cents.[68] The possibility of joining the Knights of Labor and the need for organized opposition to her working conditions motivated her, and when she joined the union in 1884 the Knights were just entering their peak years. The Knights reached an apex in 1886, were pretty well supplanted by the AFL by 1890, and were virtually extinct by 1900. Barry, therefore, was in the right place at the right time; she became president ("Master Workman") of her 1,500-member local, then president of her 9,200-member district. In 1886, she was elected to attend the national convention of the Knights in Richmond, Virginia.

At the 1885 convention a motion had been made to establish a committee to gather statistics on women's work: Where did women work, and under what conditions? How much did they earn, and how were they treated? At the 1886 convention this motion passed, and when the convention turned to Barry, she accepted and thus became the first General Investigator for the Department of Women's Work in the Knights of Labor. Her duties were complex: she was to collect data about working women (and she did compile the first nationwide statistics on women's work)[69] and to agitate for the abolition of child labor and for equal pay for equal work. She was, by all accounts, an excellent speaker, and she spent the next four years traveling from place to place giving more than five hundred lectures, a latter-day circuit rider for the causes of women.

Barry was a practicing Catholic all her life, but that did not prevent her being denounced by Catholic priests for her work: in 1888 Father Peter C. McEnroe called her a "lady tramp" and the Knights a "vulgar and immoral society." Barry defended herself and her cause as "an Irishwoman, a Catholic and an honest woman."[70] Priests were not the only ones to comment negatively on her work; she was opposed by some male Knights as well and met resistance and apathy from some of the women she was trying to help. Add to her experience the fact that the Knights themselves were suffering from internal disputes, and it is not hard to imagine her frustration: her vivid reports to the conventions (1887–89) about deplorable conditions endured by working women and children to the contrary, "She found herself unable to build up a stable membership."[71] Believing that women should only work in cases of economic necessity, Barry herself retired from the Knights of Labor job in 1890 when she married Obadiah Read Lake. She spent much of the rest of her life working for Catholic charitable causes, temperance (both as a member of the WCTU and as a speaker for the Catholic Total Abstinence Union of America), and suffrage.

If Barry was not particularly effective, it is because the organization she represented was not effective.[72] Yet women outside of the Knights of Labor had a very hard time finding a place in which to play a role in the labor movement. "Confined by their perception of the female role, male dominated unions frequently were reluctant to espouse the cause of women. As a result the most effective champion of women workers for nearly a half century was the Women's Trade Union

League."[73] While it is not clear just how effective the WTUL was in the cause of women and labor, the WTUL (like the Knights) did provide a way for women to be involved in the labor movement. Because the labor movement attracted mostly immigrant and lower-class women, its membership was largely Catholic and Jewish. The WTUL, therefore, could be an important arena in which to study the role of Catholic women in the labor movement.

If Catholic historians *do* occasionally think of a woman in the labor movement, it is Mary Harris "Mother" Jones (1830–1930). Joining the Knights in 1879 and never associated with the WTUL, she achieved fame as a wily and tireless organizer for the United Mine Workers.[74] Jones, a fearless woman, had a reputation for being an extraordinary field director and was active in strikes up into her nineties: "the image of a pink-cheeked old woman who dared to go to the center of brutal strikes was potent and effective."[75] Whether American Catholic history can really lay claim to Jones is questionable. Her background was clearly Roman Catholic, and she had an impressive, self-designed Catholic funeral before being interred, with great drama, in a coal miners' cemetery;[76] but she probably did not practice her religion much of her adult life. When she testified before the Industrial Commission in 1915, she said, "I don't go to church; I am waiting for the fellows in the church to come out and fight with me, and then I will go in."[77] As an important figure in the labor movement and as an open *critic* of Catholicism, accusing it of "abandoning the revolutionary thrust of the Gospel,"[78] Jones is an important figure in American Catholic history. Her case needs to be made, however, on the basis of her prodding antagonism toward Catholicism rather than a clear representation of its beliefs.

Unlike the suffrage movement, which involved relatively few Roman Catholic women, the labor movement, insofar as it included women, was heavily Roman Catholic. With the exception of Mother Jones, however, who is granted a page in Hennesey's *American Catholics*, no Catholic woman in the labor movement is ever mentioned by American Catholic historians. The two explanations for this omission — that women played no important role in the labor movement, or that whatever role women played is historically uninteresting — bring us again to the heart of the structural problem. Since labor historians are beginning to change the parameters of their investigations to include the work of women, historians of American Catholicism, who typically see the labor movement as a crucial chapter in American Catholic history, must begin to widen their own horizons to embrace women's role in that movement. Some of the mythology that accompanies the women's movement — for example, that women are now drawn to paid labor *because* of the women's movement — can begin to be dispelled. Furthermore, any history that allows us to imagine that women's natural place is in the unpaid labor market (the home) is probably predicated on data mostly derived from middle-class and upper middle-class women. By paying attention to the role of Catholic women in the American labor movement, perhaps we can begin to write a more inclusive history and to tap the strengths that lie in the untold part of the immigrant success story.

WOMEN ON THE FRONTIER: BUILDERS, TEACHERS, AND PIONEERS

A popular misconception pictures men moving west, taming the frontier, and being followed by women who settled into home life and brought with them a kind of moral order. In fact, women were on the frontier from the beginning; as Arthur M. Schlesinger, Jr., says, "Life could not have gone on without them."[79] American Catholic women have been pioneers and innovators on many fronts; founding religious communities, building hospitals and schools, settling the frontier, and turning aside the tide of anti-Catholic bigotry, they have built and maintained the substructures of American Catholicism, yet they are rarely mentioned in the history books, even for their most notable achievements. The care of the sick and the teaching of the young, even when done in impressive hospitals and in a remarkably successful network of schools, is unpaid labor, "women's work," devalued by both society and the church. When American Catholic historians talk about schools, they feature the foresight of the bishops, the efforts of the pastors, and the sacrifices of the families who used them, but they rarely give due credit to the sisters who staffed them. The myth of the nun as demure, passive, and delicate would be eradicated were we to look specifically at some of the independent, strong-minded, robust women who literally built schools and hospitals across the United States.

Women who were not members of religious congregations are almost totally lost to us, and women who were important in their religious sisterhoods have only recently begun to receive some of the attention they deserve.[80] Still, the visibility given to nuns in the last twenty years is only a beginning: the historians who write about them have first had to rescue them either from obscurity or from pious, sentimental (and often historically inaccurate) accounts of their lives written for the edification of the community. As the archives housed by religious congregations of women are made available to scholars,[81] historians can go beyond biography to analyze their achievements in a world suspicious of Roman Catholics (nineteenth-century America) and in a system hostile to independent women (Roman Catholicism).[82] One of the important tasks of Catholic priests and bishops in their times was building: in the New World, new buildings were required, and successful bishops were those who staked out new territory, founded new parishes, and supervised the building of new churches. It has always been assumed that along with this great building up of the structures of American Catholicism "the good sisters" followed along and took up their positions as teachers and administrators. Since women have been invisible in the books, and since men have been credited as the great builders, no one has much thought about the contribution made by women to this work. Yet, the schools, hospitals, orphanages, colleges, and convents built by woman have been an amazing part of the story of American Catholicism.

One example — not at all untypical — of a remarkable builder was Mother Mary Baptist Russell (1829–1898), the superior of the Sisters of Mercy in San Francisco from 1854. Born in Ireland to a well-to-do family, Kate Russell joined the Sisters of Mercy in 1848 and made her final vows in 1851. In 1854, the young Mother Baptist Russell traveled to San Francisco with five other sisters and three novices, commissioned to care for the sick and the poor and to minister to distressed women. Within a year she had worked in hospitals and with unwed mothers and orphans, begun a regular prison visitation to San Quentin, and made an enormous impact on her environment. She founded the first Catholic hospital on the West Coast (St. Mary's), opened a night school for adults, established a shelter for homeless and unemployed women, and in 1861 built the Magdalen Asylum, a shelter for prostitutes. She opened and staffed free schools for the primary and secondary education of both boys and girls and opened a home for the aged in 1872. When she died, the obituary in the *San Francisco Bulletin* called her "the best-known charitable worker on the Pacific Coast."[83]

In addition to the building up of charitable institutions, the Roman Catholic story has been very much one of schools. When the Third Plenary Council of Baltimore (1884) specified that each parish should have its own Catholic school, the American Catholic church embarked upon one of the most amazing building and educational programs in the history of the world, one duly recognized and praised by historians. Yet the history of Catholic education in America virtually ignores women: colleges for men are discussed at some length, but academies for girls are ignored; parochial schools are described in terms of pastoral initiative rather than in terms of the sisters who staffed them; significant educational firsts for women—like, for example, the foundation of Trinity College (Washington, D.C.), the first national Catholic college for women—are mentioned in passing. In this case, besides the reasons we have already examined for the omission of women's achievements, we must remember the pre-Vatican II ecclesiology, which did not quite consider nonclerics part of the church. When talking about *church* history, historians focused on bishops and priests: parochial schools were a testament to *their* inventiveness and savvy, not to the work of the sisters. Furthermore, the schools built by sisters were—by the same definition—independent of the normal church structure and therefore not really part of church history.

When feminist historians look at the development of women's education in this country, and when Catholic historians write a more complete account of the growth of the Catholic school system, they will have to evaluate the work of women like Mother Marie Joseph Butler (1860–1940), founder of Marymount College; Mother Mary Aloysia Hardey (1809–1886), phenomenal builder of schools and pioneer in women's education; Sister Julia McGroarty (1827–1901), first American superior of the Sisters of Notre Dame de Namur, founder of Trinity College; Sister Georgia Lydia Stevens (1870–1946), musician and co-founder of the Pius X School of Liturgical Music (1916) at Manhattanville; and Sister Madeleva Wolff (1887–1964), founder of the first Roman Catholic program of theology open to women (1943), at St. Mary's, Notre Dame.[84]

Finally, Roman Catholic women have been pioneers in the literal as well as the figurative senses. In this particular category, their work may be of more interest to feminist historians trying to enlarge their conception of women's achievements throughout American history than to historians of American Catholicism. However, I mention them here partly to draw attention to a problem historians have with the availability of sources. Though it is encouraging to know that American Catholic sisters are receiving some attention these days and may, by dint of their often spectacular achievements, find their place in the story of American Catholicism, one can still be concerned for those laywomen who have had no community to keep their memory alive. It is clear that if sisters, whose archives have been available all this time but who are only now getting some attention from historians, are obscure in American Catholic history, laywomen are almost hopelessly lost to us. When we find an unusual woman who happened to be Catholic, therefore, it is tempting to make more of her accomplishments than is appropriate.

Margaret Brent (c. 1601–c. 1671), colonial landowner and Mary Sargent Neal Gove Nichols (1810–1884), a pioneer in health reform for women, both have some interest for feminist historians.[85] Brent was the first woman to ask for a vote — two votes, really — in the Maryland Assembly; Mary Nichols was an early feminist and the first woman in the United States to lecture on diet, anatomy, and hygiene. Neither of them, however, can really be made to fit into the story of American Catholicism very clearly. Brent, because she apparently exercised wide executive powers for Lord Calvert, might cause us to ask about the position of women under a Catholic colonial administration, and Nichols, because she was a convert to Catholicism, might hold some fascination for those who see converts as evidence of Catholic success; however, neither of them changes the landscape of American

Catholicism, either as it has been defined in the past or as it might conceivably be defined in the future.

One laywoman who *might* have a place in a renewed American Catholic history is Nellie Cashman (c. 1850–1925), impressive as a woman and as a Catholic. She was a prospector and "one of the first of a band of daring women to invade the frozen, uncharted fields of the North." Her biographer, John P. Clum, said that "as a thoroughbred and seasoned 'sourdough' she had no rival among her own sex, and there were few, if any, among the male adventurers who could qualify in her class"; but he remembered her most as a good Catholic woman who "went about doing good."[86] Clum met her in Tucson, where she was running a restaurant and, unobtrusively, doing good deeds—"she has half a century of good deeds to her credit," he noted (p. 370)—and he was fascinated by her. She had joined the Cassiar fields gold rush of 1877[87] and was credited with keeping scurvy at bay by importing fresh vegetables, especially potatoes. At heart a prospector—her years of operating restaurants in Arizona were during the lulls of her life—she was quick to return to the goldfields again in the great Yukon gold rush of 1898. Clum knew her in Tombstone, where she reared the five orphaned children of her sister, and when Clum wrote about her, years later, it was with the hope that the "courageous, resourceful, efficient Nellie Cashman" would not be forgotten (p. 375). He collected stories about her, gave her most of the credit for building and financing the first Catholic church in Tucson, and recounted her role as "Mother Confessor" to condemned murderers and her apparently outstanding kindness to those in need. Clum has preserved what we know of Nellie Cashman, but his hopes for her memory have not been realized; Nellie Cashman, if she was an important Catholic woman pioneer, has been lost.

Whether or not other Catholic laywomen find a place in American Catholic history—some surely will; for example, Martha Gallison Moore Avery[88]—we need to be cognizant of the paucity of sources in this regard, to mourn what has been lost, and to be deeply grateful to the dedicated women in religious congregations who saved their letters and stories and diaries year after year even though no one asked to study them. Nuns are beginning to appear in bibliographies, but they have not yet taken their place as an integral part of the story of American Catholicism. The mistaken impression that men (priests and bishops) conquered the frontier and then sent for the sisters to carry on the work of the church derives partly from experience — in most Catholic memories, sisters were too demure, cloistered, and unworldly to have possibly done heroic deeds, building hospitals, living in huts under primitive conditions, and masterminding great school projects — but mostly from women's invisibility in the history books. Until Mary Ewens's work, *The Role of the Nun in Nineteenth Century America*,[89] no one looked seriously at the things these women did, or at how they were treated after they had done them. To have a real history of American Catholicism it is necessary to make these pioneering women a visible and important part of the story.

THE MISSIONARY MOVEMENT: WOMEN IN THE MEDICAL PROFESSION

The American Catholic church was built on the sweat and blood of its early missionaries, mostly religious order priests. Women do not factor significantly into this story until the nineteenth century when they became important in two ways: some as immigrants whose missionary work extended to non-English-speaking Americans, and some as Americans whose missionary vocation took them to mission fields abroad. When asked to name a famous missionary outside the United States, many Catholics might be able to remember Father Damien, "the leper priest," but few would mention Mother Marianne Cope (1836–1918), an equally distinguished missionary to the lepers, decorated by the king of the Hawaiian Islands and celebrated in poetry by Robert Louis Stevenson.[90] Similarly, when American Catholic historians talk about the exciting beginnings of the Catholic Foreign Mission Society of America (also known as Maryknoll), they usually discuss the splendid work of Thomas Frederick Price and James Anthony Walsh without mentioning the seven women who, under the direction of Mary Josephine Rogers, became the Maryknoll sisters.

In order to focus the discussion of missionary activity, I will concentrate on the ways that American sisters made significant contributions to the medical profession while doing historically important things for the American Catholic church. The medical profession felt the impact of nuns in two ways: in the professionalization of nursing, and in the feminization of doctoring. In both of these areas, American Catholic sisters played an important role. Their contributions during the Civil War and their establishment of enormously successful mission fields in the nineteenth century ought to be a more visible part of American Catholic history.

When one thinks of the pioneer of nursing professionalism, one thinks of Florence Nightingale (1820–1910), but "Florence Nightingale not only dervied her inspiration and encouragement from, but owed her training to, the Catholic Church." When Nightingale went out to the Crimea in 1854, it was largely with the help of Henry Edward Manning, archbishop of Westminster, who "mobilized the little force of fifteen nuns from various convents who formed not only the nucleus of the original expedition, but its backbone."[91] In a time when nursing outside the home was not thought to be an appropriate task for women, and when women who did take on the job were often morally or professionally unfit for it, Catholic sisters had the reputation of being the only trained, dedicated women in the fledgling nursing profession.

In the United States, the importance of nuns as nurses was recognized most clearly during the Civil War. American Catholic sisters were "undoubtedly . . . the best nurses of this period."[92] They responded to the needs of the country promptly and with great efficiency. Mother Angela Gillespie (1824–1887), for example, built and administered "the best military hospital in the United States"[93] during the Civil War. Her work and that of other Catholic nursing sisters made the nuns "heroines of the war,"[94] though such is not evident from the quick, anonymous mention they usually get in history books. If their work had such an extraordinary effect, why is it not a more central part of the American Catholic story? The Ancient Order of Hibernians and its Ladies' Auxiliary petitioned the United States Congress and gathered the necessary (and impressive) data to convince the United States War Department that a monument to honor the "nuns of the battlefield" would be fitting since they played so significant role during the Civil War.[95] The monument stands in Washington, D.C., but the role of the nursing sisters is still passed over swiftly by historians.

Besides bringing skilled nursing, which benefited women almost as much as the country — Inez Hayes Irwin says that experience during the war "raised nursing from a menial occupation to a dignified profession . . . and taught women how to organize"[96] — nursing sisters "changed public attitudes toward the church from hostility to respect."[97] They are often mentioned and praised for this work along with Catholic chaplains, but we need to remember that, whereas there were 84 Roman Catholic chaplains during the Civil War, there were 640 sisters. By sheer numbers, therefore, their impact was probably far greater than that of the men, but this is not mentioned or even speculated about.

In bringing professionalism to nursing, sisters were doing what women were supposed to be doing, that is, serving humanity. In attempting to become physicians, however, women had to confront a stone wall of opposition from both the medical profession and from the church. One of the most important women in the struggle to change canon law to allow sisters to become doctors was Mother Anna Dengel (1892–1980), the Austrian-born founder of the American-based Medical Mission Sisters (Philadelphia). Dengel did not come to the United States until 1923, and though she became a naturalized American citizen, her outlook, background, experience, and vision all mark her as a global personality: she was born in the Tyrol and educated in Germany and France; she graduated from medical school in Ireland and practiced medicine in England and India before coming to the United States on a trip meant to raise money for the Indian missions.

Anna Dengel's and the Medical Mission Sisters' story really begins with the life and work of Agnes McLaren (1837–1913),[98] a Scots convert to Roman Catholicism (1898) who spent her young life working for suffrage and with the poor, went to medical school at the age of thirty-nine — a pioneering venture in those days when most medical schools would not accept women — set up a practice in Cannes, and lived a relatively routine and medically useful life until retirement (1904), when she became interested in the problems of women in India. Because of religious customs, some women were not permitted to be seen by any man except a husband or close relative; these women were effectively barred from medical attention unless they could be attended by a woman doctor. Protestant missionaries, seeing the importance of this kind of work, had sent women doctors to India and were doing amazing work at their missions; they were especially useful in obstetrics and gynecology. McLaren saw that Catholic missionaries would have to do the same thing but was stunned to find out that canon law forbade nuns to be doctors or even to be aides in childbirth. The problem had two logical solutions: either change canon law or persuade laywomen doctors to serve in India. When it was clear to McLaren that the first option was not going to work, she started to facilitate the second: she established a Medical Mission Committee in England under the patronage of Cardinal Bourne with the express intention of raising money to build a hospital and to help promising young women through medical school in order to staff that hospital. It soon became clear that the problem was more difficult than it had first appeared, especially because laywomen, without community support, tended not to stay out in India. McLaren did not live to see the law changed, but before she died she had befriended Anna Dengel and sponsored her medical education.

Dengel, like McLaren, saw the problem: responding to a priest who lamented the high turnover rate of lay missionaries, she said, "It is hard to be expected to lead a kind of community life—without a community . . . and it is hard not to be fitted with the spiritual requirements for such work. . . . There ought to be a group . . . a community, trained professionally and living entirely for God and for this special work."[99] How could there be such a group when canon law forbade sisters to practice medicine? Anna Dengel was not inclined to wait for canon law to change, but proposed instead a creative, evasive strategy: laywomen—doctors and nurses—would band together not as nuns but in a kind of community of prayer and mutual support, go out to India, do their work, and see what happened. When she proposed this plan to a Holy Cross priest, he lent her the constitutions of his own community and suggested she draw up a plan. While on a speaking tour in Louisville, Kentucky, she wrote her "constitutions," and within a few months (and after a little fine tuning) she, another doctor and two nurses moved into a house together to form the nucleus of the Society of Catholic Medical Missionaries (Medical Mission Sisters). When they took their first mission oath in 1926, after a year of preparation, they "were, for the time being, sacrificing the privilege of making public vows in order not to be prevented from engaging in any kind of medical work."[100] Canon law did not change until 1936, ten years after this first group had promised themselves to this work; within another ten years there were more than one hundred professed medical sisters in this new order working, not just in mission territories, but anywhere they were needed, including Atlanta (with blacks) and Sante Fe (with Hispanic women). Dengel had a powerful intercessor in Cardinal Dougherty of Philadelphia, who later used to tell the sisters, "Your mother is a Canon Law buster."[101] As a result of her vision and the insistence of missionary bishops, Canon Law was changed to permit sisters with public vows to practice medicine and obstetrics in the mission territories.

Missionary sisters did more than medical work, but their contributions to the nursing profession and to medical missionary work are particularly strong. As those who carried the heaviest burden of American Catholic charitable endeavor, nursing sisters were especially important. "The scanty statistics available to us indicate that sisters administered at least 265 hospitals in America during [the nineteenth] century."[102] In the Spanish-American War, sisters outnumbered chaplains by a margin of 22 to 1, reflecting in part the greater number of women who were drawn to serve the church than men. As sisters flourished in this country and as the nineteenth century came to be regarded as "the great century" of missionary work, sisters spread their work to all quarters of the world. "By the third quarter of the twentieth century, Catholic Sisters in the mission fields outnumbered priests and brothers combined by a ratio of two to one."[103] The great success story of American Catholicism — in foreign and domestic missions — cannot be told rightly without a heavy emphasis on the work of the sisters.

CONCLUSIONS

By including the contributions of women to American Catholic history we will begin to expand our understanding and to resolve the distortion that results from ignoring women. We can see that the major stories of the nineteenth century — westward expansion, conflict with anti-Catholic attitudes, missionary endeavors, the Civil War — all included women in significant ways. Because the women discussed here did very much what men did, we can begin to get some data to compare the work attitudes of women with those of men. One hopes that as their stories lead to a more complete picture they will begin to stimulate some theoretical questions that will change the field.

When we talk about immigrants, for example, we know that Catholic immigrants from non-English-speaking countries were doubly vulnerable: by being both "foreign" and Catholic, many of our immigrants had an enormously hard task when it came to assimilation and upward social mobility. We have always taken pride in their story as we rehearse the triumphs of American Catholicism. But what additional questions need to be asked about women immigrants, who were triply dispossessed as foreigners, Catholics, and as women? By including their struggles in the American Catholic story, we may well have to expand our historical categories to include challenges and issues pertinent especially to women.[104] In doing these things, we can question the field as it is presently understood and work toward a more representative history. We will also have to face the sad fact that it may be too late to find data even for women in traditional categories. The stunning dedication and pioneering spirit of religious women has been recorded in convent archives, but much of what laywomen did — save for their role in the labor movement — might now be lost to us.

In the twentieth century American Catholic women were more free for some things and less free for others. Catholic women's colleges opened by pioneering nuns made it possible for Catholic women to get an education; the National Council of Catholic Women (NCCW), formed during the First World War, played a crucial role in social justice education and service after the war. In fact, the NCCW was much more effective on this front than the National Council of Catholic Men.[105] When the archives of the NCCW are finally searched, we may have some new information about Catholic women in early social reform movements.

After the First World War, sisters, who had worked energetically and with freedom, were slowly curtailed in their activities and made to conform to a role and lifestyle which defined them as demure handmaidens, delicate, withdrawn brides of Christ who were not quite human. As Catholicism became a parochial subculture after the Second World War, all women played their traditional parts: wives and mothers conformed to the stereotype supported by official church pronouncements about complementarity, and nuns became silent but efficient pillars of the Catholic school system and hospital network. Men—priests, bishops, and laymen—took the credit for running the church. By the time of the Second Vatican Council, women were almost totally invisible. It is time to question these developments: if vigorous, independent women of spirit were forced into submissiveness, able to find only an uncomfortable home in the church, something vital was lost to American Catholicism.

The remainder of this book is devoted to assessing the impact of this invisibility: by looking at some contemporary questions that can be raised in the context of Roman Catholic women's experience, we can begin to get a deeper and more immediate sense of why the women's movement is necessary within the American Catholic church. While I do not wish to highlight distinctions between sisters and laywomen, I have focused on laywomen when discussing "women in the parish" and have devoted a chapter exclusively to sisters. An examination of the history of the Women's Ordination Conference and the emergence of the Womanchurch movement reflects the collective energy of some contemporary American Catholic women. A review of the expanding and subversive insights of Roman Catholic feminist theologians and a look at some directions for a feminist spirituality can give us a deeper sense of the intellectual and religious potential of the women's movement within the American Catholic church.

This present chapter shows us that ignorance about our roles in American Catholic history is dangerous. As we see that we must include and celebrate the lives and work of women in the past, perhaps we can see that contemporary questions about women in the church must be evaluated in our own terms. If women are in the big picture—and they surely are—then we will have to help set its borders and fill in its landscapes.

2. From Immigrants to Emigrants: Women in the Parish

What the world needs is saints and unless women hold up that ideal before their children and train them to attempt it, it is extremely unlikely that we should get them.

OLGA HARTLEY

The normal call for a woman is to be a wife and mother.

ANY POPE

The Roman Catholic Church has not yet found an "ordinary mother" suitable for canonization.

SARA MAITLAND

The American Catholic church has always counted on its women. In every conceivable setting — urban, rural, suburban — women have been the mainstays of the congregation, the tireless supporters of parish life whose labor-intensive projects have sustained everything from works of mercy to the school system. There is no question that their work has been — and continues to be — done on a volunteer basis.[1] Nor is there any evidence that women in the past were inclined to rebel against a system that consistently defined their roles as auxiliary to those of men. Whether the American Catholic church can continue to rely on us in this way is questionable, not because the church has changed, but because we are changing. The feminist movement in the general culture has given women in the parish a new perspective and provided us with a means to interrogate the system. At the same time, there is some evidence that women who have actively participated in the women's movement are quietly abandoning the church in search of alternative communities of celebration and support.[2] Though it may be tempting for some church officials to ignore such women — perhaps even feeling relieved to be rid of their upsetting questions and complaints — the American bishops are worried about women leaving the church and must realistically assume that the trickle shows clear signs of becoming a flood. In the context of a changing church and a changing society, American Catholic women in the parish are in an increasingly precarious position.

In terms of the challenges they present to the hierarchy, women are the "immigrants" of contemporary American Catholicism. Like the Europeans who came to America in the nineteenth century, they are many, in great need of support, and quite capable of being "lost" to the church unless some special care is taken to identify with them and enter into their process of "assimilation" and empowerment.

As nineteenth-century bishops identified with the European immigrants, they became increasingly entangled in the battles of the burgeoning labor movement, and because labor unions often began as "secret societies," the American hierarchy sometimes had to defend these unions from Vatican censure.[3] Precisely because of the support of the bishops, however, the American church kept its laboring classes. The church in Europe—France is a case in point—whose hierarchy was identified with the aristocracy, lost its working class members.[4] We might ask: Are today's American church leaders too identified with patriarchal structures to support the women's movement? I do not think it strains my analogy to predict that if the American Catholic hierarchy does not identify the justice issues within the women's movement and support them, the church will lose its women as surely as the French church lost its laboring classes.

The analogy is not perfect, but it does offer some parallels. If the American bishops, in their forthcoming pastoral letter on women in the church,[5] make common cause with feminists on some issues, they will be vilified by conservatives and understandably draw negative attention from the Vatican. Insofar as the labor movement drew the same kind of reaction from the same quarters, the bishops have some precedent for standing with the oppressed group. In order for women's issues to be supported, however, it must be clear to potential supporters that women's gifts are crucially important to the future of American Catholicism. One could say that Catholic feminists can be ignored: a majority of American Catholics are women, but not necessarily feminists. On the other hand, can we expect those figures to remain constant? Can we not predict that the women's movement has and will continue to have an attraction for Catholic women, that it will help them to perceive their oppressed situation and give voice to their needs? I will argue in this chapter that the values of Catholic feminists — pluralism of voices in analyzing problems, direct participation in the governance and celebratory life of the church, collegial process, and a clear desire to follow the impetus of Vatican II — are the key to the future of American Catholicism. Women in the American church, therefore, like nineteenth-century immigrants, cannot be ignored.

THEORETICAL UNDERPINNINGS OF THE PROBLEM: WOMEN'S "INFERIORITY" AND POWER

In order to understand how women in an American Catholic parish might relate to the women's movement, we need to see how and why women have questioned the old stereotypes of female inferiority. Up until the American women's movement began in the mid-1840s, women had been universally described as inferior to men.[6] Physicians argued that their brains were smaller than those of men and that intellectual stimulation would have a deleterious effect on their reproductive abilities.[7] Ministers and priests, led by the texts and traditions of their religious heritage, either castigated women as the cause of evil in the world or urged them to fulfill the myriad duties of their positions as subservient wives or dutiful daughters.[8] Legally, women were barred from professional life, ownership of property, and the right to vote.[9] The Catholic Encyclopedia, in its article "Women," summarized what appeared to be an undisputed fact: "The female sex is in some respects inferior to the male sex, both as regards body and soul."[10]

While it is true that by the 1960s women were no longer barred from university education and were able to own property and to vote, the belief that women are inferior to men persisted and manifested itself most clearly in the area of sex-role identification. Male psychologists — Erik Erikson is a case in point[11] — studied boys and girls and discovered profound differences between them; sociologists of the family, like Talcott Parsons, described masculine behavior as that suited to the role of the breadwinner.[12] Men, social scientists said, were "naturally" aggressive, rational, objective, and commanding, whereas women were passive, emotional, subjective, and obedient. In short, men were suited to roles in the world; women were suited to roles in the home. Infinite permutations of this theme can be found as one traces the feminist critique of culture and society. Furthermore, the various ways in which "natural female traits" have been described all claim to be "objective," value-free accounts of reality. They appear to be unassailable.

The first works of the new wave of the women's movement challenged sex-role identifications. Far from being value-free descriptions, Elizabeth Janeway argued, they constitute a "social mythology"[13] constructed by scientists to keep women in "their place," that is, at home. Erikson and Parsons were not objectively describing female roles, she said, they were advocating them, using so-called scientific data to say what women ought to be rather than what women are. Kate Millett, analyzing the work of certain male writers, challenged sex roles by developing a theory she called "sexual politics."[14] If politics includes power relationships, sexual politics are power relationships sexually enacted. To her way of thinking, sex-role stereotypes are expressed sexually as patterns of domination and subordination; men use sexual power and definitions to control women and to keep them from achieving power of their own.

Before continuing to follow some of the directions suggested by the work of Janeway and Millett, it might be useful to examine briefly the question of power. Women tend to have ambivalent feelings about power: some know that they have none; others claim that they have some; and many are not sure that they want any. Part of the confusion lies in the definition of power, and part of the definitional confusion can be traced to the division between private and public spheres institutionalized in the eighteenth century.[15] For a number of reasons — historical, economic, and political — the eighteenth century managed to effect a clear division between the private and the public spheres. Further, the public realm was identified with masculinity and the private with femininity: men worked "in the world" while women kept the home. Gradually, citizenship became linked to participation in the public realm, which removed women further from power. The "real world" was the masculine arena of public policy; the home, tended by a devoted wife, provided a safe and restful haven from a man's daily cares. However important it was as a resting place, the home—the feminine—was fundamentally irrelevant to "real life." In this scheme of things, power took on two different meanings. Public power—"real" power—was associated with "the world" and with so-called male traits of dominance, aggressiveness, and control. Private power—a shadow reality—was associated with feminine "influence." And, just as feminine traits were often the object of suspicion or denigration, so feminine influence—female power—was considered to be seductive, manipulative, and wheedling.

Because of the separation between the private and public spheres, therefore, women were effectively eliminated from public life. Furthermore, their "own sphere" was theirs, not in the sense that it was created by them or chosen by them, but because it was assigned to them. Finally, because that assignment was backed up with divine commands and public legislation,[16] any woman seeking power—which might mean a job, fair wages, an education, or simply the right to choose her own marriage partner—was accused of taking on "masculine" traits and of stepping out of her God-ordained place.

When we think about women and power today, we encounter two interrelated problems: women seek both personal power and corporate strength. On the one hand, women long for personal power, that is to say, self-confidence and self-determination; on the other hand, they wonder how they can mobilize the power they do have in order to make it more effective in society. Since personal power is related to feeling lovable and competent, it has been extremely hard for women to find it in the public sphere. Having been told for centuries that they were incompetent in "worldly matters"; finding themselves struggling with blatant and subtle sexism from peers, subordinates, and superiors on the job; having too few role models and insufficient "permission" to claim public power; women often shy away from overt power "in the world" and from descriptions of private power that sound too domineering. Failure to find clear ways to exercise corporate power may be attributed to ignorance, and inexperience.[17] Many women do not realize that they have power already; when women do recognize it, they are sharply divided about whether and how to use it. Mostly, however, women have had relatively little experience in corporate power ventures "in the world," though they may have had some strong experiences of group power in church settings.

Paradoxically, just as churches have been the source of texts and traditions to keep women from power, they have provided women with ways to experience some collective strength. By choosing to stay within their assigned sphere of influence and to exploit the so-called feminine virtues of service and helpfulness, women in church groups have been able to use their organizations as foundations for supportive and effective means of action. In some ways, however, Catholic women's organizations, especially at the national level, experience many of the same tensions as individual women do. Organizations, too, have to decide whether or not to fight for self-determination and how to ensure that the group expresses its own concerns rather than becoming a reflection of some outside agenda. As we shall see when looking at the histories and positions of two major Catholic women's groups — the National Council of Catholic Women (NCCW) and the Grail — feminist analyses of sex role stereotypes and feminist insistence on structural change have had a major impact on Catholic women's organizations.

RADICAL FEMINIST CRITIQUE AND CATHOLIC WOMEN

Janeway, Millett, and others raised questions of definition for women. By denying "traditional" sex role stereotypes they invited women to begin to define their own experience. The practical consequence of their analyses was an organized form of resistance called consciousness raising, a process of understanding that can help participants "connect the pieces of everyday life and expand its scope, opening up . . . at least a glimpse of the whole social process."[18] Consciousness raising gave women a form in which to relate and validate their own experiences, to see what they had not perceived before: that there is a power in the commonality of women's experience. Relegated to the private sphere and meeting one another only in social settings, in volunteer or school-related groups, or in discussions about child rearing, women had been effectively isolated from one another at the level of politics. Consciousness raising groups allowed women to feel a sense of solidarity with each other with respect to their own—not their children's or their husband's—issues. As they talked about sexuality, power, feelings of frustration and joy, they found that they were not at variance with one another even if they were considered "marginal" in an androcentrically defined society. With a growing sense of solidarity, many women began to sense the political ramifications of their experience and the power of their collective energy. The slogan "The personal is political" is an indication of what these women were feeling in the late 1960s, but it was, more importantly, a direct repudiation of the split between private and public spheres that made women's lives and concerns unreal and apolitical.

Empowered by consciousness raising, women began to move in their own behalf and in pursuit of their own goals. Feminism, to borrow Linda Gordon's pellucid definition, is "an analysis of women's subordination for the purpose of figuring out how to change it."[19] Women, on the local and on the national level, began to identify themselves as feminists. In the university, they pointed to the invisibility of women in every academic discipline. In corporations and political caucuses they began to mobilize support for more equitable legislation and economic policies. Radical feminist theorists "began developing questions, categories and analyses which broke wholly new ground and irrevocably altered the perceptions of most progressive people."[20] As Hester Eisenstein says, the writing of radical feminists "represents a distinctive and original contribution"[21] to feminist thought and to intellectual history. The work of popular and political feminists was often useful and instructive for those not familiar with the women's movement: affirmative action, the Equal Employment Opportunity Act, *Ms.* magazine, and television talk show discussions about women's lives all had some bearing for them. On the other hand, these same women would probably have found the work of academic feminists irrelevant and the questions raised by radical feminists bizarre and threatening.

Still, it is to the work of radical feminists that we must now turn, if only to provide a context for contemporary Catholic interest in the issues. Radical feminist theory is at a turning point which many Catholic women might find attractive. In order to understand its current agenda, however, we must look at some of the questions raised by these theorists in the 1970s. Beginning with the fact of a fundamental inequality between men and women, radical feminists searched for the source of that inequality. In attempting to understand deeply entrenched beliefs about female "inferiority" and the almost universal relegation of women to the "domestic sphere,"[22] they gathered information from a variety of perspectives and constructed complex arguments that raised serious questions about motherhood, sexuality, and gender characteristics. However complicated the issues — and the interdisciplinary nature of the investigations as well as the technical problems of analysis ensured that the arguments were extremely complex — their rephrasing in the popular press made them look totally iconoclastic and frightening. Furthermore, the very nature of the institutions being queried — motherhood, for example — virtually guaranteed that radical feminists would be perceived in defensive and highly emotional terms. Reduced to their simplest forms, radical feminist theories questioned the "institution" of motherhood,[23] the power of "enforced heterosexuality" to support male dominance,[24] the insanity-producing pressures of traditional sex-role expectations,[25] the usefulness of rape to convince women of the need for male protection,[26] and the correlation between "scientific" (masculine) traits and the destruction of the planet.[27] To those who did not follow the steps of the arguments, as well as to those who wished to discredit the women's movement, it appeared as if feminists were those who denigrated motherhood and the family, denied their own femininity, espoused lesbian separatism, and hated men even to the extent of believing them to be naturally evil and wicked, the perpetrators of war, rape, and genocide.[28] It is small wonder that beginning feminists or casual readers of the movement wanted to dissociate themselves from the kinds of questions raised by radicals, nor is it surprising that those hostile to the women's movement found more than enough grist for their mills in the works of radical theorists.

RADICAL FEMINISM AND VATICAN II

No brief summary can capture the revolutionary power of the radical feminist analysis, nor is there anything to be gained from "defending" it against the caricatures of those who find it intrinsically wrong. It is useful, however, to draw an analogy between the women's movement and the Second Vatican Council: both ushered in an era of radical change in what appeared to be changeless institutions; both have found enormous support and have drawn highly critical responses. Because Pope John XXIII opened the council in October 1962 and Betty Friedan published *The Feminine Mystique* in 1963,[29] it appears as if both movements began in the turmoil of the early 1960s, but we know now that both had more than a century of preparation behind them.[30] Although John XXIII and Friedan initially stunned their respective constituencies, their work quickly stimulated an enormous burst of creative energy: Catholics could scarcely fail to believe that the Holy Spirit was at work in their church while women, aware of an energizing presence in their midst, were beginning to believe in the revolutionary nature of womanpower. In both movements there was some distinction between a practical issues branch and a theoretical/ intellectual branch: the practical side of the women's movement gravitated toward the concerns of the National Organization for Women (NOW);[31] the instrumental aspects of the council were worked out in tangible liturgical reforms and revised catechetical programs. The intellectual side of the Vatican II era can be found in the work of theologians, just as that branch of the women's movement can be found in the writings of academic and radical feminists: in both movements theorists can be located along a spectrum of opinion, so that in the church and in the women's movement one can find fairly standard, easygoing, palatable positions as well as more radical, difficult, and disconcerting ideas. Theorists in both groups have inspired successors to strike out in new and potentially dangerous territory, and they have drawn dire criticism from opponents who inevitably predict the end of Catholicism or of femininity.

The difficult ideas of theorists do not discredit a movement any more than do the anxious predictions of its critics. Those who hope to preserve the traditions always argue with those who wish to forge ahead into new areas: their arguments usually lead to further clarification, so that the community itself can decide matters by virtue of its support for one direction or another. In the postconciliar Catholic church, as in the women's movement, there are those who wish to return to things as they were, or to prevent any further change. Similarly, there are those who support the changes to date and believe things have gone about as far as they can (or ought to) go. Lastly, there are those who believe that the changes so far are good indications that a more radical kind of transformation is in order, that we must now be prepared to move toward thoroughgoing structural change. Furthermore, people tend to move in and out of these "camps" as they seek their own clarity of vision on the issues.

Whether we can follow the steps of their arguments or not, radical feminist theorists and post-Vatican II theologians have brought us to consider some rather similar points of view. Women in the American Catholic church have a stake in both movements, especially in some of the practical aspects of major theoretical questions. Briefly stated, both the council and radical feminism aim toward structural change; both are concerned with larger political implications of the movement(s). This is particularly evident in three areas: universalism, collegiality, and social justice. The council was careful to underscore catholicity, the universal extension of Catholicism, yet it was equally concerned to respect non-Catholic and non-Christian religions. The embracing posture of Catholicism is now characterized by a willingness to learn from other religions and to be enriched by association with radically different religious perspectives. The women's movement, too, after an initial naïve euphoria that accompanied a false sense of universalism, has realized that women need to be sensitive to diversity among women. Since Third World women and women of color in the United States do not want to be "absorbed" into the largely white, middle-class American women's movement — if only because their need to hold a negative view of the dominant culture tends to verify their own identity as a subordinate group — we have to respect their disdain for us and examine the ways in which we participate in their oppression. Both the ecumenical dimension of postconciliar Catholicism and the sensitivity to cultural diversity by women are attempts to be genuinely open to and informed by the experience of others.

Though sweeping in its reforms, the Second Vatican Council was probably most radical in its inauguration of genuine structural change within the church. Collegiality aimed at shared power: bishops were to share with the pope, priests with their bishops, and parishioners with their pastor. The changes in the church, therefore, were not simply stylistic or liturgical but were meant to alter significantly the structures of Roman Catholicism. The women's movement, too, in its radical agenda, aims at genuine structural change: radical feminists are not content with advancing a few women in the current male-dominanted structure but hope to realign the system so that there is shared power at all levels.

Finally, a very strong emphasis within contemporary Catholicism is on social justice. The council's virtual obliteration of the distinction between the secular and the sacred inspired believers to find the divine in the people and situations of the world: gospel-based Christianity demands that Catholics respond lovingly to the cries of the poor. The National Conference of Catholic Bishops in the United States has been particularly clear in its insistence on the need for strong programs to ensure social justice throughout the world.[32] The women's movement, too, is constrained to "see the women's movement as connected, both theoretically and practically, to other struggles for social justice." The women's movement, therefore, is not an isolated search for separate space, but a placing of "women's goals at the center of a progressive political program."[33] As such, it shares with postconciliar Catholicism a sense of urgency about justice in the world.

American Catholic women, therefore, have some means to relate to radical feminism. It is not necessary to subscribe to all the intricacies of radical feminist arguments in order to follow some of the creative directions of the movement. One can be an enthusiastic postconciliar Catholic without understanding the complex nuances of contemporary theological arguments. It must be remembered, however, that radicals — theological or feminist — often say alarming things: their imaginative energy about the future often sharpens the ways they interrogate the present. Their task is not to propose ways for women (or other theological perspectives) to fit into current structures but to stimulate institutions to reorganize so as to include women (or non-Christian viewpoints). As Jean Baker Miller says, when we ask questions in the "old way," we say to women, " 'How do you propose to answer the need for child care?' That is an obvious attempt to structure conflict in the old terms. The questions are rather: 'If we *as a human community* want children, how does the total society propose to provide for them? How can it provide for them in such a way that women do not have to suffer or forfeit other forms of participation and power? How does society propose to organize so that men can benefit from equal participation in child care?' "[34] Radicals, therefore, try to redefine the questions. In so doing, however, they often draw opprobrium from what might appear to be unlikely sources. Yesterday's "leaders" sometimes become today's backpedalers: Pope John Paul II appears to be retreating from some of the implications of Vatican II, and Betty Friedan has accused radical feminists of alienating the majority of American women from the women's movement.[35]

Just as the function of theorists is to imagine new structures, the role of movement "leaders" is often to remind us of the traditions. When John Paul II recalls the strengths of the pre-Vatican II church and Friedan emphasizes the needs of the family and the sanctity of private space, they offer a counterbalance to radical theories and enable the argument to go forward. Our attention, however, is probably best focused on ultimate goals rather than on the technicalities of the process. If we adhere to the general directions of post-Vatican II Catholicism, we can see ourselves, as Karl Rahner did, "in a transition from a 'western' church to a 'world church,' "[36] in which, presumably, there will be a pluralism of proclamations, a plurality of theologies, liturgies, and ecclesiastical practices, and dynamic differences of opinion about the role of the gospel in political life. Similarly, if we support the basic goals of the women's movement, we will find value in "the option of entering the world and attempting to change it, in the image of the woman-centered values at the core of feminism."[37] It is to those "woman-centered values" that we must now turn in order to address the painful realities of everyday parish life for American Catholic women.

THE DOUBLE-BIND OF WOMEN IN THE PARISH

If the Second Vatican Council and the women's movement both offer Catholic women a chance to be universally concerned, involved in structural change, and aware of a nexus of social justice issues, why should Roman Catholic women need the women's movement? We might also ask: Why do Roman Catholic feminists need the church? The questions ask us to consider the relative advantages of a particular standpoint: Should Roman Catholic women address these concerns as Catholics, as feminists, or as both? Those who suggest that we need not choose between the two apparently see no problems with the phrase "Roman Catholic feminist." In fact, however, many feminists as well as many Catholics consider "Roman Catholic feminist" to be an oxymoron. One must, therefore, choose a standpoint: All thinking (theory) needs a concrete location (standpoint) from which to evaluate, feel for, inquire about, and offer solutions to a specific problem. Furthermore, since thinking and acting cannot really be separated, we can say that theory is a way of understanding practice or experience. When we talk about Catholic women, therefore, we need to ask if their standpoint comes from their experience as Catholics (from the long, rich tradition of social justice and post-Vatican II renewal), or from their experience as feminists (from the particularities of their own oppression that enable them to empathize with other forms of oppression). The reason to force a choice between the two is that a conjunction of the two is impossible: Catholics have an impressive history of social justice advocacy and, at the same time, a depressive history of discrimination against women.[38]

Women who worked for and with the church in the exciting years immediately following the council had an experience similar to that of the women who worked for abolition in the nineteenth century and those who worked for New Left causes in the twentieth: They were crucial partners in the task (often outnumbering the men significantly), obviously full of ability, able to accomplish difficult tasks and—so long as they concentrated solely upon the issue at hand—respected by their male colleagues. If and when they insinuated their own sense of oppression into the movement, however, they were ridiculed or silenced.[39] The women's movement in the 1840s began because Elizabeth Cady Stanton and Lucretia Mott, both tireless abolition workers, were not recognized by (or permitted to speak to) the World Anti-Slavery Convention in London to which they were official delegates: "Struck by the irony of a 'world's convention' which had opened by excluding representatives of half the human race, [they] found they had a common concern to promote the rights of womankind."[40] In the 1960s, women in the New Left "became increasingly aware of their own passive position in their political enclave." They baked bread and made coffee while men discussed politics, were labeled as trouble-makers if they attempted to participate in the discussion, and so grew increasingly "irritated and restive under the domination of men who, in relation to women, differed little, if at all, from 'establishment' men."[41]

In various progressive movements of the 1960s — peace, civil rights, antipoverty — women found themselves welcome only so long as they did not raise "women's issues" or attempt to take on "men's jobs." In the American Catholic church in the 1960s women participated in renewal with passion and dedication: they worked on ecumenical committees, and interparish educational projects in hundreds of small and large ways to enhance renewal of familial, liturgical, sacramental, spiritual, and social life within Catholicism. Yet when they began to question Catholic attitudes toward and treatment of women they encountered either a chilly silence or a rehearsal of traditional Catholic teaching about complementarity. Women in the abolition and the New Left movements found eventually that they could not establish a successful women's caucus (or movement) within the setting in which they experienced discrimination: a separate women's movement was, for most of them, a painful, if obvious, necessity. Women in the parish, those who have given years of their time for "renewal" may now be finding that they, too, must establish their own movement outside the conventional structures of parish life.

COMPLEMENTARITY

Official Catholic teaching about women — complementarity — is a religious form of sex-role stereotyping. The texts, traditions, and canons of Catholicism are relentlessly sexist in language and suggestion; liturgical celebration is marred by discriminatory language and practice; pastoral concern is often either oblivious to women's problems or hostile to women's desire for empowerment within the church; and the very structures of the church may well be intractable where feminist ideals are suggested. If Elizabeth Janeway had examined papal teaching about women, or any other embodiment of official Catholic opinion, she would have found the same grounds for complaint as she did reading Erikson and Parsons: under the guise of "divine will" (rather than scientific investigation) women were portrayed as dependent, submissive, maternal, and naturally complementary to men.[42] According to Catholic thinking, the sexual differences between males and females testified to a divine intention about their respective roles. It is, as Anne Carr observed, "a kind of biological determination from which psychological, sociological and religious or theological natures and roles are derived."[43]

Those who defend complementarity often do so as a way to protect the family: women are the guardians of the family, clearly intended to rear children and to provide high spiritual and moral guidance for the next generation. Their arguments, however, are still essentially biological. As Michael Novak says:

> In past ages, for reasons rooted in biology, the male has been understood as grounding, both through his body and through his role as hunter, provider, and warrior, the image of *history*. It was chiefly men who made history, and history was chiefly about men. The female has been understood as offering through her body and her cultural roles (as bearer of progeny, nurturer, and requirer of space and time in peace) the image of *nature*.[44]

Furthermore, motherhood and the home were thought to be a woman's only means of gaining respect and protection. Pope Pius XI writing in the 1920s and Michael Novak writing in the 1980s make virtually the same argument: when women leave the home and motherhood, they lose respect, undermine the family, and place themselves in a dangerous position as competitors with harsh and rugged men.[45]

Just as feminists criticized sex-role stereotyping in the general culture, Catholic feminists have been pointing to its deficiencies as a religious value within the church. The argument is not whether there are sexual differences between men and women, but whether there are different human *natures* and whether those "different natures" dictate a divinely ordained and permanent division of labor among men and women. As we shall see when discussing women's ordination, the issue of "women's nature" undergirds many of the arguments against ordination and makes the discussion less than dispassionate: the case against women's ordination has been so thoroughly refuted at its major points that the issue now hangs on tradition and the thin thread of complementarity.

Those who extoll complementarity are usually quick to assert that differences do not mean diminishment: women are different, they say, but not inferior.[46] But we must ask what inferiority means in the church. How would it be demonstrated? Is the usual complementary choice for Catholic women — motherhood or a convent — a way to keep women in powerless positions? And is powerlessness linked with inferiority? In her assessment of universal female subordination, anthropologist Sherry Ortner offered three types of evidence to prove that a particular culture considers women inferior:

(1) elements of cultural ideology and informants' statements that *explicitly* devalue women, according them, their roles, their tasks, their products and their social milieux less prestige than are accorded men and the male correlates; (2) symbolic devices, such as attribution of defilement, which may be interpreted as *implicitly* making a statement of inferior valuation; and (3) social structural arrangements that exclude women from participation in or contact with some realm in which the highest powers of the society are felt to reside.[47]

The texts, traditions, language, pastoral care, and structures of Catholicism all contain explicit, implicit, and structural devaluations of women, and it is to them that we now must turn as we try to understand a church that claims to reverence women while actively discriminating against them.

As the British Laity Commission commented in its report to its bishops: despite the fact that "very little research ha[s] been undertaken to establish how Catholic women in this country regard themselves . . . there is no shortage of *authoritative* statements suggesting what women should or should not be doing."[48] Before the women's movement began to have an impact on the Catholic church, almost everything we knew about Catholic women — our natures, aspirations, sources of fulfillment — was written by male celibates. To a far greater degree than married men, priests and monks adhered to beliefs about female nature that imagined women to be most profoundly themselves in postures of obedient surrender.[49] Women, so far as Catholic teaching was concerned, were capable of fulfilling their "natures" in motherhood—sisters in this scheme were understood to be "spiritual mothers"[50]—or rebelling against it in harlotry. Paradigmatically, women replicated either Eve or Mary and, in either case, were responsible for male destiny:

Woman has the awe-ful choice of being Eve or Mary: she is rarely neutral. Either she ennobles and raises man up by her presence, by creating a climate of beauty and human nobility, or she drags him down with her in her own fall.[51]

Behind this schizophrenic view of woman lay centuries of misogynist writing aimed at avoiding real women by either mystification or slander. The first feminist voices raised in the American Catholic church—those of Mary Daly and Rosemary Radford Ruether—examined the Catholic texts and traditions about women.[52] Though Catholics may do better than Protestants in terms of a tradition of female saints, most of what we find about women is characterized by a high level of hostility, diminishment, frivolity, and sappy romanticization. Furthermore, most female Catholic saints are either virgins or martyrs, whereas most Catholic women are married and not likely to die defending the faith. Behind the rhetoric about Mary and motherhood, Catholic feminists found a deep well of prejudice against women: from the early church to the present, male church leaders have regarded women as naturally unclean, unfit for service on the altar, intellectually inferior to men, dangerously seductive in youth and garrulous in old age.[53] Whether they drew on biblical beliefs about female uncleanness or philosophical arguments about female identification with matter versus male identification with spirit, church leaders for two thousand years have upheld the marginalization and denigration of women as "God's will." Since God created women as inferior or complementary to men, they reason, churches are bound to uphold and perpetuate a divine (or natural) order of things by replicating God's design.

TEXTS, TRADITIONS, AND CANONS

In the Old Testament we find very few women, and no one statement that can reflect the full range of the "biblical view of women."[54] Still, it is clear that women are often considered to be the "property" of their fathers or husbands, and that women find their glory in being perfect "helpmates" of men. Since Israel understood itself largely in terms of male–dominated occupations of war and religious cult, women had very little existence outside their roles as wives and mothers. All women were legally "nonpersons" and nonsubmissive women were usually branded as loose or bad women. Feminist interpreters have begun to question these views, but we must still admit that the Bible is written (and translated) by men and about men: biblical authors believed that God ordered society in a patriarchal manner so that all power was invested in males. Though it may not be surprising that ancient Hebrew men believed and wrote such things about women, feminist critics argue with the reluctance of contemporary church leaders to abandon some of these culturally conditioned positions. The argument, in fact, turns upon profound exegetical differences: anti-feminist interpreters find God's will in the subordination of women and the hierarchical organization of society, whereas feminist interpreters locate God's will in prophetic themes of liberation and equalitarian structures.[55]

Were we to read ancient nonbiblical sources written between the Old Testament and the New, we would find an eagerness to blame women for evil in the world. During this time, Bernard Prusak says, it was apparently "necessary for men to create theological reasons for excluding women from any active role in civil or religious society in order to preserve their own dominance and cope with their sexual drives."[56] From the *Odyssey* to the church "Fathers," women's corrupting power as sirens was feared: their mysterious connections with sex and childbirth threatened men and led them to make a fundamental connection between sex and evil. Women gave men life, but at a more basic level, they contaminated them, since their natural uncleanness tainted every child.

Perhaps the sheer volume of ancient literature against women explains why the "new community" envisioned by Jesus did not endure. When we read the New Testament we perceive two lines of thought about women. On the one hand, Jesus treated women positively, calling them to discipleship and imagining a community "of men and women, Jews and Gentiles, slaves and free people, in which inequalities and injustices were removed and all persons and races were united in mutual respect and love."[57] On the other hand, we see Paul wrestling with this new vision in light of the old heritage, and we see later writers effectively telling women to be seated, subservient, and quiet. We know that many church leaders continue to focus on texts demanding subservience from women even though Catholic Scripture scholars have argued that it "is simply impossible to cite the New Testament as a document supportive of male authority."[58] Their reasons for doing this provide the focus of the current feminist debate about New Testament interpretation. Antifeminist interpreters of the New Testament are not just perverse (as Mary Daly argued in 1968),[59] they probably *are* "interested in preserving a cultural structure of male domination."[60]

Feminist interpreters like Elisabeth Schüssler Fiorenza are now interpreting the antifemale texts of the New Testament as reactionary, arguing that the egalitarian gestalt of the early Christian community was so profoundly countercultural that male leaders began systematically to subdue equalitarian impulses in order to fit the Jesus movement into a "more acceptable" patriarchal mold, one that Jesus himself had deliberately avoided.[61] The real issues, therefore, are probably more structural than textual. As Rosemary Radford Ruether observed in an essay on women's ordination: "It is not possible to imagine the admission of women to the Catholic priesthood [read: the empowerment of women in general] without, at the same time, modifying certain fundamental notions about hierarchy, theology, Church and authority. This, even more than the women, may be what the hierarchy fears."[62]

For the "Fathers" of the church (in the first five hundred years after Jesus), as for medieval theologians, the only good woman was a virgin: by renouncing their inherently evil sexuality and taking up rigorous ascetic practices, women could transcend themselves. A virgin, in effect, was no longer a woman; since she had risen above the messy, unclean, seductive, lower-order parts of her nature, she could now rightly be seen as a *man* in the eyes of God.[63] The richest vein of misogynist literature is found during this period. All great theologians of Catholicism—Augustine, Ambrose, Aquinas, Jerome, John Chrysostom, Tertullian — have something terrible to say about women. Collectively forming a significant part of the Catholic tradition, they believed that males alone are fully made in the image of God and that women are not fully persons; women are, they said, dangerous to men because they are essentially erotic, lustful, and revolting; the virtues that lead to salvation, they argued, are male virtues, and some believed that in the resurrection we would find only male bodies. Women were considered to be, for all practical purposes, whores, wives, or virgins; even nuns "never escaped the male assumption that [they were] a danger, a source of contamination."[64] According to Aquinas, a woman is "naturally defective," suspended at best in a state "of eternal childhood, in which she would be subject to man 'for her own benefit.' "[65]

The opinions of the "Fathers" along with various ancient collections of ecclesiastical regulations make up the complicated matter of canon law. Since Catholicism adheres to tradition as well as to Scripture as a source of divine revelation, it continually sifts through the traditions in order to interpret modern problems. Therefore, it is not hard to imagine that many of the laws pertaining to women reflect female uncleanness and inferiority: anthropologically and ethically women have the status of subjects who are inherently unfit for pastoral functions and liturgical participation. According to canon law, women cannot be ordained or serve on the altar. In the pre–Vatican II church, they could not "assist at Mass" (say the responses) unless no male were present, and then only "from afar" so as not to contaminate sacred space. Women are seen as biologically unclean: Erling Brodersen says "that the biological fact of menstruation is the main obstacle to women's participation in liturgical functions."[66] Women are devalued in small ways and in mortifying circumstances: priest's housekeepers must, according to canon law, be older than fifty and preferably unattractive; women being examined for nonconsummation of a marriage must bathe for thirty minutes before the exam, whereas men to be examined need not bathe at all. A female physician's evidence before a marriage tribunal must be corroborated by a male colleague, but not vice versa, and until recently women were not permitted to ride in the front seat of a car being driven by a priest.

When we examine the texts, traditions, and canons of Catholicism, therefore, we find some rhetorical exaltation of women and much actual disparagement. Almost all the texts come from men who chose celibate lives in order to be freed from contact with contaminating women. Because many of the texts come either from the Bible or from the revered "Fathers" of the church, the argument is made that they cannot change: constituting, as they do, authentic representations of the divine will, the misogynist traditions about women within Catholicism seem inexorable. We must ask, however, if the refusal to change is really located in the sanctity of the texts, especially since where "the church has wished, it has treated apostolic traditions with great freedom."[67] When we look at the past, we look at male privilege:

The operative law of the Church is designed to grant men—specifically priests—the absolute controlling position. Since it is only human to enjoy and defend power, we should not expect a radical change of attitude to come from them. Neither should we expect to find convincing reasons for a change in the historical record of canonical jurisprudence, because the few charitable voices we will hear from the past will drown in the fury of pronouncements against women. We are confronted with a system that will in every likelihood continue to write discriminatory new laws on the basis of the discriminatory old law.[68]

When we look at official Catholic teaching about women—complementarity—we find sex-role stereotyping; in the texts, traditions, and canons we find a fear of women buttressed by texts hostile to them. Modern papal teaching, centering as it often does on the sanctity of the family, takes pains to praise and honor women but primarily in their roles as faithful wives and generous mothers.[69] The Catholic church is not on record in support of "women's issues" outside their traditional sphere. When popes speak about women's "equality," they mean that woman shares with man in the redemptive merits of Christ and has, with man, an equal eternal destiny. Women are not, according to papal teaching, identical with men but have complementary characteristics that fit them to be companions and helpmates.

LITURGY AND PARISH EXPERIENCE

In moving from the relatively more abstract world of ancient texts to the weekly experience of liturgy, we enter a discriminatory territory much closer to home. Liturgical language as found in Scripture, prayers, hymns, and devotional literature is consistently androcentric. In both public worship and private prayer women are invited to become "sons of God." Admonitions are addressed to "brothers," and believers are enjoined to relate to "God the Father," whose only begotten "son" has redeemed the world. This language offends many women because it eliminates them completely; male-specific words like *brothers* are not inclusive but exclusive. The use of so-called generic male words like *mankind, all men,* and *he* are sometimes thought to be less offensive because they "include women," but if they really do include women — a debatable point — they render them invisible. There is "rather convincing evidence that when you use the word *man* generically, people tend to think male and tend not to think female."[70] As Miller and Swift have shown, the "use of *man* to include both women and men may be grammatically 'correct,' but it is constantly in conflict with the more common use of *man* as distinguished from *woman* (p. 18). The use of generic male pronouns is not "just words"; it is a political issue, "and the very ambiguity of the word [man] is what makes it a useful tool for those who have a stake in maintaining the status quo" (p. 35).

In the male-exclusive language of Scripture and liturgy, women are not permitted to name their own experiences or find images to which they can relate naturally or even supernaturally. Furthermore, since the language of divine revelation is overwhelmingly masculine and since a majority of its images for God are male, Christians are left with a distorted picture of the deity. Rosemary Radford Ruether has put the issue most forcefully:

The Christian churches have barely begun to recognize the seriousness of the feminist criticism of patriarchal religious language. It will not do simply to declare that God is Spirit, and therefore, "He" is not literally male, and then assume that all can go on as before. What is involved is nothing less than an idolatrous projection upon the nature of the divine of the characteristics of the ruling sexual group in society. This is more than just a matter of language and iconography. It also involves the fundamental way that the divine is imagined to "act" in relation to the "world," modeled after social power roles. The fundamental authority of the Biblical revelation is at stake. If this tradition is based on a symbol-system that reflects the conquest of women by men, then its revelatory authority is tainted by social ideology. Its images of God, creation, redemption and future hope are interwoven with characteristics oppressive to half of the human race. Such characteristics are not only evil, but blasphemous, since they act as *sanctions of evil* in the name of the Divine.[71]

Feminist critiques of biblical language and imagery argue that the traditional reading of the texts has been incomplete and biased. The language of the Bible and of liturgy are culturally conditioned, they say, following the same kind of argument exegetes use when explaining why Paul's directive about women covering their heads reflects a custom of the time rather than a divine imperative. When the cultural-conditioning argument is applied to male God-language, however, the consequences are more threatening. Krister Stendahl, former dean of Harvard Divinity School, makes the point quite clear:

The masculinity of God, and of God-language is a cultural and linguistic accident, and I think one should also argue that the masculinity of the Christ is of the same order. To be sure, Jesus Christ was a male, but that may be no more significant to his being than the fact that presumably his eyes were brown. Incarnation is a great thing. But it strikes me as odd to argue that when the Word became flesh, it was to enforce male superiority.[72]

If male God-language is a "linguistic accident," the ramifications for the whole theological enterprise are enormous. What do we do, for example, with the traditional formula for the Trinity? Can we change "Father, Son, and Holy Spirit" to "God, our Creator, Jesus, our Saviour, and the Spirit who is holy?"[73] Margaret Farley, of Yale Divinity School, says this:

"Fatherhood" is the image traditionally used for the first person of the Trinity, and "sonship" for the second. But only in an age when the male principle is thought to be the only active principle, the only self-contributing principle, in human generation, is there any necessity for naming the first person "father" and not also "mother." And only in an age when sons are given preeminence as offspring is there any strong constraint to name the second person "son" and not also "daughter."[74]

The issues raised by questions of sexist language are theologically complex and liturgically complicated. Though many people have no objection to changing hymns where possible and eliminating hymns that cannot be easily altered, they resist changing the sacred language of biblical texts. It may help to translate "feminine" passages with feminine words—Deuteronomy 32.18, for example, ought to say "the God who brought you to birth" (a mothering image) rather than "the God who fathered you" (a masculine image)— but most feminist critics agree that a more radical approach is necessary. The Lectionary Committee of the National Council of Churches made just such a revolutionary step when it agreed to retranslate the Lectionary readings from the original languages into "sex-inclusive English," a language fundamentally different from the English we now speak.

Discriminatory language is only one reason why many women feel liturgically alienated from the Catholic church. The prohibition against girls serving on the altar confuses not only the children involved but their parents: it is no longer experienced as "God's will" or as "the way it is" (a sacred tradition) but is increasingly felt as discriminatory.[75] As parents attempt to explain to their children why Simon can be an altar boy but Molly cannot be an "altar girl," they find themselves hard-pressed to find an adequate religious reason for the difference. Most of all, women find very little opening for themselves in the church outside of traditional role-identified tasks like cleaning, baking, arranging flowers, and running bazaars to support the school. Since their role in church is closely related to their experience with pastors, we need now turn to women's relationships with their priests. As noted earlier, very little research has been done on this subject, though thanks to the pastoral initiatives of Archbishop Rembert Weakland (Milwaukee)[76] and the British bishops,[77] we do have some information supplied by women themselves. Since my focus is on the American church, I will rely on the Milwaukee report, noting only that the British publication generally corroborates the American findings.

In 1981 Archbishop Weakland established a task force to examine the role of women in the local church. Composed of priests, sisters, and laypersons, the task force agreed to concentrate on *listening* to women. In ten general sessions throughout the diocese, they heard from women in the parish, and in seven special interest sessions they listened to women employees of archdiocesan agencies, representatives of women's organizations, young adults, minority groups, and women active in the Women's Ordination Conference. While the task force recognized its failure to "hear from large numbers of the most invisible of women: the poor, racial minorities, those who have already left the institutional Church, those who are without hope,"[78] it was nevertheless convinced that its report was accurate and generally reflective of the views of women in the church. If anything, the collective opinions in this document represent a more sanguine and positive response than could have been anticipated had all the women in the parish been available for consultation.

Within the local church, according to the Milwaukee report, women feel invisible, powerless, unwelcome, and trivialized. They experience the sexist language of the liturgy as rejecting and hostile and believe that the church's refusal to ordain women is a "reminder of division and inequality" (p. 7A). Those women who still feel hopeful admit to being "mighty tired [and] not nourished in any proportion to being drained" by their work within the church (p. 8A). Since the "climate for women in the Church is set to a great extent by the attitudes and behavior of members of the clergy," the task force was particularly interested in women's relationships with their pastors.[79]

Many of the women and members of the task force were prepared to admit that priestly insensitivity toward women is partly the result of general cultural formation, but they also believe that seminary training and enforced celibacy exacerbate the problem. The counseling of women, they noted, "has nearly always been done by men, sometimes by men with a narrow view of womanhood, men who have been taught from seminary days to be leery of women, men who consider women seeking guidance as hysteric and/or sexual threats." Many women felt that priests are uninterested in and unprepared to deal with family violence, rape, divorce, unwanted pregnancy, single parenting, birth control, widowhood, and other "women's issues." In fact,

women representing various centers for victims of domestic violence said that the predominantly male image of the Church causes women to hesitate in asking help from the Church. In instances where they have sought help from Catholic clergymen, almost without exception battered women have been counseled to return to the abusive situation. Many women who have been unwilling to follow this advice have left the Church. Persons involved in centers for victims of domestic violence pointed out that, for the most part, Catholic clergymen do not recognize family violence as an area of concern and have not been responsive to invitations to become better informed about this area of neglect.[80]

What role seminary training plays in priestly insensitivity is not entirely clear, but women feel that seminary training makes priests suspicious of or patronizing toward women.

Though it may be true that some women in some parishes experience none of these problems, they would have to admit that their good situation is directly related to their pastor. The parish system is still priest-dependent in the sense that "father" specifies policies. Mary O'Connell has identified seven ways that priests "pastor" a parish,[81] but the differences in style only underscore the point: another priest could change the whole parish style, so that any "gains" women made could disappear.

Some women would argue that they do not want to change and are content with things the way they are. Because more women are active in parish "ministry" today, and because 75–99 percent of those women identify themselves as "helpers," content in their role as handmaid to the clergy,[82] it is tempting to think that there are no real problems and that the kinds of attitudes gathered by the Milwaukee task force are out of line with general opinion. Before concluding that women in the church are really content, however, we need to examine some statistics and to question the paucity of roles available to women in the parish.

The CARA study, *Women and Ministry,* sponsored by the Leadership Council of Women Religious, found a remarkably high number of laywomen in parish ministry in the United States.[83] Though the study clearly had problems of design and definition,[84] one can still see what these women are doing: they are volunteering their services to a church in need. Of the women active in some kind of parish ministry, 92 percent earn no money at all, and of the 8 percent who do receive a salary, precious few earn more than $10,000 a year (13%). Of those who are paid, 67 percent earn less than $5,000 a year. These women are from the middle and upper middle classes, generally involved in religious education and liturgical ministry, and so fill the spaces left by sisters and priests while, at the same time, fulfilling the traditional Catholic definition of woman as auxiliary. More significant than their salaries, however, are their ages: more than 67 percent of the women actively working in the parish at this time are over forty years old. Since they were reared in the pre-Vatican II church, they were taught complementarity along with the meanings of Catholicism, and though they may have embraced the spirit of the council, they may also be somewhat leery of feminism. Furthermore, since their voices are heard only when they agree with the status quo, it may be hard for church leaders to hear any dissonance unless, like Archbishop Weakland, they make an effort to seek a wider range of women's voices.

The women in the CARA study appear to fit happily into the parish model and into traditional roles, but we must wonder if a new generation of post-Vatican II women will be so eager or able to work for low pay in jobs with little status and no decision-making opportunities. Whether or not the parish structure is changing—as Joseph Fichter predicted it would in 1965 as he marked the new emergence of the laity[85]—women are changing, and it is likely that the Milwaukee report is much more representative than the CARA study. We can expect, therefore, that the parish might change after all, demographically if not structurally; that is, if the parish does not open itself to women's questions and begin to accommodate women, they will leave it. As William McCready of the National Opinion Research Center says, "Women are voting with their feet, they are leaving the Catholic church in significantly large numbers—especially women under forty—and in numbers far disproportionate to men leaving."[86]

Yesterday's parish clearly offered women a special, if secondary, place, but it is difficult to imagine that the system as we have known it can endure and keep its women. The whole concept of parish embodies structures that relate more to the needs of nineteenth-century ethnic groups than to modern American Catholics. In the rush of immigration during the last century and in the face of nativist threats to "foreign" Catholics, parishes were havens of protection. Priests, the best-educated members of the parish, were there to lead and protect their people: the old image of shepherd and his flock was an apt one. Parish organizations supported a system of Catholic social, spiritual, and intellectual life operated by the laity in cooperation with the pastor. As such, parishes were organizations of male dominance in which men constituted the cultural norm and were considered to be the creative, authority-bearing, justice-dispensing agents. Women in this model were helpers, subservient agents whose lives derived their meaning in relation to men. This combination of hierarchical order and complementarity was seductive to women in the past because they did not question its assumptions: complementarity gave women a place to interpret their lives, was supported by almost everything popes said about women, reflected traditional images of Mary as the handmaid of the Lord, and was incarnated in the lives of dedicated, self-effacing female saints.

Once women begin to perceive Catholicism as a hierarchical structure with a misogynist tradition still invoked to support discriminatory practices, they can question the secondary status offered them by way of complementarity. When they see that restrictive roles, negative definitions (or stultifying mystification, as in "women are so mysterious"), and debasement of "women's work" are necessary consequences of a hierarchical arrangement, they may see that they have a stake in structural change within the institution.[87] Or, as we shall see in subsequent chapters, they may find the present situation irredeemable and choose to seek alternative communities or choose to claim the Jesus traditions as their own, denying validity to the patriarchal institution that oppresses them. Until women in the parish are ready to make one of these moves, however, they will find themselves faced with traditional roles and will have to decide whether to embrace them, subvert them, or survive in spite of them. How long any of those strategies can endure is problematic.

At the present time, women in the parish are in a tragic double bind: whatever choice they make forces them to deny some part of their identity. If they stay within the institution they have to repress any consciousness of women's questions (about language, discrimination, opportunities) and embrace a tradition that defines them without consulting them. If they leave it, it appears that they have given up on their heritage and denied their Catholicity. We shall see that many American Catholic women have found a way out of this dilemma by way of the Womanchurch movement, a "gathering of the ecclesia of women,"[88] but first we must examine more closely the logical outcome for women choosing to remain within the Catholic church at this moment.

In today's world one cannot make a case for the church as an exciting career option for women. "At one time, the church was the only vehicle open to women who wanted to use their talents beyond the home. The world was closed to them. Now the reverse is true. The world is opening and the church remains calcified in the traditional child/church/kitchen roles assigned to women."[89] Women in the parish who embrace the traditional structures and roles either have to cast a blind eye to the social changes for women in the world around them, or they have to use a significant portion of their liturgical energy ignoring sexist language, discriminatory practices, and the invisibility of women's talents, ideas, and status. They will have to explain to their daughters that they might one day become a justice of the Supreme Court, but never a priest, and in searching for an explanation of that ban they will confront a tradition that perceives women as unclean and unfit for sacramental service. Whether or not they can accept the traditional explanations is not so important as whether their daughters will. They will live in a country where Title IX legislation has made women's sports an exciting reality, so that they may be rooting for Molly's softball team on Tuesday and Simon's on Thursday, but they will attend a church where Molly has to sit with her mother in the pew on Sunday while Simon is welcomed on the altar as a server. Every Mother's Day, "Father" will tell them what motherhood is about and they can bask in the glow of a tradition that elevates womanhood while it denies power to real women and stifles their possibilities. And if, in this sad scenario, cognitive dissonance sets in, who can be surprised? Cognitive dissonance is the disruption of one's framework of perception by a jarring encounter with another one: in some ways consciousness raising (on any issue) is designed to bring one to a point at which the old system simply does not make sense any more. It is here in this tragic place, full of anger and frustration (as the Weakland task force found), that many Catholic women attempt to survive.

CATHOLIC FEMINIST LITERATURE

Though it would be unfair to characterize Catholic women since the Second Vatican Council as moving from hopefulness to despair, one can trace developing clarity in women's perception of the problems. From Sidney Callahan's *The Illusion of Eve* (1965) to Mary Bader Papa's *Christian Feminism* (1981), we can see a change in tone and strategy. Callahan, writing in the expectant atmosphere of the council, perceived a church willing to open itself so that women could take their rightful places within it. Admitting that women have been victimized by distorted exegesis, she concluded with a vision of community "knit together in charity," in which "married women can respond to their responsibility for family, Church and world in many new and different ways." Callahan assumed that a changing church would be more inclusive of women and that women would rise to "face many new and disturbing challenges of Christian freedom and charity."[90] Papa, on the other hand, frustrated with the realities of the present situation, perceives a church *un*willing to empower women, and she has no hesitation in naming the problem with the word *sexism*. Assuming little or no goodwill on the part of church leaders, Papa tries to give women some idea of how to cope with the present situation and how to build a church in which partnership between men and women, clergy and laity, is a real possibility. If Callahan's hope was in "the church," Papa's is in women. Where Callahan ends with a gentle reminder that new days will bring new challenges, Papa ends with a strong, direct challenge to women: "Victim, and collaborator in her own victimization, the woman in the church has a special challenge to defy the sexism that defiles her."[91]

A parallel development can be traced in comparing Sally Cunneen's *Sex: Female; Religion: Catholic* (1968) to Kaye Ashe's *Today's Woman, Tomorrow's Church* (1983). Here we can see a similar method—gathering of data from women about their lives in the church—but a difference in attitude and demand for a solution. Cunneen, like Callahan, wrote in the glow of the council, but her book, full of women's own voices, is not sanguine. Her statistics show women encouraged by the council, more active in American life, and altogether willing to find a way to voice their complaints about clerical complacency and lack of genuine communication in the church. Unhappy with being put on a pedestal in a tradition of discrimination, the women in Cunneen's book want honesty and change: they believe in "the power of the Spirit" to "bring joy" along with the pain of new life.[92] Fundamentally, however, the tone of Cunneen's book is hopeful: the women represented here are unhappy with the way things have been and sense the possibility of change. The women who responded to Ashe's survey are considerably more angry, and Ashe herself is sharp in her assessments and summaries. "While women do not want to grab power," she says, "neither do we intend to wait patiently to be told what we will be allowed to do, and where and under what circumstances." Cunneen saw a church making enormous changes whereas Ashe sees a church trying to negate some of those changes. She predicts that those church leaders "who listen, however, are likely to discover women who may be angry, yes, but who look past anger to . . . a future not of revenge, which would reproduce the past in reverse, but of freedom and independent action, and the creation of something new."[93] Cunneen believed the church would change with the impetus of Vatican II, whereas Ashe sees that it has not changed enough. Both realize that women must voice their own protests and raise their own questions. The central difference between these two books lies in the respondents to the survey: the first group is clear, cautious, and hopeful; the second is angry, much more likely to seek alternatives beyond the church, and much more strident and demanding about implementing the communitarian possibilities of the council.

One of the clearest expressions of the problems and possibilities for women in the parish is Joan Ohanneson's *Woman: Survivor in the Church* (1980). Ohanneson has no hesitation in naming the issue: "I am tired of having God used against me in the politics of exclusion, when I am told, at the same time, that I am a pearl of great price."[94] Women must name ourselves, she says, echoing Mary Daly a dozen years earlier.[95] When women say who they are, they realize that they are essentially *survivors*:

On reflection, it seems to many that they have survived the impossible! They have survived the messages they have received about their bodies, the guilt which almost drowned their souls. They have survived the roles of servant, slave, institutional "sufferer." They have survived as long-suffering mother, silent sister, dutiful daughter, uncomplaining domestic worker. They have survived their silence, their humility, their subservience. They have even survived their own church history which, until now, has largely been a legacy of anonymity.[96]

If women have survived all this, it is only to go forward, says Ohanneson, and her book presents strategies for survival along with descriptions of oppression. She recognizes the courage of those women who have been speaking out within the church, but also notes their potential loss: "Their numbers will either grow or they will vanish. Having cried out with the collective pain of centuries they will decide that the church, the Body of Christ, has no ears with which to hear them. And in despair, they will walk away" (p. 184).

Ohanneson understands those women who have left the church and those who have stayed. She knows that things will not change for women until "women love themselves enough to make [them] happen. That is why the greatest challenge facing the female population in the church today is a public ministry to women: a ministry to women, by women, for women. It is critical because only women can declare, first to themselves and then to each other: This is who I am; this what I need; these are my dreams." Women must "trust their own questions," she says, but more importantly, they must begin to network, to find groups of like-minded women with whom to talk, plan, and take action (p. 185). Alive to the possibility that increasingly, "the Gospel ministry will be exercised apart from the institutional Church" (p. 90). Ohanneson points Catholic women to groups and strategies that ensure women's survival as well as the future of the church.

Women have gifts that are not used within the church. They have experience which is not called upon, and they have power they have never used. In order to make their presence felt and their gifts available to the community, they need freedom and self-determination, neither of which is fully available to them in the present parish situation. Like women in the abolition movement and the New Left movements who realized that they could not change the order of things from within because they did not really have any place or power "within," women in the parish may well find that they want to consider alternatives. As they grow more aware of the negative texts, traditions, canons, and language and the discriminatory practices of Catholicism and at the same time urge their daughters to seek equity and opportunity in civil society, women in the parish will have to wonder why they do not find more justice, charity, honesty, and accountability in the church. What will they do then?

CONCLUSIONS

Women in the parish are in a precarious situation. If middle and upper middle class white women (the majority of the sample in the CARA study) continue to be happy to be "Father's helper," in the parish, we can wonder what the complexion of "women in ministry" will be like in a church that seeks to involve all its women. The pedestaled promises of traditional Catholic teaching are not meant for "bad girls, poor girls, and independent women."[97]

Although the women's movement has challenged sex role stereotyping, the Catholic church continues to proclaim it, by way of complementarity. Whereas feminist theorists frighten some women with their hard questions, and feminist theologians make the clergy nervous, both groups attempt to redefine essential issues and confront the status quo. At some levels the concerns of radical feminists are parallel to those of post–Vatican II Catholicism: both aim at real, nuanced universalism, at structural change, and at social justice. If Catholic feminists sense an affinity between the work of the council and the agenda of feminist theologians, they are not surprised that the institutional church resists the kinds of changes demanded by feminists and prefers to define women in secondary roles with inferior status.

Can a woman be a practicing Catholic and a feminist at the same time?[98] Will the frustrated women represented in the Milwaukee report simply choose to leave the church and seek another community? Will the contented women in the CARA study continue to serve a church that gives them no vote and precious little voice? Do women really have to choose between leaving the heritage of their religious tradition and remaining in it by repressing everything they hear and know about women's autonomy, their needs to name their own experience and to share power?

Though women in the parish have many questions and practical problems, they have no effective organization with which to build an alternative for themselves. Unwilling to relinquish their faith or to sever themselves from an ambiguous tradition rich in spiritual symbolism, Catholic women in the parish often see no real alternative to the situation they find themselves in. If they cannot get what they need and want in the present structure, they remain within it simply because they can see nowhere else to go.

As we shall see in the next chapter, however, sisters have many of the same questions as women in the parish, and they *do* have a massive network of communication and mutual support. As we examine their power in today's church, we will see that it is rooted in the painful experience of their own powerlessness, an experience that women in the parish can easily understand. If we can see sisters as in a position to lead the women's movement in the Catholic church, we might also see that women need an alternative that offers them community, a link with their tradition, a chance for experimentation, and a place where they can really count. The fourth chapter, therefore, will examine the various networks of American Catholic women and look at the Womanchurch movement, which is beginning to provide women in the parish with a real choice by offering them a way out of their double bind. In the Womanchurch movement, Catholic women can abandon the oppressive institutional structures in order to find the power of the gospel. They can deny the power of misogynist traditions and texts in order to celebrate those stories that valorize women. Most importantly, they can begin to get in touch with their own power and to feel the stirrings of the spirit in the collective voices of women. If they were hopeful after Vatican II and then disappointed with the sobering realities of the contemporary situation, they can find in Womanchurch a postconciliar ecclesiology which allows them to say—as the laity did in the early sixties—"We are the church."

3. Inside Outsiders: Sisters and the Women's Movement

The appropriate renewal of religious life involves . . . an adjustment of the community to the changed conditions of the times.

DOCUMENTS OF VATICAN II[1]

We have to get out of our nunny little world.

MARYELLEN MUCKENHIRN

If the church is going to be saved, it's got to make use of its womanpower.

ANITA CASPARY

American sisters have many of the same frustrations as women in the parish: they have been confined to certain roles by way of sex-role stereotyping; their lives, wardrobes, spirituality, and behavior have been set for them by far-removed males; and they have power within the church only insofar as they conform to traditional expectations and do not try to gain a hearing for any of their own issues. Their problems are exacerbated by their history of isolation, as well as by a tradition of superiority and an illusion of power. Up until the Second Vatican Council it would not have occurred to most laywomen to attempt a personal conversation with a nun: sisters lived in consecrated space, closed off from contaminating contact with the world and effectively discouraged from dialogue with other women. Rather than suggesting deprivation, their isolation projected an image of superiority. Sisters were incarnations of the "eternal feminine,"[1] chosen by God to be brides of Christ. They were heroically dedicated to a materially austere but spiritually rich life that—as official church documents made clear many times—was far superior to ordinary life. "Although the term 'religious' has been a juridical and canonical designation used in canon law to distinguish between 'religious life' and the secular life, it has in effect perpetuated a caste system between religious and laity."[2] Whether laywomen were angered, or intimidated, by religious aloof ness, the effect was the same: sisters and laywomen had minimal con-tact and seldom met or interacted as one woman to another. Lastly, sisters were perceived as a force within the church, believed to have moral power based in sanctity and to enjoy a quasi-clerical status.

While sisters did not have "priestly powers," they were thought to be members of the club, part of the institution. In its radical reevalua-tion of traditional Catholicism, the Second Vatican Council attempted to disabuse Catholics of their perception of nuns as clerics. Sisters, the council said, are laywomen, so defined by canon law. "Yet this asser-tion never makes much sense to laywomen since it is obvious that, if nuns are technically 'laywomen,' they are not exactly 'laywomen' in the same sense as women who do not belong to any religious congrega-tion."[3] Sisters, therefore, though defined as laywomen, are still per-ceived by many women in the parish as officials within the institution.

In fact, however, sisters have very little power in the institutional church. Rosemary Radford Ruether maintains that "the present insis-tence of canon law that nuns are laywomen represents the end process of a long effort by the hierarchy to demote nuns from their original status as members of the clergy."[4] Less influential than they were in the ancient church or during the Middle Ages, "religious women" have found themselves continually reminded of their vulnerability in the last twenty years. Their postconciliar renewal process showed them how limited their own decisions were when in conflict with any male authority; the mandated revisions of their constitutions are now being submitted to obdurate scrutiny in Rome;[5] and their attempts to exam-ine and reject their "superior state" have met with resistance not only by clerical officials but by laypeople with a stake in the myth of the otherworldly innocence of religious life.

Sisters are done a disservice both by those who want to fix them on pedestals *and* by those who embody their Catholic grade school memories in angry plays about sadistic nuns. Pedestalization robs the object of devotion of any real freedom of movement and is not sought by those who want to define their own lives and work. Hostility can also be paralyzing, and is often punitive. Does a patriarchal culture imbue us with unconscious desires to punish what appear to be inde-pendent women? Nuns have, in much of Western history, been the only organized group to provide a separate role for women.[6] If this distinction has given them some power and independence, they have also been punished for daring to go beyond patriarchal definitions. In literature and popular culture sisters have suffered outrageous idealization and pornographic appropriation: the nun as eternally sweet and uncomplaining is a ready-made sexless virgin "who will work men's salvation for them and love it,"[7] whereas the nun as whore, the sadist in habit complete with boots and whip, is the dangerous, seductive, insatiable, and malicious femme fatale whose cruelty is interlaced with religious themes. On the one hand, therefore, nuns have been pedestalized, appearing to have transcended the tribulations of ordinary womanhood; on the other, they have been standard symbols for the two most pervasive and vicious female stereotypes, virgin and whore. Precisely because they are not mothers, wives, or young daughters, nuns are an ideal symbol for misogynist projections.

Contemporary sisters are moving into yet another phase of their own renewal process, but recent Roman directives to American bishops are designed to thwart any further "progress." Subject to absolute episcopal control, nuns are not "quasi-clerical" and do not have even the limited powers priests exercise over their own lives. At heart, sisters have an interest in the same issues as radical feminists and women in the parish: they care about universalism, structural change, and social justice. More importantly, however, nuns have organizations and organizational skills, networks that women in the parish do not have and that radical feminists are trying to build. Because of their experience with "religious life," sisters have a deep understanding of bonding, and they know how to work collectively to attain their goals. Their experience in the last thirty years has also taught them how powerless they are in a male-dominated, hierarchical institution: they have little to lose and much to gain by challenging the system.

SUBVERSION OF TRADITIONAL ROLES: "THE OUTSIDERS' SOCIETY"

Like female children in Victorian society, nuns have been cast in the role of the "dutiful daughter." Writing in the mid-1960s about the

"changing sister," Angelica Seng discussed the obstacles to be over-
come in establishing better relations with the rectory. "Many sisters,"
she said, "have been conditioned, in the name of a pseudo-reverence
and obedience, to regard their relations with priests and especially with
the pastor as one of silence, obedience and dependence. Perhaps it is
something akin to a father–daughter relationship, in which the daughter
never even reaches the adolescent stage."[8] Derogatory roles can be
subverted or made powerful by sheer dint of numbers, but willingness and ability to experiment with new roles usually comes only when
one can become free of an imposed stereotype. One way to achieve
this freedom is to perceive oneself as outside the system, since outsiders are usually in a much clearer position to oppose an institution.

In 1938, in an angry, creative response to a request for financial support from a pacifist organization, Virginia Woolf defended her unwillingness to join their group and outlined a radical feminist tactic. In
proposing an alternative society to respond to a variety of the world's
needs, she wittily but unwittingly described a vantage point to which
many American sisters can probably relate. Women, she said, have four
great teachers that, properly adhered to, become virtues: by accepting *poverty*, they promise to earn enough to be independent but no more;
by living a life of *chastity*, they refuse to sell their talents or brains for
money and prefer to pursue a work for its own sake; by living with
derision, women refuse to advertise themselves, holding "that ridicule,
obscurity and censure are preferable, for psychological reasons, to fame
and praise"; and by staying *free from unreal loyalties*, they rid themselves
of national, religious, or family pride, so as not to be co-opted by those
who would seduce or bribe them into captivity. According to Woolf,
these virtues prove that women do not have to *get* outside the system;
they are already outside it and form the cornerstones of a new society:
"If name it must have, it could be called the Outsiders' Society. That is
not a resonant name, but it has the advantage that it squares with facts —
the facts of history, of law, of biography."[9] Woolf's reasoning was simple: since women are not permitted to be educated, or ordained, or to
take part in the professions, since they are at the mercy of laws written
to their disadvantage and are ruled by tyrannical fathers or husbands,
they are, in fact, not part of the system. Women are, perforce, outsiders.

Woolf obviously was not referring to sisters but to all women, and although some of the specifics of her argument no longer obtain — women today are permitted to get an education, for example — her point about women as outsiders is still persuasive. If women are really outside the system, however, we can ask why they do not admit it and bond together to form a collective alternative to an oppressive society. This question is central to Carolyn Heilbrun's advocacy of the reinvention of womanhood. Women, she says, organize their lives so as to avoid the acutely painful recognition that they are outsiders, and in ignoring this fact, they cooperate in their own oppression. "To perceive their own suffering would be to open them to other suffering, to rob them of the protection they have carefully built up against the experience of pain. Women have avoided adventure, risk and opportunity because they have been taught that suffering, the shaking loose of the comfortable foundations of one's life, must be avoided at all costs."[10]

Dorothy Sölle's stages of suffering help to explain the avoidance. In its first stage, suffering is mute, isolated, and accepting; in its second, it is lamenting, aware, and articulate about the pain; and finally, suffering leads to change by way of solidarity, organization for the conquest of powerlessness.[11] Most women have become fixated at stage one: they are "dominated by the situation . . . and see [their] proper action as submissiveness and powerlessness."[12] Ironically, nuns, who might have been characterized as saintly inhabitants of stage one twenty years ago, have been directed by their oppressors to move through the remaining stages. When Pope Pius XII mandated adaptation to the modern world and upgraded education for sisters, he began a process of self-perception that led to articulation and change.

In the late 1940s, as sisters began the long process of looking at themselves and their place in the church, they found themselves in the very situation that Woolf described. Education had been closed to them or kept to a bare minimum; ordination was out of the question; they were usually forced into stereotypical lives, even though a few of them were allowed to pursue "male" professions in intellectual or administrative life; they were bound by unfair laws written against them and for them with no consultation whatsoever; and they were at the mercy of the "fathers" in Rome. They were outsiders with an insider's profile. In terms of their relationship with the women's movement, their recognition of outsider status was crucial: "one does not apparently awaken to the awareness of being a female outsider, unless the condition of 'outsiderness' has, through other means, entered one's consciousness."[13] Though Woolf recognized the connection between bonding and becoming a force within society, she also knew that women's first task was to recognize themselves both as outsiders and as having some status independent of that granted to them by fathers and husbands.

Increasingly, women in the Catholic church may be forced to claim Woolf's insight, to perceive themselves as outsiders whose true affinity is with the active wing of the women's movement. They may even see the logic in Woolf's program for her society's members: to work for peace, liberty, and equality; to investigate and criticize universities and churches; to support women's education and professional life; to promote women's sports for their own sakes; and, perhaps, to create a new religion.[14] They may also find that in order to be effective they must not repeat the words and follow the methods of the system, but find "new words and creat[e] new methods," and be most helpful "not by joining . . . society but by remaining outside" it (p. 143). Whatever American Catholic laywomen discover about themselves and their position within the church, sisters may well have discerned it first. In a fascinating conjunction of papal directives, personal experience, and conciliar urgings, American sisters were moved in the 1950s to look squarely at themselves and their status. Their renewal process led them more deeply into a discovery of themselves as women even as it gave them new theological skills and spiritual insights. The renewal of religious life prepared great numbers of American sisters to assume positions of leadership in the postconciliar church and in the emergence of Catholic feminism.

GETTING FREE FROM ENCUMBRANCES: RENEWAL OF RELIGIOUS LIFE

From ancient times, membership in the body of Christ was conferred through baptism so that there were no distinctions of Christian dignity or destiny among members. Nevertheless, as the early community moved from an apparently equalitarian structure to a hierarchical arrangement,[15] differences arose between clerics and nonclerics that eventually led to a notion of clerical superiority. At its worst, clericalism appropriated the church for the clergy, so that the church was defined as the pope, bishops, and priests, with the laity supporting the work of the church by cooperating with the clergy. The preconciliar understanding of Catholic Action, for example, assured the laity that they could participate in the work of the church by helping the bishops. The post-Vatican II slogan "We are the church," therefore, expressed both a surge of power felt by the laity in the sixties and a reaction against an ecclesiological model that identified the church with the clergy.

In its early stages, religious life developed in a context of moral superiority and was supported philosophically by a dualism that separated the secular from the sacred. Eventually, the sacred became the realm of those in "religious life," but the term laity, encompassing as it does all nonordained persons, did not originally support internal distinctions of merit, even though it was apparent that some Christians were more dedicated, more heroic under torture, more given to prayer, fasting, and almsgiving than others. Gradually, however, especially in the context of persecution—when heroism and cowardice were manifestly visible—differences between ordinary and extraordinary Christians began to emerge. The designation "confessor," for example, was reserved for those survivors who had endured torture without rescinding their belief in Christ: confessors were a people set apart, honored for their strength and recognized as vessels of divine grace. Their distinction, therefore, was based not on office, but on merit and achievement. When the persecutions ended in the early part of the fourth century, those searching for alternative ways to demonstrate their total and heroic dedication to God fled to the desert in order to confront the demons through prayer and fasting.[16] Adopting practices of asceticism, a system of discipline devised by Greek philosophers and others to combat vice and enhance virtue, these early Christian monks and nuns understood themselves to be aiming for perfection. When a literature began to build up around this new eremitical life, interpreters recalled a second-century penitential text that made an extraordinary promise: good works *beyond the commands of Jesus* win more glory.[17] Since one interpretation of the gospel admits that Jesus demanded total surrender to God, it may be hard to imagine what good works were possible beyond that command. Yet within a short time, a distinction was made about the requirements for the Christian life that separated "commands" from "counsels." The former applied to all Christians, whereas only those seeking perfection were called to observe the latter. These so-called counsels of perfection—poverty, chastity, and obedience—formed the basis for "religious life" in the church, a state existing somewhere between the laity and the clergy yet superior to both, since neither laity nor clergy were called to or vowed to follow the counsels of perfection.

As religious life was increasingly understood to reflect the spiritual rather than the material world, the distance between "religious" and laity widened: spirituality became the province of those vowed to religious life, and the laity were gradually disenfranchised from an increasingly clerical and monastic church. If religious life was also essentially "masculine,"[18] that only meant that women who wished to lead lives of perfection had to deny their sexuality with sufficient fervor to inspire the compliment reserved for the most heroic female saints, namely, "she has become a man."[19] Nuns, therefore, called by God to lead a life of perfection, fled from the world, the flesh, and the devil by promising to be poor, chaste, and obedient. The rewards for such heroic self-sacrifice were closeness to God—obviously impossible in "the world"—and a strong sense that one was living in a superior way of life.

So long as the church maintained the antagonistic dualism of secular and sacred, those closer to the sacred realm were part of an elite. As more complex modern developments blurred, perhaps even obliterated, the distinction between the secular and the sacred, however, the supports for an elitist interpretation of religious life disappeared despite the fact that many of the trappings of that life remained. Mid-twentieth-century sisters were challenged to understand themselves as laywomen who were also members of religious congregations. No longer extolled for having chosen a superior way of life, they had to reimagine religious life in secular terms, a long and gradually radicalizing process of renewal that began long before Vatican II.

Renewal is often thought to be a synonym for the changing lifestyle of sisters. Indeed, the dramatic changes in clothing and behavior were long overdue. Before the renewal process began every detail of convent life was dictated with equal firmness:

Being dressed in a particular way, walking always in icy cloisters, eating at scrubbed tables—all these things came to constitute the very identity of nuns themselves. Although a founder might have been a woman of quite staggering courage and independence in her time, her modes of thought and behavior were bound to lose their pioneering flavor with the passing of centuries. But her community continued to cling to the old observances. So the original spirit of her order—the fearless innovation and the brave initiative—was lost, drowned in a welter of archaic absurdities: refectory regulations patterned on the eating habits of eighteenth-century French peasants, stilted recreational practices of a Victorian household, clothes of sixteenth-century Belgian widows.[20]

The more dramatic aspect of renewal, however, was educational. Higher standards in the American school system, augmented by papal encouragement to adapt to modern times, moved sisters toward dynamic change.

EDUCATION AND FORMATION

For a number of reasons, Americans in general took a greater interest in education after the First World War. No longer was an eighth-grade certificate sufficient for advancement in our society: from the early 1920s on, the goal was secondary education for everyone. When a high school diploma became a minimum requirement for young people, an enormous burden was placed on the nation's teachers. Those who taught in private or small country schools were shocked to find that they now needed a baccalaureate degree to teach high school and a two-year certificate (plus summer school until the baccalaureate was completed) to teach elementary students. "State and regional accrediting agencies that made college degrees for teachers . . . mandatory had somewhat the effect of an earthquake in the hitherto tranquil lives of Sisters in the immediate pre- and post-World War period."[21] Sisters had been accustomed to on-the-job training: they had been teaching for years on a combination of goodwill, self-education, tutorial supervision, and holy obedience. Because they concentrated on basic skills and had a reputation for teaching them very well, sisters lived in an unreal educational world in which college degrees were luxuries and the intellectual life always a little suspect. Where state requirements allowed five to fifteen years experience to count in place of a degree, older sisters could operate within the system until younger ones received at least a two-year certificate. Many of these younger sisters then took another twenty years to complete their college education. "The whole educational process of the times became a rush for credits, seen as a necessary expedient, but a fact that was to militate for many years . . . against a love of knowledge for its own sake and an appreciation of the life of the intellect."[22]

Because of the anti-intellectualism of religious life in general and the excruciating demands the obtaining of an education placed on a sister trying to live within the rules of a medieval cloister, college degrees were, as often as not, experienced as penitential. Furthermore, the financial burden on religious congregations for hundreds of college degrees was prohibitive, and many communities found themselves caught between state requirements and the demands of bishops and priests who disagreed with the requirements and/or found their own immediate need for teachers more important than teacher preparation.

The problems facing American sisters in terms of education were, therefore, enormous. Beginning with Pope Pius XI and extending through the time of Pope Paul VI, papal support was necessary in motivating sisters to adapt to the modern world and to upgrade their educational background in order to be able to stand in the forefront of the church's apostolic life. The real power for renewal, however, lay in the initiatives of American sisters themselves: they identified the problems, sought concrete help, and worked collectively to redress the situation.

In 1941, Sister Bertrande Meyers published her St. Louis University doctoral dissertation: *The Education of Sisters* was an appraisal of twenty-five years of part-time attendance by sisters at colleges and universities.[23] Meyers interviewed sisters all over the country and pointed to the deplorable schedules they were trying to follow. More importantly, she attempted to assess the effects of higher education, acquired under appallingly rigid circumstances, on the religious, social, intellectual, professional, and apostolic facets of religious life. The results of her study were predictably dismal: sisters had not lost their fervor, but neither could they identify any positive results of their exposure to higher education. "As a matter of fact, in the majority of cases, the experience seems to have destroyed rather than nurtured any love of learning."[24] There appeared to be no discernible growth in leadership qualities, spiritual outlook, or intellectual awareness. Furthermore, superiors of congregations found themselves facing what appeared to be insoluble dilemmas: they were almost completely isolated from other communities and so had no support network, and they were criticized by "bishops [and] priests [who] could not quite grasp the necessity of holding a young Sister back until she was fully formed, academically and spiritually, to enter the profession of teaching."[25]

In 1949, as part of a panel discussion at the National Catholic Educational Association (NCEA), Sister Madeleva Wolff presented a paper later reprinted and widely distributed as a booklet, *The Education of Sister Lucy*: she argued that young sisters were treasures, not machines, and that an integrated, well-paced, clearly designed training program was necessary if sisters were to take their most helpful place in the American church.[26]

The work of Meyers, Wolff, and others was evidently noticed in Rome, where Pope Pius XII redoubled his efforts in the interests of educating sisters. In 1950 the first International Congress of Religious met in Rome. Sisters were told "that the shortage of vocations was not a cause but rather an effect of individual Communities clinging to antiquated customs."[27] The Sacred Congregation of Religious, they were told, "would look favorably upon requests for any changes in constitution, rule, custom and ascetical practices that would modernize the spirit and works of the individual Community" (p. 46). More importantly, the congress supported collaboration among communities and helped sisters lay the foundations of collective interaction.

Fired by official support and eager to adapt to the demands of the modern church, American superiors held their first National Congress of Major Superiors at Notre Dame in 1952. The desire for further collaboration was apparent, and the continued interest in sister education led to discussion of new concepts: the "words 'formation' and 'houses of formation'— new words in their new contexts — were being proposed, described and discussed." The fact that "these rich developments of the religious life were entering . . . convents by the 'oblique route of education' took nothing from the glad tidings" (p. 49).

A month later, the second international congress was held in Rome, this time with an emphasis on education. Roman officials supported the new idea of congregational "juniorates" to educate young sisters, and they helped sisters to resist bishops who wanted to bypass the process: from the secretary of the Sacred Congregation of Religious, "Superiors received authority, which might be called a mandate, to withhold young Sisters from the apostolate until the spiritual and religious formation, begun in the novitiate, had been integrated with the intellectual and professional" (p. 56). *Aggiornamento* (modernization, bringing up to date), a word not heard until the Second Vatican Council a decade later, was thus officially under way in religious congregations of women in the mid-1950s: higher education was essential to its process, and Roman officials were demanding and supporting a well-paced, modernizing evolution of religious life.

In its practical aspects, renewal began with a revision of the *horaria*, the hours of a "typical day," and a questioning of traditional but outmoded customs. In an effort to integrate education with formation so as to develop the sister as a "a *whole* person, thus eliminating the dichotomy of the interior and the exterior life, of work and prayer, which gives rise to so many anxieties in a Sister's mind and inhibits her full development" (p. 105), the Sister Formation Conference (SFC) was established in 1954. Headed by Sister Mary Emil Penet, and sponsored by the National Catholic Education Association and later by the Conference of Major Superiors, the SFC received a $50,000 Ford Foundation grant in 1956 to develop a college curriculum appropriate to and specifically for sisters. Almost overnight, 150 Sister Formation Centers sprang up in the United States and were instrumental in persuading bishops to endure a three-year wait while young sisters finished their education. In terms of renewal, as Meyers has noted, the "decade 1950–60 was to make the greatest changes in the active Orders of women during their more than three centuries of existence" (p. 59).

LEADERSHIP AND BONDING

In fact, the 1950s were only the beginning. Led and supported by the pope and the Sacred Congregation of Religious, American sisters in the 1950s responded enthusiastically to challenges of formation and sister education. By the 1980s, however, sisters were increasingly identifying their own issues, embracing feminism as a social justice concern, and were, by various ways and means, being opposed by the pope and the Sacred Congregation.[28] The change, over thirty years, was gradual and logical. The 1950s were devoted to organization: the Conference of Major Superiors of Women (CMSW) began in 1956 as a national forum for the exchange of ideas and as a way to coordinate the professional, apostolic and religious life of sisters. It was approved by the Holy See in 1959 and the decade ended with a real sense of accomplishment because genuine renewal had begun.

The 1960s began with cooperation between sisters and Rome but ended with some skepticism. Early in the decade the Vatican asked 10 percent of American sisters to volunteer for service in Latin America and received an overwhelmingly generous response as twenty thousand American sisters were trained for and sent to work there; the radicalizing impact of the Latin American experience was and continues to be a crucial part of the development of American sisters. In the middle of the decade, CMSW sent a unanimous petition to Rome asking to be represented on commissions dealing with the lives of sisters and received no reply, chillingly reminded that communication between Rome and American sisters was meant to be one-way. By the end of the decade, sisters were finding themselves inspired not only by the energy of the council but also by the vision of their founders and the objectives of the newly burgeoning women's movement. Sisters were moved to claim their own voice and shape their own destiny.

CMSW began to branch out in the 1960s and to examine the major effects of the Second Vatican Council on religious life. At an "official" level, Rome sent a questionnaire to assess the "actual conditions" of religious life for American sisters, and the council "fathers" invited the president of CMSW, Mary Luke Tobin, a Sister of Loretto, to the last two sessions of the council as an auditor. In the arena of social justice, CMSW supported sisters marching for civil rights in Selma, petitioned for "just salaries" for sisters, and hired a management consultant firm to help with geographical realignment and governmental reconstruction.

The major undertaking of CMSW in the 1960s, however, was the National Sisters' Survey, commissioned by the conference and directed by Sister Marie Augusta Neal, a Harvard-trained sociologist at Emmanuel College in Boston. Neal, with help from a committee of professionals, designed a massive questionnaire and received an 88 percent response: her statistics and interpretations helped to explain what would later be a key issue in the sisters' involvement in the women's movement, namely, the relation between religious belief and support for structural change.[29] In some ways, it could be said that Neal tallied the effects of the council on American sisters: she compared differences in beliefs characterized as pre-Vatican II and post-Vatican II and found that those sisters who preferred older theologies also tended to perceive their own goals as adjusting to existing conditions within church and society, whereas those sisters who read postconciliar theologians and imbibed the spirit of Vatican II were more likely to aim at the transformation of society. Her work also showed how powerful an influence the Sister Formation Conference had on American sisters: by insisting on proper professional training of sisters, SFC supported the "massive education of religious women in liberal arts colleges and professional schools, and the personal encounter with the meaning of the new theology," which, in turn, showed "how effectively religious had been co-opted by established institutions resisting change."[30] Neal's work was sobering and challenging; CMSW responded to it in different ways throughout the next decade.

In 1970 CMSW underscored its commitment to social justice by calling for a shift in priorities away from internal reorganization toward service to others. A distinctive symbol of a changing perspective was its change of name from Conference of Major Superiors of Women to Leadership Conference of Women Religious (LCWR), signaling a public acknowledgment that their thinking about authority had changed and that their structural self-perception did not find its best expression in notions of "superiors."[31] More importantly, it allowed them to name themselves, to state their own identity as they experienced it. Whatever their reasons, the changes were not welcomed in Rome, and the Sacred Congregation for Religious and Secular Institutes (SCRIS) withheld formal approval of the name change for three years.[32] LCWR used its new name from the beginning (1971), and it is important to note their persistence in the face of official opposition.

The decade of the 1970s was devoted to world solidarity, liberation themes and women's issues. LCWR endorsed and supported Network, a Washington-based lobbying group of sisters interested in social justice and feminist issues; they initiated a large-scale collaborative conversation of national sister groups in "Sisters Uniting"[33] and supported the Center of Concern, an "independent, inter-disciplinary team engaged in social analysis, religious reflection and public education around questions of social justice with particular stress on the international dimension."[34] Their executive officers began going places besides meetings of sisters: they attended meetings of American bishops as observers, went to Russia to explore the plight of Soviet Jews, sent representatives to International Women's Year in Mexico City (1975) and traveled throughout the world of social justice concerns. Led increasingly by their own agenda, LCWR endorsed the Equal Rights Amendment, joined the ecumenical committee for support of the ERA, sponsored workshops on consumerism and economic justice, wrote and distributed consciousness-raising packets on world hunger and feminism, and grew increasingly interested in Third World issues. The Inter-American conferences have had a tremendous impact: these periodic meetings of representatives from LCWR, the Conference of Major Superiors of Men (CMSM), the Confederation of Latin American Religious (CLAR), and the Canadian Religious Conference (CRC) have helped to bring the Latin American situation to the attention of sisters in the United States and have had the effect of making social justice a more global concern. More aware of themselves as women — as outsiders — LCWR requested the appointment of women to the Synod of Bishops and to SCRIS, even though their appeals were repeatedly ignored. More directly, one of the "assembly goals" of the 1976 meeting was "the empowerment of women," and in 1978 LCWR unveiled a five-year plan to promote study, prayer, and action on women's issues.

The decade ended with the president of LCWR "greeting the pope in Washington": Theresa Kane urged the pope "to be mindful of the intense suffering and pain that is part of the life of many women . . . to hear the call of women . . . [to be] included in all ministries of our church."[35] The papal response to Kane was similar to the Vatican response to CMSW in 1965: silence, this time made awkward by the glare of publicity. To many it may have looked as if Kane had overstepped her bounds—some sisters were quick to make an apology to the pope and to disavow any connection with "the public rudeness shown him by Sister Theresa Kane"[36]—but to those in the conference, it was the needed rupture of a long silence.

Since 1972 LCWR had consistently requested an audience with the pope and just as consistently been ignored. It is difficult to imagine a more convincing evidence of "outsiders' status." Kane's petition called attention to a glaring injustice in the Catholic church, but it also set up her own congregation, the Sisters of Mercy of the Union, for special disciplinary scrutiny and inspired a new wave of negative attention from SCRIS to American sisters.

In the 1980s renewal is a radically new endeavor, because the numbers are changing so dramatically and because sisters themselves have developed into a genuinely new breed. From a peak of more than 180,000 sisters in 1966, membership in religious orders has dropped to 130,000 in 1985 and some predict a drop to 60,000 by the end of the century. The sociologist Andrew Greeley believes that "in the long run there will be no more orders of women in the United States."[37] His prediction, however, begs the question: What constitutes a religious order of women, and how might alternative communities be imagined? In many ways, that is the challenge of renewal in the 1980s.

Sisters' experience in the 1950s taught them the value of collective work and networking: long before the women's movement was advising women to "network for strength," sisters in SFC had formed a background of association that would later solidify in LCWR.[38] Nuns in the 1960s took a long look at themselves in community meetings, through a spate of books describing "the new nuns,"[39] and by way of the National Sisters' Survey; in the end, they saw themselves as change agents, women capable of naming themselves, setting their own agenda, and collaborating for justice in the world. Their efforts in the 1970s to secure justice in civil spheres taught them that real justice was linked to systemic change: the principles of justice, they learned, could be used to evaluate structures as well as individuals. The 1971 Synod of Bishops emphasized what many sisters were coming to believe, that ecclesiastical credibility depended upon the church's own accountability to the principles of justice.[40] The church, therefore, was not immune to social justice analysis.

Renewal in the 1980s has been bound up with ministry to the marginalized: contemporary sisters make "good copy" for major metropolitan newspapers because many readers are not accustomed to thinking about nuns running drop-in centers for bag ladies, acting as attorneys in slum neighborhood storefront offices, and being tortured and killed in Central America.[41] If sisters have found more satisfying ministries, however, they have also found less satisfying places within the institutional church. Sisters, like many laywomen who are leaving the church, have problems living within a sacramental structure that is clearly sexist and apparently oblivious to feminist questions. Sisters, like many laywomen, have found themselves relating to each other for spiritual direction, theological insights, and liturgical celebration, thus displacing "father" as a central authority figure in their religious lives. Their work in social justice arenas has, by logical extension, drawn them to a deeper commitment to the women's movement: the "feminization of poverty" has led many of those ministering to the poor to examine the structures that impoverish women and children first. Most of all, however, sisters have experienced profound changes in their understanding of authority and church.[42]

Old concepts of authority rested on the belief that God is absolute truth, that the Roman Catholic church has a direct line to the deity and therefore speaks for God. When these values were internalized, they demanded obedience without question and gave believers a sense of security that rested on belonging to an institution with a divinely guided teaching authority. Contemporary understandings of authority, however, lead people to question everything, to understand as much as possible, and to see that security is sometimes another name for stagnation. The old injunction to "obey in all things but sin" bypasses questions of truth and suggests that making decisions, especially about religious matters, is dangerous. Contemporary understandings of spirituality and theology, on the other hand, stress the importance of context and relationship—with others and with God—and point to the fact that nothing is accomplished without risk. Authority, finally, if it is to stand in the stream of the Jesus tradition, must be linked with service.

During the twenty-fifth anniversary celebration of LCWR in 1981, a panel of past presidents presented a historical recapitulation: Mary Luke Tobin spoke about the Vatican II years, the hopefulness after the council and the empowerment sisters felt when they understood themselves to be change agents; Margaret Brennan expressed the acute pain sisters felt as Rome continually refused to meet with LCWR, and concluded that it was the leadership of *women* that put sisters into some conflict with the institutional church; Joan Chittester voiced the anger and urgency many sisters felt at being ignored by Rome and at being put into a conflict situation by the simple fact of having a feminist consciousness in a sexist church; and Mary Daniel Turner, analyzing the differences between power and violence, urged sisters to begin to develop a theology of power in order to resist violent uses of power by anyone, even church officials.[43] Their recapitulation is reminiscent of Woolf's "Outsiders' Society," expressing hopefulness gradually stifled by male authority. Recognizing the conflict they are in—seeing themselves as outsiders—they have bonded together and now look for the possibilities inherent in their collective strength.

As sisters have grown more restive and challenging in the last few years, hints of disapproval have begun to come from the Vatican: communities have been indirectly warned that the Vatican might not approve their new constitutions or might withdraw approbation from LCWR. These "suggestions," experienced by many as veiled threats and as a misuse of power, put sisters in an awkward yet potentially creative position. Most sisters do not want to lose their connection with the church: if they did, they might not find locations for their ministry, they might lose the support of bishops and people. On the other hand, sisters have read enough new theology and have had enough collective experience in the last thirty years to question ecclesiological models before they capitulate to fears for their institutional lives. If their connection with the institution has always been with the hierarchical church, they wonder if they might try to forge a link with a different model.

Greeley's prediction about the end of religious orders of women is based upon the past, in which groups of women relate to a patriarchal model of church, seek its approval, agree to be circumscribed by its limits, and allow themselves to be subjected to whatever sanctions the institution issues. Sisters today show a strong unwillingness to align themselves so uncritically with that model: LCWR is clear about its sense of growing consciousness and conscience, articulate about itself as prophetic, and willing to bond and to take risks. Sisters' values are no longer totally consistent with the hierarchical model: nuns seek autonomy and self-definition, freedom, commitment to key issues, affirmation of themselves as change agents. They also face pain with strength and courage. Though they did not sense or intend that their own perceptions of themselves would come into conflict with the institutional church, they now know that sisters *are* in conflict with the Vatican authorities. Their present position and the wrenching questions it poses come not only from the process of renewal, but also from a new consciousness of themselves as women. The other side of the renewal process shows how sisters have come to be feminists.

FROM RENEWAL TO RADICALIZATION: SISTERS AS FEMINISTS

Renewal was clearly aimed at adaptation to the modern world in terms of education and organization; its predictable outcome was a radical consciousness raising about the nature of religious life in a patriarchal institution. Perhaps Vatican officials so needed the resources of American sisters that they were blind to the risks of the educational experiment,[44] or perhaps they believed that sisters were too docile to be empowered by collective action. Whatever the reasons, church authorities encouraged the very education and collaboration that eventually led, paradoxically, to significant involvement of American Catholic nuns in the women's movement.

SOCIOLOGICAL ANALYSIS

In the various books about the "new nuns" written in the 1960s, sisters used sociological analysis to understand their past and imagine a new future. Goffman's analysis of "total societies," explained one sister interpreter, "is hard to match . . . as a guide to the perversions of community."[45] Goffman was interested in asylums, not convents. His insight was that total societies handle human need by way of bureaucratic organization—a large managed group with a small supervisory staff and with little social mobility between them, and in which each group imagines the other in terms of narrow, hostile stereotypes. This idea resonated with what many sisters had experienced as religious life. The very notion of "management" requires steps to make people manageable: the inmates Goffman studied were forced to break with the past, had little or no contact with their former world, were dispossessed of their own clothes, names, and keepsakes, were divested of adult self-concepts by being forced to ask permission for almost everything, and were subjected to a total invasion of privacy. Once an inmate was made pliable, he or she could be reconstructed: habitually deprived persons obtain gratification from small gifts and permissions.

When Sister Aloysius Schaldenbrand used Goffman to interpret convent life, she noted the central difference between nuns and inmates: sisters chose their life freely, had theological reasons for self-mortification, and understood themselves as opening the self to God's transforming grace. At the same time, she pointed to the fact that Goffman was interested in effects rather than motivation and that convents, regardless of the motivation of their members, needed to understand the "total society" model, be aware of its tendency to control members, and listen to the voices of social scientists. Religious life, she said, though not always approaching the extreme model of Goffman's asylum, did have "total society" tendencies that needed to be continually interrogated: high-handed "superiors" who understood themselves as managers, a reward system based on conformity, the equating of humility with inferiority, overemphasis on rule observance, arid life conditions, denial of human dignity, and the attempt to exist as a self-contained unit with no interest in "the world." All these tendencies had to be criticized as nuns learned to adapt to the modern world. How far Goffman's analysis described life in convents is not as important as the fact that sisters often found quite a resemblance. Schaldenbrand and others opened sisters to a new self-understanding and to the importance of sociological insight.

Much of the early work of Marie Augusta Neal echoed the need for sociological analysis that can show how social control operates and how change is possible.[46] Neal's interests were twofold: to challenge the traditional "family model" of religious life and to criticize sisters' minimal response to social needs. Sisters, she said, had to build new models of community in the modern world. By abandoning a model that relied on gratefully obedient "children" ruled by a superior "mother," nuns could empower themselves to reconstruct the social order. Until sisters were in a position to ask structural questions, she argued, they would always be caught between the poor, to whom they ministered, and those on whom they relied for financial and emotional support: those who had rich patrons would become servants of the rich, content to staff benevolent institutions rather than to follow the gospels and social encyclicals of the church, which demanded a more radical response to social disorder.

Helen Rose Fuchs Ebaugh's work in the late 1970s reported on the changes religious communities had made on the basis of sociological analysis. Her study of organizational dilemmas charted the progress communities made from a "total society" model to a type of voluntary organization in which members joined together to achieve a common purpose. Her conclusions are worth quoting at length:

The most tenuous and challenging area for religious orders presently is a redefinition of organizational goals, especially in terms of apostolic commitments. . . . It is perhaps time for religious orders to undergo a succession of goals and to discover a unique role for themselves in the current church and larger world. While teaching and nursing were primary needs of an immigrant, rural church in eighteenth and nineteenth century America, issues which are just as real and poignant in today's church might well be the needs of minority groups and the white poor and the political and radical injustices prevalent in society. Or, perhaps, it is time for American religious women to begin . . . to think in terms of service to the Third World, where the impact of a group of highly committed, dedicated women could be dramatically felt. It is also possible that religious orders will need to refocus their goals away from service tasks and toward an emphasis upon creating a supportive community for members. . . . The goal of religious orders, therefore, becomes group centered rather than service oriented. What members do jobwise becomes far less important than their sharing together a supportive group life that meets the needs of the members. When this occurs, religious orders become part of the larger communitarian movement increasingly evident in the Western world in the past decade.[47]

Part of the renewal process, therefore, was a new self-understanding made possible through sociological analysis. Knowing what religious life had been gave sisters some power to imagine what it could be in the future in terms of both community life and community goals.

AWARENESS OF VULNERABILITY

Another side of renewal, however, was a heightened awareness of vulnerability: those sisters who attempted to "renew" themselves beyond the boundaries set by local authorities were forced into serious confrontation with their bishops. The "outsider" status became devastatingly real and was experienced corporately and personally. On a personal level, those sisters who were sent away to study often met sisters from other places, encounterd new ideas, and found themselves so changed by their experience that they became outsiders in their own congregations, forced to fight the hierarchy in their communities in order to achieve structural change. In the corporate clash with the hierarchy, sisters were told to choose between obedience and loss of canonical status. They were thus placed in a double bind: if they followed the mandated renewal process to rid themselves of those religious restrictions that interfered with their ministry, they would lose ecclesiastical approbation. The Glenmary Sisters in Cincinnati, who worked among the rural poor in Appalachia, chose to redefine themselves as a community of laywomen working with the poor. "In September 1965, Cincinnati Archbishop Karl Alter restricted the sisters' hours, table reading, educational courses and contacts with nonreligious," all of which inhibited their ministry. "The once 102-member Glenmary order will dwindle to about 15 sisters in August when 50 nuns leave to work together as laywomen," a Catholic newspaper reported.[48] It was the first major departure of nuns from an American religious order, but it was not the most famous: in 1968 the Immaculate Heart of Mary Sisters in Los Angeles (IHM) "defied their cardinal by refusing to retract any of the reforms on which they had embarked in response to Vatican II."[49] Their forced decision to leave religious life en masse shocked the American Catholic church and made clear sisters' vulnerability to male authorities.

The IHMs, founded in Spain in 1848 as a semicloistered community, had come to California in 1858 and promptly built schools and adapted to the new mission territory. By 1924, they had changed sufficiently to be virtually unwelcome in the Spanish motherhouse and so became an autonomous American community. "As early as the 1940s, the California community was becoming increasingly progressive, to the point where it was criticized by churchmen for giving courses philosophically ahead of Catholic teaching." When their local male superior, Cardinal McIntyre, visited the community in 1962, it was not in friendship: he "questioned the community's theological training, pointing out that it should be following not the thinking of recognized contemporary theologians, but his own." His message to the community was frighteningly concise: conform or get out. He disapproved of their experimentation and changes and "gave the sisters sixty days to conform to traditional religious practices." His demands placed the community in an awkward position, since the changes had been approved by their general chapter, a forum immune from his "approval." When Anita Caspary, then Mother Mary Humiliata, the superior general, appealed to Rome with questions, McIntyre toned down his demands. When a subsequent general chapter looked to further modifications, however, "he took the new decrees as a statement of defiance .. and insisted that if the decrees were not dropped the sisters must withdraw from the schools in the archdiocese."[50]

The ensuing conflict did not just touch the IHMs, but struck a major nerve in the renewal process of American sisters in general. The IHMs found themselves supported by progressive theologians and condemned by others who accused them of emptying religious life of all meaning. Roman authorities sided, not with the sisters, but with the archbishop: the changes in their governmental structure and formation process were said to be causing scandal and were summarily forbidden. Furthermore, the Sacred Congregation dispatched a set of directives for the sisters to follow that directly conflicted with their own renewal decisions. When a pontifical commission of four American bishops reviewed the case, they advised the sisters to "pay lip service" to the directives and cause no further trouble. Perceiving this advice as hypocritical, the community split: fifty older sisters remained, and four hundred followed Anita Caspary to become the Immaculate Heart Community. All four hundred sisters "requested" dispensation from their vows and became the largest group of American sisters "to be reduced to the status of laywomen again."[51] Today they call themselves a "community without walls," admit married couples to full membership, and think of themselves as a network of people who share similar ideas but not similar lifestyles.

The Glenmary and IHM communities clashed with male authorities who did not want sisters to govern their own lives. All sisters learned something about institutional vulnerability in these confrontations, and they began to sense the wisdom in collective strength. Having been approached by fifteen or more religious orders having trouble with Rome, the Leadership Conference of Women Religious established a consultative panel so that no group of sisters could be forced to capitulate to official sanctions without recourse to the collaborative strength of American sisters. While LCWR presents a relatively calm appearance in their public positions on these problems, it is clear that they are experiencing a growing sense of anguish over some of the tensions between Rome and American religious communities.

An additional "lesson" from the "loss of canonical status" conflict lies in questioning the value of that status: official approval of a religious order gives that order position within the institution, but it also subjects the members of that community to disciplinary control. One group that has, from its inception, been a noncanonical community is Sisters for Christian Community (SFCC): its experiment with modern and modified "religious life" may prove to be quite useful to American sisters.[52]

Founded in 1970 by Lillanna (formerly Sister Audrey) Kopp, Sisters for Christian Community is a fast-growing group of former sisters attempting to live an unstructured community life: SFCC allows sisters to create their own commitment formula and decide the length of time they serve; sisters may or may not formalize their dedication, and they interpret the traditional vows—poverty, chastity, and obedience—as serving, loving, and listening. The sisters are self-supporting, pay taxes, and make their own arrangements for insurance, medical care, and retirement, since the community has no motherhouse or any other official structures. Kopp, a sociologist interested in systems, believes that bureaucratic models are dysfunctional and that "hierarchy doesn't work."[53] She defines the impetus of Vatican II as away from elitism and supportive of collegial process, diverse, noninstitutional ministry, and constant change. Whether SFCC will survive into the future remains to be seen. Since its members are mostly former sisters, one can expect it to decline just as sisterhoods in general are expected to decline. Yet the very success of the experiment, in terms of increasing membership and the possible future move to loosen the structure by making vows optional,[54] makes SFCC something of a showcase for experimental, noncanonical communities. The decided advantage of the community's noncanonical status is its immunity from Roman control. At the same time, however, SFCC appears to have no collective leverage within the church and gives little evidence of political power. It may be that "outsider" status, in order to be effective, must be experienced paradoxically, from within the institution.

The renewal process radicalized sisters through sociological analysis and the confrontational experience of one or two highly publicized encounters with religious authorities. In a more discreet way, however, each community moved to its present status of safety or danger by its own internal process. If one can divide religious communities into three categories—emerging, renewing, and diminishing[55]—one can make fairly accurate predictions about the relationship of each group to political radicalization and feminist principles. Emerging groups will be small and innovative and can be expected to be relatively insignificant politically, since they seldom come into any direct confrontation with bishops. Diminishing congregations will continue to resist change and can also be expected to be nonconfrontational and politically inactive; the only interesting question such groups pose is whether or not their strategy and their essentially conservative framework will survive and attract new members.

Renewing congregations —"inside outsiders"— will be the groups to precipitate significant change for religious life, because they are in a position to be frequently at odds with church authorities over issues of authority and apostolate as they attempt to implement their understanding of Vatican II. Renewal, besides involving sister education, encouraged experimentation with community life, mission, and self-understanding. Some groups were more daring than others, some quicker to reform their structures of government, some more concentrated on community identity.

When the history of American sisters is written in the future, some congregations will stand out as beacons of renewal, able to combine traditional understandings with innovative ideas. The Sisters of Charity of the Blessed Virgin Mary (BVMs), for example, were an early-changing group that developed a successful democratic community model.[56] As they have lived with self-government, the BVMs have steadily become an example of feminist collegial process. The Sisters of Loretto (SLs), led through their renewal by Mary Luke Tobin,[57] also changed early and creatively but are particularly important because of their commitment to social justice. When the community brought a lawsuit against the Blue Diamond Coal Company (1979), for failing to list the SLs as "shareholders of record," the company responded with a typical trivializing question about what "the good sisters" ought to be doing with their lives. The sisters responded by defending their action in terms of the gospel: the Beatitudes demand, they said, "a sharing in the struggles of the world against all the evil afflicting our sisters and brothers everywhere."[58] The Maryknoll Sisters (MMs) moved from traditional missionary strategies to the Latin American-inspired "basic Christian community" model in order to respond to the suffering of oppressed peoples. Their reading of the gospel has inspired certain kinds of action on behalf of the marginalized: social justice and liberation from oppression are, for them, constitutive elements in the following of Jesus. Their commitments to structural change and social justice have led them into highly controversial and dangerous situations. Two of the four American women killed in El Salvador in 1981 were Maryknoll sisters.[59] Their work with the poor has increasingly demonstrated that most of the poor of the earth are women and children, a perception that has led the Maryknolls to ask deeper questions about the sexist roots of oppression.

These few examples serve to highlight some of the quiet, persistent ways in which some religious communities experienced renewal as a means toward radicalization. Other communities undoubtedly have other stories reflecting different facets of the renewal process. One thing appears to be clear: the closer a group gets to issues of structural change — externally, through social justice work and political involvement, or internally, by way of challenging institutional structures — the more dangerous they appear to authorities and the more they draw Vatican opprobrium. Two groups of sisters have raised important questions in these regards for the future of religious life: the Sisters of Mercy of the Union (RSMs) have been visibly involved in politics, and a progressive group of contemplatives has challenged medieval enclosure rules to claim their right to form associations.

A CASE OF OFFICIAL REPRESSION

Many of the sisters who have been in highly publicized "trouble" with the Vatican in the last few years have been RSMs: Theresa Kane challenged the pope on the issue of women's ordination; Agnes Mary Mansour was given an ultimatum from the pope to resign from her post as director of Social Services for the state of Michigan or be severed from her thirty-year relationship to the RSMs; Arlene Violet, Republican nominee for attorney general of Rhode Island, was ordered not to run for public office and so chose a "temporary leave" from her religious congregation; and Elizabeth Morancy, a three-term Democratic member of the Rhode Island House of Representatives, tried to stay in both politics and religious life but finally chose to ask for a dispensation from vows in order to spare the RSMs further trouble from

Rome. All these sisters, in some way, raise questions of power and politics. Sisters' were the only voices of public challenge raised during the pope's visit to the United States. When Theresa Kane, speaking for LCWR in 1979, dared to confront the pope, she showed, if nothing else, that the old reputation for docility and meekness no longer obtained for American sisters.

The Agnes Mary Mansour case has attracted considerable attention from theologians precisely because it raises the issue of "due process" in a church supposedly moving toward collegiality.[60] In her statement to the press, Mansour said this:

From the beginning . . . I have acted in good faith seeking the necessary approvals . . . I have attempted to be faithful to my vow of obedience by discerning honestly with my religious community and others. . . . I believe in a tradition of obedience more fully developed . . . since Vatican II . . . an obedience born out of mutual dialogue and openness to seek the truth. . . . The directive I received . . . was not the result of a dialogic, objective process, but of a unilateral one where neither I nor my religious superiors were ever given the opportunity to appropriately present our case.[61]

Mansour was not the only Catholic ever to have been in the sensitive position of opposing abortion personally while being responsible for the administration of public funds that would finance abortions for poor women. Joseph Califano, former secretary of HEW, Mario Cuomo, governor of New York, and the Catholic layman who was Mansour's immediate predecessor in the Michigan post did not provoke the sanction visited on Mansour, nor were their policy views the locus of harassment by the local bishop. So far as Rome was concerned, the crux of the matter was not the position itself, but the fact that it was taken publicly by a nun. The papal representative told Mansour it was her "ecclesial identity" that required strict adherence to magisterial teaching. As the 1984 elections have shown us, however, it was the fact that the position was taken publicly by a *woman* that rankled the Vatican: Geraldine Ferraro's position on abortion, not unlike that of some Roman Catholic senators and representatives, was signaled out for relentless attention by some American Catholic bishops. The Mansour case, as well as the experience of Geraldine Ferraro, raises fundamental ecclesiological questions along with serious legal ones.[62]

The Morancy and Violet confrontations focused more directly on politics, but were also ecclesiological. After United States representative Robert Drinan, a Massachusetts priest, was told to leave political office because it was inconsistent with his clerical vocation, bishops began to put pressure on sisters who were holding public office at state and local levels. Most of the sisters refused to resign, on the basis that, unlike Drinan, they were not "clerics" and therefore were not bound by laws written for priests. In the revised *Code of Canon Law*, however, the old legal directives lost all ambiguity: any member of a religious order — all nuns — were forbidden to seek or hold public, political office.

In the face of specific and clear legislation, nuns could comply, defy the law, or seek to escape through a legal loophole. Violet chose the loophole of temporary dispensation from her vows, fully intending to return to conventual life when her political career is over.[63] Morancy, on the other hand, tried to win approval from her bishop and attempted to run for office without seeking dispensation from her vows. Her decision challenged the church by making a case for the validity of political ministry, and she cited Pope Paul VI's *Call to Action*, which encourages religious involvement in world problems, as her support. Her argument turns on the nature of religious life, which, according to Morancy, should not be lived apart from the world.[64] The Vatican response was negative: her bishop did not support her; Rome, therefore, simply repeated its directives, and she resigned from her order to continue her ministry. The "principle" that priests and nuns ought *not* be engaged in politics does not quite fit Roman Catholic history. In fact, to quote Rosemary Radford Ruether, it "seems to have been invented primarily for a new situation where church leaders begin to act as reform or revolutionary change agents, rather than sanctifiers of the political status quo."[65]

In striving to be faithful to the mission of the church and to the traditions and goals of their founders, sisters have consistently found themselves involved in situations demanding action for change. "And they have found that in a modern context, with its pluralism, with its interaction between public and private sectors, their social ministries are rapidly translated into political challenges."[66] The mixture of religion and politics in America is problematic for Catholics at least in part because traditional Catholic positions are at odds with American values of freedom, pluralism, religious diversity, and the right to dissent. Sisters in political life force the issue: Is religious action in the political sphere to follow a hierarchical model of social and political reform from the top down? Or will nuns in political life, women active primarily at the state and local levels where they are in touch with grassroots needs, carry the day in American Catholicism? Sisters come to politics from a background of education, health care, and social services. When Sister Clare Dunn, minority leader in the Arizona state legislature, died in an automobile accident in 1981, she was eulogized by her peers as "the conscience of the House and a champion of the poor."[67] Why, then, are sisters forbidden to follow a political ministry?

The level of harassment directed at the RSMs in the last six years leads me to believe that their challenges to religious authority are particularly troublesome. The flagrant lack of due process, not only in the celebrated Agnes Mary Mansour case, but in the less well known tubal ligation controversy,[68] testify to an obdurate, reactionary response on the part of church officials. Is their defensiveness a reaction to Theresa Kane's challenge to the pope in 1979? Have the RSMs been singled out to show other sisters what can or might happen to religious women who act too independently? Or does their new conception of religious life simply make the Vatican nervous? "Sisters today are still feeding the hungry and clothing the naked," says Betty Barrett, a 63-year-old RSM peace activist, "but we're also addressing the issues that result in people being hungry and homeless. It's social sin we're fighting now."[69] In other words, many sisters, typified by the Sisters of Mercy, are committed both to social justice and to structural change; they are striving to create a new society and have been encouraged to do so by the conciliar support for a new church. In confronting the old church, however, sisters challenge "the world's oldest and most entrenched living bureaucracy."[70] The RSMs have learned how perilous such dissent is and also how their own survival empowers others.

All active sisterhoods in various stages of renewal can learn from the experience of the RSMs: political ministry, especially, is a pertinent question as nuns understand religious life as living among the marginalized. The experience of progressive contemplatives is harder to assess in terms of immediate relevance, but not at all in terms of feminism. In a time when most people think of nuns as activists or teachers or nurses, it is sometimes difficult to remember that "real nuns" are those enclosed in contemplative monasteries. Since these women are the last "angels in the house," the institutional church seems to be especially invested in curtailing any moves they make toward greater freedom and self-definition, as if "nuns" may not drift toward being "sisters."

A SURPRISING SECTOR FOR RADICALISM

Sisters are a relatively new invention in religious life: the idea of a group of women who pursue a ministry "in the world" was foreign to church officials and was resolutely opposed each time it was suggested. Pious cunning was required to bring active orders into existence. Women in religious life, unlike their male counterparts, were never permitted to work in the world. On the contrary, "all nuns, collectively and individually, present and to come, of whatsoever order of religion, in whatever part of the world they may be, shall henceforth remain in their monasteries in perpetual enclosure."[71] When Boniface VIII issued this decree in 1298, it was ostensibly to protect women, to construct safeguards against frail, feminine nature. Papal enclosure rules, written only for orders of women, included minute prescriptions for supervision and separation and ensured that religious life for women would be lived according to rules set forth by men. Nuns were told when to rise and retire, what to wear, when and what to pray, what they could read, hear or see, and what they were to aim for. In order to serve God in religious life, nuns had to sever all contacts with the outside world and forfeit their freedom.

When Angela Merici attempted to establish the Ursulines as an "active" order in 1544, she and her sisters were forced back into the cloister. It was not until Vincent de Paul and Louise de Marillac combined patience and shrewdness in 1633 that the first uncloistered religious order was established: the Daughters of Charity devoted themselves exclusively to works of mercy, did not take solemn vows, and were not considered to be nuns. Active sisters took "simple vows" and, with little or no official encouragement, proliferated in the eighteenth and nineteenth centuries. They were given grudging acceptance by popes, but they were not considered to be true "religious" until the beginning of the twentieth century. Furthermore, most papal declarations of tolerance or legitimation stressed the ways in which the group should follow the spirit of enclosure.[72] Official resistance to active women needs little explanation from a feminist perspective. It is not hard to explain why Vatican officials did not encourage apostolic orders; neither does one have to reach very far in order to account for the intense reaction contemplative sisters received when *they* made their first overtures toward self-determination.

Whether contemplative sisters are understood as dutiful daughters, angels in the house, or brides of Christ, their role has been the same: in the words of a contemporary sociological analyst, they are "to have no needs or demands, to renounce everything for the benefit of others, to bear all things patiently, to lend a helping hand to every need, to be invisible yet always there, to stand passively ready, to endure, and to be disciplined."[73] Yet, led principally by a group of progressive Carmelites in the United States, many American contemplatives resisted this stereotypical description and bonded together in 1969 — without official approval and in spite of official opposition — to form the Association of Contemplative Sisters (ACS).

Contemplatives were caught up in the ambiguities of the postconciliar era to a greater extent than other sisters. Encouraged as early as 1950 by Pope Pius XII to form federations and to reevaluate their formation programs, contemplative sisters could not readily understand how leaving the enclosure — breaking with ancient laws and customs — could be appropriate. Isolated for centuries, many of these sisters did not want to form a federation, perceiving it to be a form of modernity that was ultimately threatening to the vocation. The papal initiatives of 1950, therefore, did not mobilize these nuns. By the time of the Second Vatican Council in the early sixties, however, it was becoming increasingly clear that renewal would require collective vision and energy. *Perfectae Caritatis*, the conciliar decree on the renewal of religious life (1965), called for modification of papal cloister and the elimination of outmoded customs. Furthermore, it said that "in such matters, consideration should be given to the wishes of the monasteries themselves." Contemplative nuns, like other sisters, were encouraged to return to the sources of their strength—the gospels and the vision of their founders—and to adjust themselves to the conditions of the times. Prudent experimentation was the order of the council.

Less than a year after the promulgation of the conciliar decree, however, and just as nuns were warming to new ideas, a directive for implementation was published that restricted the extent to which papal cloister could be modified and insisted that "material separation" was an essential constituent of contemplative life.[74] How broadly the term "material separation" could be interpreted was not altogether clear, and many sisters looked forward to opportunities to discuss the guidelines and to begin some implementation of renewal. What those interactive forums would be was not clear, however, since contemplative nuns had no right to free assembly. After they attended one meeting of the Conference of Major Superiors of Women in 1965, contemplative sisters were forbidden to attend another one, and the president of CMSW was told not to allow contemplative sisters to become even associate members of the organization. When members of various contemplative orders met for mutual support in 1966, they were told by the apostolic delegate that they could hold no future meetings and seek no further consultation.[75] The Vatican response to requests for an association of contemplative sisters was a Bishops' Commission headed by Cardinal Carberry of St. Louis.

When a major meeting for contemplative sisters was planned for 1969—at Woodstock, Maryland—and after the invitations had been sent out, Carberry wrote to all contemplative convents and discouraged them from attending meetings. In May of that year, Carberry sent a questionnaire to all contemplatives for the purpose of gathering information from them about their lives and hopes for renewal. In July, right before Woodstock and long before that questionnaire could be processed, the Vatican issued a decree, *Venite Seorsum*, stating that those who oppose papal enclosure "can develop another kind of religious life, leaving the traditional form of papal cloister."[76] In other words, those who wish to experiment must be dispensed from their vows: those contemplatives who wish to test their experience of the Holy

Spirit, or follow the impetus of Vatican II, must leave contemplative life.

Obviously issued without consultation of nuns themselves, *Venite Seorsum* was published to intimidate the nuns at the Woodstock seminar in August. When a Latin text of it was studied at the meeting, most of the 135 contemplative sisters at the seminar signed a letter of protest against its norms.[77] To what extent *Venite Seorsum* was experienced as a threat is not clear, but the founding of the Association of Contemplative Sisters at Woodstock was a strong signal from the sisters that they would not be intimidated by it. Woodstock deepened the nuns' awareness of their need for mutual support and introduced them to new forms of repression. ACS, founded at that meeting and respectfully announced to SCRIS, has never been approved or recognized by Roman officials. The degree to which Vatican bureaucrats were surprised that the angels in the house shed their wings is not clear: four centuries earlier, the great Carmelite reformer, Teresa of Avila, experiencing similar opposition from male authorities, said, "That I am a woman is enough to make my wings droop."[78]

The enclosure conflict made entry–level feminists of many contemplative sisters. ACS was founded as an association of sisters who had a distinctive experience of repression in the church, an experience that might be called that of "outside insiders," confined to the cloister without power and without voice in their own future. In spite of the polite letters announcing its founding, the very existence of ACS was a clear act of defiant self–determination, and its six–week educational forums—held during four successive summers in the early 1970s—were an attempt to heighten awareness, not only of contemplative life, but also of issues and events in theology and the world at large. ACS operates simply as a forum of exchange and has usually resisted extension to include non–nuns, because the sisters prefer to channel their energy into those issues that have a direct impact on their community life. One indication of the effect of these past fifteen years on progressive contemplatives is the creative leadership they are showing on the issue of religious language: many progressive monasteries have changed the language of the prayer book to eliminate sexist language altogether. As one sister explains, "What happens when you begin to make the language universal is you begin to see the loving, nurturing, more feminine side of God."[79]

The other side of the renewal process, therefore, whether experienced in quiet, contemplative environments or in the public forum of political involvement, has been radicalization. Sisters have been through a laborious and liberating process in the last thirty years. With promptings from the Vatican, they have upgraded their education, adapted themselves to the modern world, and formed a strong collective identity. With the help of new theology, expanded horizons of experience, and sociological analysis, they have come to a new understanding of themselves in the past and in the present: in their new ministries and self-understandings they relate to the prophetic justice themes of the Bible and have a strong sense of themselves as women of the gospel. Individual communities have made significant contributions to the future of religious life, whether or not that life continues in its present forms.

CONCLUSIONS

Although the Vatican and the council originally encouraged the renewal of sisters, SCRIS and the present pope are not supportive of the directions taken by American nuns. For Roman officials, religious life is set apart from the world, lived in "canonically erected communities" (convents), distinguished by religious garb (the habit), and presided over by rightful authorities (superiors).[80] Frequently repeated themes of dependence, authority, obedience, and surrender signal a return to the mentality and politics of the preconciliar era and are aimed at sisters because women are usually perceived as being in the most vulnerable position within the church. The directives against the sisters, however, are really aimed at all those who have supported the progress of the American church in the last twenty years. Whereas the document from SCRIS insists that religious life cannot be lived "in the world," American sisters and many American Catholics believe that religion is embodied precisely in the tensions and opportunities of daily existence. The values adopted by many of these sisters are pluralistic and feminist ones that challenge the way religious influence operates in a society. In adopting feminist values of collective experience and collegial process, American nuns challenge the very *modus operandi* traditionally used by Catholics in political situations, namely, decree. If traditional Catholicism is willing to be political only through the directives of popes and bishops, American Catholic women—religious and laywomen—are determined to add many more voices to the discussion. Vatican displeasure with these women, as with liberation theologians, is rooted in a hierarchical ecclesiology and a fear of losing control.

The surface issues appear to be almost trivial: for example, by insisting on nuns wearing habits, Roman officials put themselves in the awkward position of claiming more expertise in matters of appropriate clothing than those wearing the clothes. The real issue, however, is control. Sisters, who have been obedient and cooperative throughout their history, now find themselves at odds with the Vatican. "Faithful to the church's call for renewal, we now find ourselves repudiated by the same church," said the National Assembly of Religious Women (NARW) at its 1983 convention. When a group of sisters from the Leadership Conference of Women Religious met with SCRIS to protest the insistence on religious garb, "several Vatican officials responded that if the Americans insist on wearing 'purely secular garb' they might consider joining secular institutes,"[81] a response reminiscent of Cardinal McIntyre's ultimatum to the IHMs two decades earlier. Typically, the Vatican did not consult with sisters before writing the new directives, nor did they explain the reasons for appointing Archbishop John Quinn to head a mandated study of United States religious life. Though Quinn and LCWR have put the best face on the commission—both saying that it will give sisters and bishops new avenues for dialogue—the sisters clearly perceive the directives and the commission as "symbolic of the subtle ways by which the church seeks to maintain traditional control."[82] The Vatican may make it appear as if they are disturbed by a vocation crisis, but "American sisters . . . clearly understand that the root of the problem does not lie in the presumed disobedience, dissent and defection of American sisters, but rather in the collision course of following two diametrically opposed models of religious authority and obedience."[83] The positive result of the Quinn commission has been the highlighting of the differences: it is now much easier to perceive the different ecclesiologies espoused by each group.

Those two models, embodied in the pre- and post-Vatican II church, are the hierarchical and the collegial. Through its directives on the "essentials of religious life," the Vatican has called sisters back to a pre-Vatican II church and decreed that the age of experimentation is over. For sisters, however, continual evolution is crucial for survival. In many ways, the *success* of experimentation in discovering more gospel-centered ministries and in reconstructing religious life to enhance freedom and human growth, has led sisters to believe that experimentation is just beginning. If Muckenhirn was right in 1967 when she was talking about internal renewal—"Now is the time for intelligent and courageous experimental action"[84]—many American sisters would be inclined to think that her words could be even more forcefully invoked in the 1980s. Sisters have always had to break through barriers in order to create new forms of life and to respond to the needs of the world. "If 'ecclesiastical authority' had really held sway [in the past]—if the bishops had been left to coordinate the church's energies, as the pope puts it—none of the teaching sisters who did this work in the past would have been available. Their religious communities would not have existed."[85]

The ironies in the situation are numerous. Sisters have achieved a kind of power among themselves by realizing that they have little power within the institutional church: their self-perception as "outsiders" has been crucial to their decision to bond together for strength and to pursue a social justice ministry. Their power, therefore, lies in their powerlessness, and their outsider status in the hierarchical church gives them insider status in the women's movement. At the same time, sisters have some real power of their own: they are highly educated, committed, and bonded. Their peculiar strengths, indeed, may be necessary for the survival of the American Catholic church. They are an existential manifestation of the connections between death and new life: the "dying" experienced by religious orders is happening at a time when sisters are growing closer to the laity and when a new kind of bonding coupled with a post-Vatican II ecclesiology offers new possibilities for growth. Still, at the peak of their power, they are imperiled by repressive papal directives — a fact which is probably more predictable than it is ironic.

If it is true that laywomen have many reasons to challenge the structures of the church, that is also true for sisters. It may be that laywomen are not as clear about their own powerless position as they might be, but sisters are: they know women are in a precarious situation and are convinced of the need for collective action. Sisters need laywomen — their numbers and their support — and they have something to offer them: as laywomen look around for organizational support in their own struggles, they can look to sister support networks as welcoming rather than excluding them. How well a national coalition of sisters and laywomen can function remains to be seen, but Catholic women, like women in general, are increasingly sure that hope lies in collective strength. The renewal process has made feminists of many sisters and has placed the American Catholic church in the fascinating position of being prodded or led into new territory by its "dutiful daughters."

4. Ordination, Collective Power, and Sisterhood: Foundations for the Future

If we ... don't create our lives ...
we shall thirst in Hades,
in the blood of our Children.

DENISE LEVERTOV

A new God is being born in our hearts to teach us to level the heavens and exalt the earth and create a new world.

ROSEMARY RADFORD RUETHER

Your daughters shall prophesy.

JOEL 2:28

The problems addressed thus far have been universal; women's invisibility in history, the encroachments of cognitive dissonance as women attempt to live within a sexist system, and the dispiriting realities of outsider status are not peculiar to Roman Catholic women. The solutions suggested in this chapter, however, though not exclusively Catholic, have originated within the Catholic community. Since nuns have been in the ironic position of finding strength in their very powerlessness within the church, it may appear as if they offer the only correctives to the current malaise. In fact, however, American Catholic women have found several ways to test their collective strength as they attempt to remain within their tradition. Collaborative models of parish leadership, and participation in ecumenical groups like the Sojourners community are two ways Catholics have found to implement the structural goals of collegiality in their religious lives; although both are lively, creative alternatives, neither is discussed here. In this chapter I will describe the women's ordination movement as it moved from demanding "equal rights" to calling for fundamental structural change; the development of collective strength in a wide variety of Catholic women's organizations; and the emergence of the Womanchurch movement. Because of the enlivening experience of their new corporate identity, Catholic feminists have been tempted to use the vocabulary of "sisterhood" to explain themselves and set goals for their future. I will argue, however, that sisterhood is an inadequate metaphor to use in our present conflictual situation.

In the long history of Christianity, women have been *defined* (as sources of evil in the world or as complementary helpmates), *described* (as frivolous minors or mysterious creatures), and had their lives *determined* by males who claimed to speak for God. The relationship between women and God, therefore, has been distorted by those who project their own misogynism onto the deity. Catholic feminists have now moved into a position from which they can argue that sexism is sinful and that the structures of the church must be changed in order to accommodate a more just and grace-ful embodiment of the Jesus traditions. These claims have been a long time in coming into focus; the history of radicalization of the Women's Ordination Conference and the varied experience of women's groups offer ways to understand the perspectives of American Catholic feminists. A look at the emergence of the Womanchurch movement and an argument for the limits of sisterhood as a strategy provide insights for the future.

WOMEN'S ORDINATION:
FROM EQUAL RIGHTS TO STRUCTURAL CHANGE

Ordination of women to ministry is not new, even though the arguments are relatively recent within Roman Catholicism. By 1970, virtually all Protestant churches admitted women to the ministry. This practice did not particularly disturb Roman Catholic officials, since "the ordination of women to the pastoral office seemed to raise no strictly theological problem, . . . these communities had rejected the sacrament of Orders at the time of their separation from the Roman Church."[1] Setting aside for the moment the ecumenical offensiveness of that reasoning,[2] and taking Roman logic at its face value, we see that women's ordination presented no threat to Roman Catholicism until women were ordained in churches with a specific ministerial *priest-*

hood: Vatican officials could ignore ordination so long as it had no relationship to what they recognized as the celebration of the Eucharist. When Anglican bishops ordained women in the early 1970s, however,[3] the issue was raised within the context of eucharistic ministry and so moved Roman officials to react vigorously against it. The specific reactions of Roman Catholic officials, therefore, are relatively new.

In 1962, on the eve of the council, Gertrude Heinzleman, a Swiss lawyer and member of St. Joan's Alliance,[4] submitted a petition about women priests to the preparatory commission of the council. At about the same time, one of the earliest scholarly works on the state of the question was written as a doctoral dissertation under the direction of Karl Rahner.[5] That dissertation, by Haye van der Meer, was the first of several studies in the 1960s culminating with Ida Raming's dissertation (1970) on the refusal of canon law to admit women to the ministerial priesthood.[6] These works, plus a growing fear of the question by church officials, prompted reactions and calls for study: in 1972 Pope Paul VI issued an apostolic letter excluding women from the priesthood and from new lay ministries of acolyte and lector.[7] That same year the American Catholic bishops issued a report that rehearsed the traditional arguments against ordination for women and called for a study of the issue.[8] Van der Meer's work was translated into English in 1973, because the translators believed it would "be of immense assistance in this forthcoming study."[9]

Van der Meer wrote not to solve problems but to raise questions. Indeed, the last line of his book ruefully admits that the question is difficult, valid, and almost insoluble. He did, however, give a painstaking analysis of Roman Catholic arguments from Scripture, tradition, the magisterium (the teaching authority of the church), and theological speculation. None of the arguments, according to him, was conclusive, since all rested on dubious assumptions about female nature, outdated biological concepts, and inconsistent theological symbolism. It is "amazing," he said, "that there is no formal declaration of the *extraordinary* magisterium of the Church in reference to the question of priesthood for women" (p. 90).

Van der Meer's work appeared in English at a propitious time: the Second Vatican Council had set the Roman Catholic church on a major program of ecclesiastical and liturgical renewal, and feminist theologians like Mary Daly had urged Catholic women to examine their peculiar status in a church "which at the same time idealizes and humiliates [them]."[10] Women, quite apart from Catholic ecclesiastical contexts, were beginning to ask questions about equality between the sexes: encouraged by Protestant women and schooled by the civil rights movement, Catholic activists were ready to press the women's issue. Furthermore, in 1972 the United Nations declared that 1975 would be International Women's Year.

It is not surprising, therefore, that Roman Catholic women began to move on their own behalf in the 1970s. We have already seen that the Leadership Conference of Women Religious urged its members to seek justice for women throughout the 1970s: its 1974 annual meeting resulted in two important resolutions, one supporting the principle that all ministries in the church be open to women and men as the Spirit calls them, and one affirming women's rights to active participation in all decision-making bodies in the church. Thus when a Roman Catholic laywoman, Mary Lynch, called thirty-one friends together in Chicago in December 1974 to ask whether the ordination question ought to be raised during International Women's Year, she did so within a burgeoning spirit of consciousness and challenge.

The Chicago meeting, along with other developments, led to what was to be the first national women's ordination conference in the United States.[11] That meeting, which had to turn away five hundred people for lack of space, gathered twelve hundred participants to hear papers, celebrate liturgies, and lay the groundwork for what would eventually become the Women's Ordination Conference (WOC). One month before the Detroit meeting, Archbishop Joseph L. Bernardin, then president of the National Conference of Catholic Bishops, issued a statement affirming the traditional ban against women's ordination in the Catholic church.[12] The first meeting of WOC, therefore, occurred in a highly charged atmosphere in which participants questioned not just the technical problems of women's ordination, but the very notion of priesthood and the structure of the church itself.

At the conference bishops were criticized for their lack of openness on the issue. Elizabeth Carroll, former president of LCWR, called for honest discussion by reminding participants that the "bishops acknowledge the benefit of discussion . . . but apparently not at women's initiative." They have not, she said, "entered upon serious, continuing dialogue with women about women."[13] Five years after Carroll made this observation, and mostly because of the persistent lobbying of WOC, a two-year dialogue was established between a committee of bishops and representatives from WOC, but little came of it. In Detroit Rosemary Radford Ruether challenged women to consider whether or not they really wanted to be ordained within the present hierarchical church. There is good reason, she said, "to think that the present clerical and institutional structure of a Church so constituted is demonic and itself so opposed to the Gospel that to try to join it is contrary to our very commitments." If women want to be ordained, Ruether argued,

they must demystify in their minds the false idea that priests possess sacramental "power" which the community does not have. The sacramental power of the priest is nothing else but the sacramental expression of the life of the community itself in Christ, which the community has designated him or her to express for, and to, the community. The alienation of sacramental life as a power tool to be used over and against the community is the basis of all false clericalism; such clericalism is deeply rooted in sexist symbols of domination and passivity. Women cannot ask to be ordained without questioning fundamentally this concept of clericalism.[14]

Margaret Farley, too, urged women to "challenge [the] hierarchical concept of orders" and claim a "moral imperative" for ordination, since philosophers have given "women a rational base from which to challenge vague feelings among both men and women that women are indeed somehow less suited than men to enter into the realm of the sacred."[15]

Throughout the conference proceedings, one can find two dominant themes: an equal rights perspective elaborated in criticisms of past practices and a motivation for change located in "the sake of the Gospel itself."[16] Participants were reminded that laws against the ordination of women were rooted in "a false interpretation of the nature and role of women . . . [which] engages the Church in a speculative falsehood [and] entails harmful consequences for individuals in the Church and for the Church as a whole."[17] Participants called for new images of church in which there would be full collaboration between men and women, since only "with mutuality of relationships at all levels in the Church will we be able to open to a Christian life which is characterized by creative union, by a life which is modeled on the life of the triune God."[18] Ordination of women, therefore, was set within the context of a new theology of the church as sacrament, a "church [which] would embody the Christian message of equality, freedom and love as a causally effective sign to itself and to the world."[19]

If the Detroit conference was marked by positive enthusiasm, the Baltimore meeting of WOC in 1978 was more consciously feminist. The Detroit meeting was called in hope; the Baltimore conference occurred after that hope had been dampened by the Vatican decree against the ordination of women.[20] The Vatican declaration rests on arguments from tradition and Scripture that can be summarized easily: the church has always opposed it; Jesus did not do it; no one has a "right" to it; the priest, acting in the name of Christ, must represent him physically; and whether or not there were deaconesses in early Christianity has no bearing on ordination as such. All these arguments, rooted in a long tradition of practice and interpretation, can be reduced to the antagonism between the authority of the past and the challenges of the future. In important ways, the declaration raises serious questions about the nature of women, the image of God, and the structure of the church, all of which were addressed at Baltimore and, earlier, in a series of counterarguments by respected theologians.

Almost immediately after the publication of the Vatican decree, Leonard and Arlene Swidler published *A Catholic Commentary on the Vatican Declaration*, which included the decree itself along with the "mimeographed and unsigned" commentary provided simultaneously by the Sacred Congregation for the Doctrine of Faith, as well as the Biblical Commission report on the ordination of women. Confusingly, the report from the Biblical Commission says that Scripture leaves the question open, whereas the declaration itself argues that Scripture definitively refuses ordination to women.[21] Whatever the conflict between these two Vatican documents, however, the declaration carried more weight and was the one addressed by the commentators.

The Swidlers solicited essays from forty-four theologians, Scripture scholars, and WOC activists, all of whom argued against the interpretations, conclusions, and presuppositions of the declaration. As Leonard Swidler noted in his introduction, the old slogan in regard to Vatican decrees — *Roma locuta, causa finita* (Rome has spoken, the case is closed) —"might in the matter of the Roman declaration on the ordination of women priests more accurately be stated: *Roma locuta, causa stimulata!*"[22] The spirit and decrees of the Second Vatican Council, with the consensus of major Catholic theologians, demand collegiality: theologians have not only a right, but a duty, to probe, contradict, and engage in dialogue with official church statements.[23]

In a very real sense, the denial of ordination to women is another way of saying that the American enthusiasm for the post-Vatican II church has gone too far, and that the influence of the women's movement on American Catholicism needs to be curbed. The Baltimore conference, therefore, took a more consciously feminist approach and was more geared to structural analysis. The Vatican had attempted to settle the argument by decree and by a proof-text interpretation of Scripture, but nearly every major theologian in the world had opposed both the decree and the tactic. Furthermore, the scriptural foundations for opposing women's ordination had been denied by Catholic biblical scholars.[24] The participants at the Baltimore conference, therefore, responded to Roman interpretations of tradition and to what they believed were false and malicious assumptions about the nature of women.

Those meeting in Baltimore came with a vision of pervasive renewal in the church based on a clearly feminist critique of church and culture. The title of the conference proceedings — *New Woman, New Church, New Priestly Ministry*[25] — indicates the breadth of the critique. In Baltimore, efforts were made to assess sexism within the context of racism and classism; opposition to the traditional view was made on the basis of structural renewal and an interpretation of institutional sexism as sinful. Mary Hunt contrasted the "patriarchal past" with the "feminist future," and Elisabeth Schüssler Fiorenza argued that the pressing task was not to comfort but to challenge. Representatives from all over the world situated the question within an international perspective and theologians — male and female — argued, not just for ordination, but for the gathering of a new church already present in our midst.

The vision of a new church built on arguments that had been going on long before Baltimore, especially in relation to the role of the priest. In an article published even before the Detroit conference, the Jesuit theologian Edward J. Kilmartin drew on historical and theological sources to say that "the narrow concept of priestly character as participation in the priesthood of Christ with special reference to the power of consecrating . . . is unsatisfactory."[26] The eucharistic event, as Kilmartin and liturgical theologians know, depends not on the powers of the minister but upon the faith of the community. The "power" of the priest, therefore, is the sacramental expression of the faith and life of the community, not juridical clout based on the notion that the priest is "another Christ." In fact, Kilmartin said, because "the priest does not directly represent Christ, he cannot act to distribute the spiritual blessing derived from the Mass as affirmed in the traditional Scholastic theology of the fruits of the Mass." If this is the case, then "one should not argue that Protestant Eucharists are defective." Furthermore,

since the priest directly represents the Church united in faith and love, the old argument against the ordination of women to the priesthood, based on the presuppositions that the priest directly represents Christ and so should be male, becomes untenable. Logically the representative role of the priest seems to demand both male and female office bearers in the proper cultural context; for the priest represents the one church, in which distinctions of race, class, and sex have been transcended, where all are measured by the one norm: faith in Christ.[27]

The theological critique of the role of the priest was meant to reaffirm the tradition at its best and to reemphasize the teaching of Vatican II that all believers have the task of representing Christ to one another and to the world.

The Baltimore vision of a new church extended this view. Anne Carr, recognizing diverse opinions within the church and among women themselves, urged conference participants to find unity in diversity, to affirm the need for a principle of openness and self-criticism, and to welcome the variety of visions bound to emerge on the issue.[28] Richard McBrien, re-echoing the theology of the council, noted that the "Church understands herself today as People of God, and not simply as a hierarchically-structured society to which people belong and from which people receive spiritual benefits."[29] Conciliar theology continually found expression in Baltimore. Margaret Brennan, former president of LCWR, focused on "the shared faith experience of the Christian community [as] a source of continuing revelation," and reminded the largely Western audience that the new church would have to "have a new face, contour, texture — due to cultural differentiation — becoming even more explicit than it is now, due entirely to new pastoral needs — ethnic, racial, third and fourth worlds."[30]

For a variety of reasons, partly involving structural changes in WOC itself, the anticipated national conference for 1981 gave way to a series of local meetings. This change, disappointing as it was to some of those working for women's ordination, signaled an important new dimension in methodological thinking about the issue, specifically, the attempt to move from woman to women. The title of the Baltimore conference proceedings was New Woman, New Church, New Priestly Ministry, whereas the title of a conference organized by the Center for Concern in Washington, D.C., was Women Moving Church. It may well be that a future conference will define itself as "new women, new churches, new priestly ministries." The shift from singular to plural is significant and radical: it has echoes in the history of the women's movement and in the ways feminists increasingly find themselves working. As Carolyn Heilbrun noted in relation to the Yale French Studies issue on feminist texts, "The editors . . . found themselves participating in what may be seen as a countertradition in academia, or a new tradition emerging in feminist studies — that of reading collectively, or speaking in a plural voice, or contributing individual work to a group product."[31] The decision of WOC to defer a national conference so that diverse voices could be heard in multiple local meetings was, in part, a serious recognition of the need for broader participation not only in ordination but in the gathering of new churches.

The movement for women's ordination, therefore, has raised arguments from praxis, and from the nature of the pastoral office, within the context of justice in an institution marred by the sin of structural sexism.[32] The pressure to change official policy has found worldwide support both from the women's movement and from the enormous pastoral needs generated by the severe shortage of priests. Pastoral experiments in missionary contexts may point to the need for the ordination of women, but at another level—like the women's movement itself—they urge a radical rethinking of the church and its mission.[33]

Theological arguments against the predominantly "First World" understanding of the Eucharist from "Third World" theologians may support the position of those who favor women's ordination; but at another level, they demand consideration of diverse eucharistic theologies so that the Roman Catholic church can reflect in its practice and teaching the plurality of its membership.[34] Women's ordination, therefore, is part of a nexus of major theological and practical issues within the Roman Catholic church that reflect the conflict between those whose primary goal is to guard the tradition and eschew change and those who hope to explore new paths and welcome the future. As such, women's ordination joins the larger issue of demand for inclusiveness and renewal.

THE POWER OF THE COLLECTIVE: WOMEN'S ORGANIZATIONS IN THE CHURCH

Organizations of Catholic women in the parish have traditionally followed the cultural lead in sex-role stereotyping, so that women have usually been encouraged to join service-oriented groups. Though theological developments in the twentieth century—especially the stunning encyclical of Pope Pius XII, *Mystici Corporis Christi*—stimulated the laity to become more directly involved in "the work of the church," even those organizations that provided opportunities for study and direct action tended to relegate women to secondary roles. For the most part, organizations of Catholic women have focused on prayer, cleaning, teaching catechism, and other nurturing tasks: the Altar and Rosary Society, found in virtually every parish in the United States, sums up the opportunities given to most women to be of service to the church.

Besides confining women to traditional, auxiliary jobs, Catholic women's groups have typically been directed by men—priests and bishops—who set the group's agendas and welcomed their help as long as they remained obedient daughters of the church. Catholic women were especially useful in directing the attention of their men to the church: in the preconciliar days of "missions," traveling preachers would often begin their week in the parish with a "women's mission," relying on the women to cajole male attendance later in the week.

When we move to national organizations of Catholic women, we find many of the same patterns: the National Council of Catholic Women (NCCW) was founded by the bishops in 1920 in order to unify women and broaden the scope of episcopal influence.[35] Similarly, the Grail Movement, an international group of Catholic women, was founded in Holland in 1921 by a priest who hoped to use women's untapped capacities to facilitate a worldwide spiritual renewal.[36] In the more than sixty years of their existence these two groups have developed along radically different lines, so that today the Grail is a strongly feminist group whereas NCCW has taken positions against the Equal Rights Amendment (ERA) and women's ordination. A comparison of these two organizations can tell us something about the relationship between self-determination and feminism.

NCCW AND THE GRAIL

Since the National Council of Catholic Women was founded almost immediately after the passage of women's suffrage in the United States, and since the American bishops were clearly opposed to votes for women, it is logical to wonder if the bishops' initiative in convening NCCW was related to their desire to harness women's voting power for their own causes. NCCW has consistently reflected the American Catholic experience, espousing causes dear to the hearts of the American hierarchy: their strong opposition to communism and feminism and their support of Radio Free Europe and the Hatch amendment against abortion follow the lead of the bishops exactly.[37] In their pamphlet defending their stand against the ERA[38] and in their case against women's ordination,[39] they espouse the traditional hierarchical view of women as different from and complementary to men. If they see women as "a powerful force for good,"[40] that force is directly related to service and volunteerism: "from its beginning, NCCW has recognized that giving service and advocating for justice are interrelated."[41]

In many ways, NCCW has done exactly what the bishops hoped they would do. At the first annual convention in 1921, the keynote address was given by Bishop Joseph Schrembs of Toledo, who told the assembled women:

We trust you. That is the idea. If we did not trust you, we would not have called you. We trust to your own good sense, we trust to your wisdom, we trust that your own experience in the past will serve you well as guidance for the future. We trust you to always prove yourselves obedient children to the Church, always receptive to its divine guidance.[42]

If NCCW has proven itself receptive to guidance by the bishops throughout its history, it has received only scant recognition from the bishops for that industrious obedience. As Esther MacCarthy has shown, the bishops told women that opportunities had arisen for them that "are among the most wonderful in the history of the world," and then recruited them to be nurses, aides, and helpers. When they responded by working tirelessly, they were not even praised for it, save at their own annual meetings, and nothing was done to promote their political or economic equality. Their activities "were not self-chosen but, rather, were imposed by the parent organization [American bishops] which later took full credit for the results . . . apparently, the women who elected to join this organization were quite content with subservient or supportive roles."[43]

As a women's organization, NCCW has been supportive of women's issues, but never by way of structural analysis. When they say that their "commitment to justice for women is evident in [their] history,"[44] they mean that they have worked within the system to improve the status of women. In the first twenty years of their existence they supported equal pay for equal work, adequate working conditions for women, nondiscriminatory immigration laws, and the improvement of health care. In more recent years they have successfully supported a breast cancer education program and parenthood education.

Though their political activity has been mostly informational, they actively lobbied for the Hatch amendment against abortion, again reflecting the priorities of the American bishops. And while they have resolved "to encourage generous acceptance of responsibilities in the catechetical ministry of the Church,"[45] they have followed the official church in refusing to support efforts for the ordination of women. Their position against women's ordination is a direct quotation of the Vatican declaration against it and so reflects a preconciliar mentality. When they argue that "the ordained ministry is a calling that is authenticated by the Church, rather than an inherent right of the individual,"[46] they apparently do not see that the statement begs the question: Who is the church?

When NCCW called for disarmament and the abolition of nuclear weapons in 1981, it was "the strongest statement ever adopted by [the] organization,"[47] and so constituted a bold step for the group. Because many of the white, middle-class married women who constitute the bulk of the organization saw the resolution as a choice between the policies of the Reagan administration and the teaching of Pope John Paul II, they were troubled about the decision and appeared not to want to make it. Nevertheless, their adoption of the resolution was impressive, especially because it *preceded* the similar stance of the American bishops. Historically, NCCW has called for study of an issue rather than for the passage of strong resolutions. Furthermore, the organization has been specifically patriotic and supportive of a strong defense program and has rarely recommended real involvement in a political conflict.[48] Their commitment to work actively for disarmament, therefore, is, as their president said, "just one more sign of growth among our members."[49] The resolution was not, however, a declaration of independence; if anything it strengthens their alignment with the program of the American bishops, who also have supported the abolition of nuclear weapons.

In the final analysis, NCCW operates as a liaison between the bishops and American Catholic women. As such, it is part of the hierarchical structure of the church and follows goals set by the bishops. It boasts eight thousand affiliated Catholic women's groups, but it is not clear how many members it has since, as a federation, it includes in its membership count all the members of affiliated groups: if an affiliated parish has fifty women in its Altar and Rosary Society, all those women are counted as members of NCCW. The accuracy of its claim to have millions of members, therefore, is questionable.

At the same time, it is the one large national organization of Catholic women in America and includes a significant sector of American Catholic women. Like the women in the CARA study on ministry, NCCW members appear content to identify themselves as helpers and to undertake roles that reflect female complementarity. There is no question that NCCW has given women a way to assume some power in the church, but in a patriarchal institution that power comes at the price of autonomy. The group began as an organization dominated by the concerns of the American bishops and continues to mirror the bishops' agenda. The organization's choice to remain in this position has prevented any possibility of taking even moderate feminist direction and has guaranteed a traditional, conservative stance on women's issues. In contrast, the Grail movement, begun at approximately the same time and also dominated, in its early years, by the concerns of the institutional church, has deliberately moved away from hierarchical control in order to take on an explicitly lay direction and, later, a strong feminist orientation.

The Grail was founded in the aftermath of the First World War, when secularization and the waning of religious influence on society stimulated the Roman Catholic hierarchy to devise new strategies to make the church's presence felt in the world. Since the social hopes of Pope Leo XIII—articulated in the late nineteenth century and tied to the parameters of Scholastic philosophy—had largely gone unfulfilled, the Vatican was searching for ways to implement a new social order using the power of the laity. When Pius XI was elected in 1922, he tied that vision to the strategy of Catholic Action, "nothing other than participation of the laity in the apostolate of the hierarchy."[50] From now on, the laity, under the vigilant direction of bishops and priests, would do those things that the leaders had been unable to accomplish. "While it can be argued that the Papal program of Catholic Action was as much a grasping for political leverage as a concern for social reform, Pius XI repeatedly called for a 'renewal of the Christian spirit' as a prerequisite for any viable social reconstruction."[51]

The response, which was part of the historical context for the Grail, was overwhelming: the spiritual vision of lay Catholic intellectuals like G. K. Chesterton, Hillaire Belloc, Christopher Dawson, and Jacques Maritain, with the impressive work of communitarian priests like Romano Guardini, moved postwar Catholics to seek a dynamic synthesis of Catholicism and humanism. Catholic Action provided a new, active way to be a Catholic and was distinguished by hallmarks of holiness, an understanding of church as the mystical body of Christ and a heroic self-conception of Catholics as representatives of a universal spiritual order. In the United States, the official response of the bishops, inspired by Monsignor John Ryan, led to a "Program for Social Reconstruction" that drew Catholics to support President Roosevelt's New Deal.[52] The NCCW was founded by the bishops at this time as the ladies' auxiliary to Catholic Action in America. At a broader level, the success of the Catholic Worker movement,[53] the liturgical movement,[54] Friendship House,[55] and the National Catholic Rural Life Conference[56] all contributed to the "renewal of the Christian spirit" by providing extensive possibilities for active lay involvement. The Grail offered women the opportunity to participate in this more expansive and somewhat less official understanding of the lay apostolate.

When Jacques van Ginneken founded the Society of Women of Nazareth in Holland in 1921, he had a sense of the church on the brink of exciting new possibilities. This particular group changed its name to the Grail in 1929, and became an idealistic youth movement that eventually flourished and became an international group of Catholic laywomen destined to "lead the way in the development of the apostolate of women." Their founder believed that women understood Jesus before men did, because they had subtle, intense emotional characters, exactly what was needed to convert the world:

Jacques van Ginneken saw the conversion of the world as a task for the laity — especially, since they had retained the spiritual qualities which men had lost — for laywomen. He knew that it would be difficult for lay people, and women in particular, to achieve the autonomy which they would require to carry out their mission. He therefore conceived a strategy for the Grail to use in relating to Church authority, an authority which had announced that it wanted an active laity but was wary of anything which might get beyond its control. The strategy was a modified version of that of van Ginneken's own Society of Jesus: relate to the highest level of authority and this level will protect you from the intermediate (and closer) ones. In the Grail's case, the highest level was not to be the Pope . . . but rather the local bishop. The intended result, however, was the same: priests (men) would be prevented from exercising their clericalizing and masculinizing control over the movement . . . the American Grail . . . cultivating only those bishops and priests who admired the goals of the movement and would assist without trying to control it, remained free by keeping "out of the environment" of ecclesiastical authority.[57]

Despite the Grail's managing to achieve a kind of autonomy from ecclesiastical control, it did not, until the 1960s, attempt to restructure itself so that it could follow the impetus of the women's movement. The Grail continually worked to become more truly a lay organization, more collegial and democratic, a desire that preceded its feminist consciousness and made way for it.

In some ways, the Grail resembled "religious life" more than it did the laity, which may be accounted for by the unmarried status of its members. Van Ginneken's original idea was hierarchical: a core group of women, dedicated in virginity, poverty, and obedience, who would both "carry the spirit" and also hold the main positions of leadership in the movement. That core, originally known as the "women of Nazareth" later became the "kern" or nucleus of the Grail. In the 1960s in the United States, Grail members began to question the identification of virginity with functional leadership roles, and in the International Assembly of 1965, began the process of separating the two, making it possible for Grail members to hold responsible positions in the movement regardless of their "vocation." It has never been easy for the Roman Catholic church to relate to single women, since they are, by definition, not controlled by husbands or male religious superiors.[58] As a group dedicated to the lay apostolate, the Grail tended to organize itself along the hierarchical and religious lines traditionally supported by the church: they had "formation" programs and made promises of "obedience" to the International President and members lived lives of chastity and simplicity, undertook serious programs of meditation and spiritual renewal, and were sent out on "missions."[59]

At the same time, they frequently ran afoul of hierarchical authorities precisely because they wanted to set their own goals. In 1942, Cardinal Stritch, upset by some of the Grail publicity and feeling responsible for them because they resided then in his diocese, wrote to them to say that they needed to be clear about their subordination to the hierarchy: they should not try to plan their own programs, he said, but should realize that the hierarchy gives groups a program and then supervises them as they carry it out.[60] In 1955, when they had moved to Cincinnati, Archbishop Alter asked them for their "rule" and conducted an investigation that concluded that they were pious but liable to experience conflict when the "trained mind of the priest is forced to determine certain unavoidable matters, which are likewise dealt with by the untrained mind of the layman." When he examined their program, Alter found it fundamentally sound but lacking in spiritual direction: "We cannot forget," he said, "that they are a group of women being led by women, with a great deal of female emotions and instincts guiding them."[61]

Led by women or not, the Grail was not politically feminist until the late 1960s. Up to that point, despite their trust in the leadership potential of women, their beliefs about feminist issues paralleled those of the official Catholic church. Janet Kalven's pamphlet *The Task of Woman in the Modern World* (1946) supported the notion that women had virtues of love, compassion, and self-sacrifice and so "should create a vital current of womanly virtues" in the world.[62] An article in *America* (1947) praised the Grail, saying that the young women there "could learn the value of their traditional womanly role."[63] And so they could. On farms, away from the cares of "the world," the women of the Grail were liturgical pioneers whose self-sufficient zest for life was embodied in folk dancing, bread baking, meditation, and practical work. Most of all, life at the Grail was characterized by impassioned discussions of books, theologians, ideas, and the future.

On the tenth anniversary of their American foundation (1954) they sponsored a conference at Grailville, The American Woman, that explicitly opposed the feminism of Simone de Beauvoir and supported traditional complementarity: in their view, Adam and Eve were equal, but not identical, since Adam was the dominant one and Eve was naturally receptive, dependent, and suited to be the keeper of the home. Their praise of women as blessed with intuitive gifts and capacities for love led to the conclusion that women's natural role was maternal, and that a life of consecrated virginity allowed women to share in a union with Christ. All of these views were ultimately rejected in the 1960s when the Grail, like other sectors of the Catholic church, was forced to confront its identity in light of the modern world. The Second Vatican Council articulated problems that the Grail—like other groups, especially sisters—had been discovering for themselves: Grail members, beginning to wonder about authority and about their relationship to the world, saw the need for a new outlook long before most other American Catholics.

In 1962, in their new oratory, at their first national conference, and led by their first American president, Grail members began to question their past in order to prepare for the future:

In light of its conviction that personal relations (which were felt to have been sacrificed along with the need for personal competence) and communal solidarity (which was felt to have been distorted by being hierarchically structured) were the things which really required attention, the Grail set out in common search of "the human." The new strategy was "openness"—to all women in the Grail (married and unmarried, the fully committed, those still searching, and those in full rebellion against the past), to contemporary society, and to the religious experience of women outside the Catholic tradition. It proved to be an agonizing process, characterized by a powerful determination to shed the old limitations and an unyielding insistence on setting no new ones. As with other American Catholics of the 1960s, the romance of certainty was transmuted by the Grail into a romance of risk.[64]

True to its original vision, the Grail remains rooted in Christian faith and called "to participate in the transformation of the world," but it now attends to that task "ever more aware of the relations of domination and submission which are embedded in our social, political and economic structures."[65] Their completely decentralized government is now shaped by the three task forces that describe their priorities: the bonding of women, the search for God in traditional and nontraditional ways, and liberation.

Their commitment to women has resulted in some stunning and influential programs. In 1972 and 1973 the Grail sponsored consciousness-raising workshops in conjunction with Church Women United: these Women Exploring Theology conferences brought women together from all over the country in order to discover and articulate the need for a more inclusive theology and liturgical language. The Seminary Quarter at Grailville program, which lasted from 1974 to 1977 involved women from twenty-eight seminaries and five universities in studying a theology "in which women's concerns are central rather than peripheral"[66] to the task of church renewal. As such, the Seminary Quarter broke new ground for women and supported an emerging feminist theology that begins, not with God, but with a theological reflection on women's experience. The books that have been published as a result of these and other workshop experiences have interrogated traditional theological education and liturgical practice and the parameters of the quest for God.[67]

The Grail is small — claiming approximately two hundred members — and officially invisible, as contrasted with NCCW, but it is significantly more influential as a forum for Catholic feminist thought and experience. It operates as a nonhierarchical collective committed to structural change and so, unlike NCCW, is not part of the patriarchal structure of the church. Furthermore, it sets its own goals and reflects a more radical approach to women's issues than NCCW: the Grail is concerned with women's crisis problems, whereas NCCW tends to focus on women's health and parenting skills; the Grail is committed to feminism, whereas NCCW has explicitly withheld support from two important feminist causes, ERA and ordination; and the Grail has taken on the issues of liberation, economic justice, and structural change, whereas NCCW waits to see what the bishops will recommend. If NCCW has given women power in numbers, it has been at the price of autonomy and a denial of feminist perspectives. The Grail, on the other hand, has claimed its autonomy at the price of numbers but without relinquishing its influence.

SELECTED ORGANIZATIONS OF CATHOLIC WOMEN

Groups and organizations of Catholic women that work from within a feminist dimension have adopted their positions because they believe that the Spirit moves within the church today in the lives of the marginalized. Far from seeing the women's movement as a luxury in a world full of problems, they perceive the real issue as the need to see the links between their own oppression and the horrors that plague the disenfranchised people of the world. Catholic feminist organizations attempt to make the connections between the lives of women and world problems so that the women's movement cannot be accused of being provincial. As Catholics, these women have raised new perspectives from which to analyze historically ubiquitous problems of ecclesiology: from the early community experiments until today, Christians have asked certain questions over and over again and answered them within the framework of their own time. Who is the church? What ought it to be doing? Who speaks for the church? How does the church best embody the values of Jesus? Organizations of Catholic feminists attempt to answer these questions in a new way by looking first to the experience of women and then using it to take a prophetic stance against a sexist structure. Many of them refuse to relate in a formal way to what they consider to be an immoral institution, preferring to bond around gospel values as they see them operative in the lives of the disenfranchised. Since most of the world's poor and dispossessed are women and children, and since women have only secondary status in the Catholic church, these groups see feminism as a valid way to live the gospel in the modern world. Since change most often occurs to counteract great pain, these groups are determined to persuade leaders that the church is hurt when it denies the voices of women: Catholic feminist groups work to alleviate women's oppression and to spread the word that the church as currently constituted does not reflect the full power of the gospel.

Many groups of Catholic feminists have emerged in the last fifteen years, beginning with the *National Assembly of Religious Women* (NARW) formerly the National Assembly of Women Religious (NAWR), founded in 1968 as a grass-roots alternative to the Leadership Conference of Women Religious, an attempt to give ordinary sisters a national voice. Its membership, now open to all Catholic women, is explicitly feminist. As their "vision statement" says: "We are religious feminist women committed to the prophetic tasks of giving witness, raising awareness and engaging in public action for the achievement of justice."[68] By engaging in justice ministry and articulating a political spirituality, NARW stands against the Vatican position on religious life as lived apart from the world. On the contrary, according to NARW, the gospel can be lived only in the midst of the world's most glaring problems.

Through writing and action, NARW has addressed women's issues like welfare, endorsement of the ERA, women's economic rights, and providing of shelters for battered or displaced women. It has paid particular attention to political causes like world hunger, the plight of farm and sugar cane workers, nuclear disarmament, and justice in Latin America. Through its newspaper, *Probe*, NARW has been especially articulate about the situations in El Salvador and Nicaragua and deserves some credit for keeping those issues alive in the public consciousness. By reaching out to sisters and laywomen who work in justice ministry, NARW has been able to influence public policy through education and action. Its commitment to justice for women has led to analyses of hunger and poverty and has consequently moved its members to see that bonding on the basis of feminist identity is insufficient in the face of enormous political problems. Its sense of world vision and awareness of the need for strong bonds with the poor give it a way to "break with the old and bless the new"[69] both in the lives of women in general and in the lives of women in the church.

Though the *National Coalition of American Nuns* (NCAN), founded in 1969, has never claimed to represent more than two percent of American sisters, it has, nevertheless, made its voice heard on a wide variety of social justice issues and in causes in support of the rights of women. Many of NCAN's causes are directly relevant to the lives of American sisters, but the organization has also staunchly supported civil rights actions, unions, the decriminalization of prostitution, Women's Peace Education conferences, and passage of the ERA. Since NCAN has always opposed rule without the consent of the governed, it has spoken out in situations where authority — civil or ecclesiastical — attempts to impose its rule without consultation.[70]

Its most famous altercation occurred in 1982, when it not only publicly opposed the Hatch amendment against abortion (in opposition to the National Conference of Catholic Bishops) but went on the "Phil Donahue Show" to publicize the decision.[71] The NCAN statement was not the first to come from a Catholic source, but coupled with an appearance on a popular national television show, it was wildly newsworthy and drew Vatican opprobrium. It was also instructive: of the 540 responses to the show received, 355 (66%) were positive and 185 (34%) negative, reflecting Gallup Poll statistics on the issue. Most of the respondents were women, and, as Ann Patrick Ware pointedly mentioned in her analysis of the responses, "Not one mentioned a single case where the church was of any help. People *did* tell of receiving comfort and understanding from their women friends, their mothers, their married relatives, but clearly they did not consider these friendly voices 'church.' "[72] Though NCAN's membership is mostly nuns, their commitment to feminist self-determination has drawn them into some of the most controversial issues within the women's movement.

The *Institute of Women Today*, founded in 1974, is an expressly ecumenical group that focuses on the religious and historical roots of women's oppression. Designed for International Women's Year as an education program, the Institute collected faculty members from the fields of law, psychology, theology, and history in order to present coherent workshops for women on some of the most important aspects of their lives. In 1975 they conducted thirty workshops in as many cities. A significant part of their goal was follow-up: they attracted an interfaith group in a city; sponsored sessions on women and the law, values clarification, new ministries, and history; and concluded with a practical strategy session geared to the local situation.

The Institute has done some Title IX education in public schools and participated in other workshops, but its most extensive ministry has been to women in prisons.[73] Through a remarkably effective network of professionals and volunteers—nuns and laywomen; Catholic, Protestant, and Jewish—the Institute provides educational programs, visitation, opportunities for inmates to support themselves while in prison through cottage industries, and chances to learn new skills—welding, for example—that will place them in a better position to obtain well-paid employment on release. As in its other workshops, the Institute's aproach to prison workshops is essentially practical: members teach inmates how to use law reference books, conduct intensive journal courses, help the women with preparation of writs, and visit women privately in order to assess their needs and connect them with other organizations that can help them. The Institute has used the prison environment to address issues important to other feminists: the sexual abuse of women inmates, for example,[74] or the filing of class action suits complaining that women "oftentimes receive more severe sentences [than men] because as women they are expected to have better conduct; when convicted, their breaking of 'the code' is considered a more serious infraction simply because 'women don't do such things.'"[75] Through the efforts of Institute members, some women in prison have had their poetry published,[76] and many more have found legal, spiritual, and practical help. The Institute's involvement with women's issues is highly practical and feminist in its grass-roots involvement, its eagerness to give women in prison equal opportunity to defend themselves, and in the attention given to the experience of women.

Other organizations have formed, related to specific issues of importance to women. Catholics for a Free Choice [77] and New Ways Ministry,[78] both headquartered in Washington, D.C., address problems of abortion and gay ministry. Both groups have male and female members and confine themselves to the questions and controversies surrounding these heated topics. The Conference of Catholic Lesbians,[79] a relatively new group, is a support network for Catholic lesbians — nuns and laywomen — and sponsors workshops and awareness sessions on a topic too seldom addressed by the Catholic church except in negative and condemnatory terms. Two groups of Catholic women who address other discriminatory practices are Black Sisters[80] and Las Hermanas: the first, made up only of black sisters, concentrates on racism within the church and society, whereas Las Hermanas, including both nuns and laywomen, focuses on class discrimination and the failure of white Catholics to acknowledge and understand the problems of their Hispanic sisters. Lastly, there are two feminist groups that have taken on higher profiles as part of the Womanchurch convergence: the Women's Alliance for Theology, Ethics, and Ritual (WATER) in Washington, D.C., and Chicago Catholic Women (CCW).[81] Both support a variety of liturgical and experiential activities for women in their geographical areas. Many of these groups along with LCWR and two Washington-based social justice centers, the Quixote Center and the Center of Concern — are part of the Womanchurch movement.

THE EMERGENCE OF WOMANCHURCH

Although the Womanchurch movement is too young to discuss in great detail, it can be set within the context of Roman Catholic feminism and the concerns raised by the various organizations of Catholic women so far discussed. If the 1970s saw the formation of several new groups of Catholic women united around one or another cause, the decade of the 1980s has been a time of coalition in which efforts have been made to bond together to form what Elisabeth Schüssler Fiorenza calls "the gathering of the ecclesia of women." Born in front of the Palmer House in Chicago in 1977, the "Women of the Church Coalition" has drawn representatives from several different organizations into dialogue and collective action.[82] Founded to replace Sisters Uniting and organized to include a variety of activist groups, the coalition survived in its early years through the energy of its founders and the determination of member groups. For the first few years, members of the coalition met regularly to exchange information and devise strategies, but it was not clear what their best course might be. Then, in 1981, a coincidence of events laid the groundwork for the 1983 Womanchurch conference.

The absence of a national WOC meeting in 1981 led many women to urge some kind of national event: there was the desire and the energy for a national conference. Also in 1981 the Washington-based Center of Concern, using an explicitly feminist process to involve grass roots participation, sponsored Women Moving Church to listen to the movement of women in the church. The Center "gathered reflections of people's experiences from across the country, provided analyses of these responses, focused [them] in a conference and continue[d] with the networking of women's base communities."[83] The meeting, which brought two hundred women and twenty-five men together in May 1981, provided a forum in which women could tell their stories, name the issues, share spiritualities, celebrate liturgies, identify important feminist and political issues, and identify resources for future empowerment. The success of this process and the continuing dialogue of the coalition led to plans for a Womanchurch conference to be held in 1983.

Sponsored by eight of the coalition members[84]—WOC, NARW, NCAN, CCW, the Quixote Center, WATER, the Institute of Women

Today, and Las Hermanas — From Generation to Generation: Woman-church Speaks was held in Chicago in November 1983. The headline in the *Washington Post* story was, "U.S. Catholic Feminists Gather to Counter Papal Conservatism," and the article spoke of participants wearing buttons with the words, "I'm Poped Out." Indeed, amid the hopefulness of the conference was the clear impression, articulated by Elisabeth Schüssler Fiorenza, that "women simply are leaving the church in growing numbers because it has become irrelevant to their lives."[85] As far as these twelve hundred women were concerned, they had reached a crisis point in their lives within the church. Many felt that the conference represented "a face of revolution occurring in the structured church" and shared the conviction "that perhaps only women, out of their traditional powerlessness, are strong and free enough to try to set things right."[86]

The key to understanding Womanchurch, however, is its claim to *be* church. The participants in Chicago did not see themselves as exiles from the church but in exodus from patriarchy. As Rosemary Radford Ruether later analyzed it, "This means women engaged in liberation from patriarchy declare this community of women's liberation to be theologically, church, that is to say, a community of redemption." Womanchurch makes no claim to "leave the church" or cut itself off from historical Christianity, but rather points "toward the beginning of a process of renewal which must include men and historical Christianity, but only when these, too, recognize the exodus from patriarchy as essential to the meaning and mission of the church."[87] As I said, it is too early to make predictions about the Womanchurch movement. The success of local conferences in 1984 — three hundred women in Chicago, for example — point to continuance and growth, and the intellectual support of Catholic feminist theologians provides the movement with a ballast to its political activism.

On New Year's Day 1984, the original coalition broadened to include newer — and older — groups of Catholic women and become the Women in the Church Convergence. The Convergence has since then become part of Womanchurch, a broadly inclusive movement that is expected to become ecumenical in the future. Its concerns reflect the issues near and dear to its member groups and so manage to provide political, activist, spiritual, and liturgical possibilities for almost every Catholic feminist still trying to make sense of her tradition. Although the presence of Catholic lesbians and those favoring a pluralistic understanding of Catholic teaching on abortion may frighten some more conservative women's organizations, the inclusion of these groups gives Womanchurch a very broad power base and makes it possible for those of different backgrounds and beliefs to meet one another in dialogue and explore bonding possibilities that go beyond their immediate differences. The decided efforts of Womanchurch to be bilingual in its meetings and publications—11 percent of the participants in 1983 were Hispanic—to collect money for "scholarships" for poor women, and to provide child care at meetings give the movement an edge over the institutional church in attracting marginalized women and those often unable to attend conferences because of financial or nurturing constraints.

American Catholic women—laywomen and nuns, from largely different backgrounds and with significant differences of experience—have learned some important things about themselves in the last thirty years. Far from being confined to complementary status and relegated to traditional roles, women have begun to engage in difficult practical and political work with other women. Against a traditional interpretation that confines nuns to convents and women to the home, Catholic women have bonded with those who believe that the gospel is to be found in the lives of oppressed peoples. Surprisingly, they have discovered that, as women, they themselves are among the oppressed and so can look to their own marginalized situation as a locus of divine revelation. Through their participation in Catholic feminist organizations and their support of the Womanchurch movement, they have radicalized yesterday's questions and imagined a future in which patriarchal institutions cease to exist. Those meeting in Chicago in 1983, for example, were not overconcerned with the question of women's ordination: for them it was a given that women could and would celebrate the Eucharist, and their actions (there, and later in small groups all over the country) questioned, not so much whether women could be priests, but whether priests, as presently constituted in Roman Catholicism, were necessary. The Second Vatican Council's slogan for the laity—"We are the church"—has been taken seriously by women as they leave the patriarchal institution but refuse to leave the community of Jesus. By claiming to be church, those in the Womanchurch movement react against a patriarchal ecclesiology and express their own power as they refuse to be marginalized or squeezed out of the community on the basis of androcentric regulations. Many women do leave the church and seek no Catholic alternative, but those who remain within the system and identify with Womanchurch become as subversives in a corrupt society.

Women in Catholic feminist organizations understand that they are gifted but not wanted unless they aspire only to secondary status. That being the case, many of them have given up hoping that anything will happen for women in the church, yet they have not given up on historical Christianity or on a Christianity for women. In the face of increased opposition—the papal directive to American bishops to withhold support from anyone who supports women's ordination, for example[88]—women realize that they are powerless in isolation and so need to bond for survival and power. Learning their lessons from the women's movement, Roman Catholic feminists presume alienation from the patriarchal structure and embrace their powerlessness within the institution as a paradoxical source of strength. Knowing the values of collective leadership, they perceive the patriarchal model as dangerous and have been moved to challenge the hierarchical church as an inefficient and illegitimate expression of Jesus' intentions. From the women's movement and from liberation theologians, Catholic feminists have acknowledged that the personal is political and that the fundamental option for the poor that connects the Gospels with the marginalized also connects women with oppression on the basis of race, class and sex. Having learned to respond to each other, Catholic feminists and those in the Womanchurch movement see the value in building coalitions and support networks in which women can minister to other women, experience collegial support, and reimagine themselves either in a base community or as part of a gathering of the ecclesia of self-identified women and women-identified men.

As women revise the literature, criticize the structures, and form new communities, they broaden their liturgical experience and deepen their political understanding. Those young women now leaving the church because it has no meaning in their lives might find an alternative in the Womanchurch movement, but it is too early to make predictions about those who have experienced the disjointedness of attending a church that denies self-determination to women while working in a society that tries to promote it. The Womanchurch movement, like religious congregations in the sixties and the Grail movement in the seventies, sees that women can still take on the grand tasks of the church—to transform the world, for example—but can now do so by way of feminist collective energy.

Finally, however, the Womanchurch movement is an ecclesiological challenge to traditional Catholic configurations. The gospel as preached in the institutional church, along with sexist language, exclusive liturgy, and dehumanizing role models for women, is not "good news." The patriarchal church has betrayed the vision of Jesus by constructing and supporting an institution that demeans, in subtle and glaring ways, more than half its membership. In face of the lopsided religious vision of Catholicism, some might fantasize about the last judgment:

Sometimes I have an apocalyptic vision of Christ addressing a group of goaty pastors that He has shoved off to the left during the Last Judgment. Christ says, "I was divorced and you shunned me and my children, muttering about broken homes, because you couldn't face my pain; I was old and in a nursing home and you denied me communion because there were no ordained ministers to be entrusted with the Host; I was pregnant and you told me abortion was a mortal sin but you didn't tell me how to cope with a child after I had it; I was poor and you kept your friendship to yourself except to smile at me when I came to a rummage sale; you denied me the handshake of peace because I was a different color, or because you hadn't seen me before. And because you didn't recognize me in anybody but white, Anglo, theologically-trained males, you clods, you can spend the rest of eternity with them alone: and that should be hell enough for anyone."[89]

Focused more upon the present than upon eschatological possibilities, however, Womanchurch attempts to embody the Jesus traditions—equalitarian structure and ministry to the marginalized—here and now, offering an alternative to patriarchal Catholicism to both women and men and seeing in itself a community of redemption.

FROM SISTERHOOD TO ALLIANCES:
STRATEGIES FOR THE FUTURE

Women in the Roman Catholic church — in parishes and convents — have discovered the necessity of the women's movement. They have encountered opposition within the church whenever they articulated their own needs or desires, and they have found it nearly impossible to change the order of things from within the institution, precisely because they have no place within that order whence to effect change. Clearly perceiving the need to bond together, Catholic women, like other women, have been led almost logically to use "sisterhood" as description of their bondedness. The women's movement has led us "to rediscover a conspiracy so vast that we are simply staggered by the number of problems that need to be addressed."[90] In this context, it is understandable to latch on to the concept of sisterhood in order to feel close, connected, and bound together in the same fate. Yet I think sisterhood is an unmanageably complex, hopelessly idealistic, and impractical strategy in the present situation. Sisterhood is difficult to oppose since it is a word that does not lend itself to critical examination: like the word, *commitment, sisterhood* is mythic, a word that mystifies analysis by living off of its own evocative power. The word *self-exploitation,* on the other hand, is inherently critical, and when used in place of *commitment* can lead us to perceive some of the conflicts we invoke as we attempt to live it. I believe we need to substitute the term *alliance* for *sisterhood* in order to place ourselves more clearly in the struggle and enable ourselves to pursue a more effective strategy for dealing with the patriarchal institution.

In Catholic circles, the desire for sisterhood has been problematic from the beginning, because "sister" describes both "sibling relationships" and "religious life." The desire to "reject the title sister and to recapture it as a name inclusive of all women"[91] has led to controversy and conferences between nuns and laywomen. Understanding the "ecclesia of women" as a "feminist Catholic sisterhood," Elisabeth Schüssler Fiorenza has drawn the controversy to a clear head by refusing to use the word, *sister,* for anyone in religious life: she uses the terms *nunwoman* and *laywoman* to underscore the differences between the two groups and to encourage a rejection of clerical privilege so that all Catholic women can be sisters. Though Schüssler Fiorenza has clearly opened debate on an extremely sensitive issue and has posed questions that have led to reflective discussion and national conferences,[92] she has not pointed the way, in my opinion, to the best strategy for Womanchurch. Sisterhood, I believe, is an inadequate model for the task at hand.

Sisterhood is not really descriptive for our reality, although it worked for many years to give nuns a way to assume a sibling identification as they left their real families behind. Sibling sisters share common experiences and many common value systems and memories and often have fairly similar perceptions of reality. Given the broad-based ambitions of Womanchurch, the attempt of radical feminist Catholics to embrace a real, diversity-respecting universalism, we cannot claim to be sisters in a familial sense. Secondly, much of the rhetoric of sisterhood is mythic or romantic, qualities that do not usually have staying power in a revolutionary movement. Sisterhood in too many families has not a been a cozy experience but a competitive one lived out in a patriarchal structure. If the media are filled with stories of sisterlove and natural, permanent bonding, folktales are just as replete with wicked stepsisters and rivalry. We might want to redefine sisterhood as Barbara Deming did: as the ability "to see ourselves in each other,"[93] but if we choose to do that, we need to be very clear that such self-knowledge and extension into another's experience calls for a major commitment of time and energy. Small religious communities choose to pursue this kind of sisterhood, as do small sectarian groups, but all evidence points to their spending an enormous amount of time and energy doing it; I am not persuaded that spending our energy in this way will make us any more effective in the arenas of power we need to enter together in order to create basic justice, let alone dramatic change.

Thirdly, sisterhood is an emotional concept. It strains relationships by investing them with personal values and feelings, so that we tend to think that all of us must like one another in order to get something done. In this way, sisterhood leads to emotional disappointments rather than intellectual disagreements. And if emotional disappointments are costly, we do to ourselves what the patriarchy wants to do to us, we weaken our own power and our effectiveness. Sisterhood does not give us a model for relating to one another that allows us to continue our work through serious and fundamental disagreements without purges. This is not to say that the "piss and vinegar" of the women's movement or Womanchurch are not emotional or that revolutionaries do not need to love some of their fellow revolutionaries, but only to suggest that sisterhood is an emotional unit rather than a working relationship. Even nuns have given it up as an ideal. Since we have friends we love more than our sisters and colleagues with whom we agree more than our sisters, we might ask why sisterhood is an attractive model for our interaction.

Finally, sisterhood leads in a curious way to horizontal hostility. Because we become involved in an emotional unit, we are prey to playing some of the games we could only play with our real sisters, that is, games we would not dare to play with colleagues: we ask our "sisters" to prove their love and loyalty. Lesbians, injured by heterosexual privilege, sometimes ask heterosexual women to give it up in order to prove their sisterhood. Along parallel lines, we ask nuns to give up clerical privilege[94] in order to prove their solidarity, thus engaging one another in the danger zones of sisterhood. Whatever the reasons for such requests, the results are predictably tragic: we hurt each other because we feel powerless to hurt the oppressive powers.

Womanchurch perceives its strength in collective power and understands that traditional Catholicism has put a membrane of mystification around "mysterious" female nature so that women cannot articulate their own social and religious reality. We also know that a hierarchical viewpoint maintains oppressive structures by defining everything in its own terms, creating a hierarchy of values that simultaneously sustains, and camouflages, the isolation of individual oppressed people. Bonding, therefore, and the sharing of experience, are necessary to the health and future of the Womanchurch movement. I think it is more realistic and effective to imagine ourselves as allies rather than as a family and so believe that we need to think about strategy in terms of alliances rather than sisterhood.

Whether a conflict model is understood as rhetorical flourish, or as genuinely descriptive of the present situation, collective strength is the only possibility for women in the church. If we believe that a patriarchal institution is, of itself, oppressive, then we may perceive also that it will use various means to retain its own power and to keep the subordinated members of the group — in this case, women — in a powerless position. Ironically, promoting sisterhood could become a patriarchal strategy, since it tends to set women up for horizontal confrontation. An effective patriarchal ploy pits one group against another so that the antagonists will self-destruct. Particularly invidious and maliciously effective, horizontal hostility, encouraged by those outside the struggle, has brought some great movements to their downfall — a history of the American labor movement shows that the Knights of Labor and the IWW both died from self-inflicted internal wounds — and it is dangerously myopic to think that Womanchurch is above this kind of internecine obliteration, or that sisterhood can prevent it.

From its beginning, the women's movement has been plagued by divisions. Marxist feminists and radical feminists differ seriously over the roots of oppression and continue to be engaged in a long-standing and perhaps unresolvable argument. Fearing contamination from each other, lesbians and heterosexual women sometimes avail themselves of ancient patriarchal concepts of purity and danger and so damage or destroy the possibilities of working together. White women and black women, wealthy and impoverished, Hispanics and Anglos — all the divisions that plague the general society are potentially capable of fracturing the Womanchurch movement. Although the nunwoman/laywoman identification is a religious way to embody horizontal hostility, it also gives Catholic women a way to resist the obliterating strategies of the patriarchy: by refusing "sisterhood" and by bonding through alliances, we might avoid some of the dangerous aspects of the argument and attempt to resolve our differences in intellectual and spiritual, rather than emotional, ways.[95]

In promoting alliances, I am suggesting that women have a common task. In *Reinventing Womanhood* Carolyn Heilbrun says we must learn from male lessons of achievement, supporting other women, identifying with them, and imagining the general achievements of women. "The male model of autonomy and achievement," she says, "is, indeed, the only one we still must follow."[96] Though I would contest Heil-brun's statement that achievement is a "male model," I have to agree that it has always been perceived that way. And though I agree with Carol Gilligan's observations that women are usually more interested in relationships than in autonomy,[97] I do not believe her observations are based on innate characteristics or that they inevitably lead women to a sisterhood model of collective interaction. I prefer to look at what we have to do as a project in which we must first set goals and then find an effective *modus operandi* for achieving them. In that process, ambition, achievement, and strength are neither bad words nor "male" words: they are the qualities of effective alliance.

Because women have been motivated historically to keep their rela-tionships protected, there may be some aspects of an alliance model that seem foreign to us, especially in the light of sisterhood. For ex-ample, alliances require us to learn to work effectively with people we fear, dislike, are angry with, or do not respect. Involved as we are in a mortal conflict on basic issues, and caught up in the struggle between competing models of church, we are called to cultivate new virtues, one of which may well be creative conflict. Jean Baker Miller says that "conflict is a necessity if women are to build for the future," and pro-ceeds to tell women to "wage good conflict." In this essentially posi-tive task which involves "reclaiming conflict," we can also move without guilt from sisterhood to alliance without losing the emotional energy necessary to change things.[98]

If women form alliances, we must be prepared for opposition: the patriarchal church will attempt to prevent us from organizing ourselves in order to serve the real interests of women. Patriarchal strategies in the church, like antifeminist ploys in the general society, will range from "guilt-tripping" to misuses of power: when women's concerns emerge at meetings in the church, someone will invariably attempt to rank oppressions and put women at the bottom of the list by saying, "Yes, but what about men? or world hunger? or nuclear warfare?" If those strategies fail, co-optation can be used: the church can elevate a few women to minor power positions in order to let the few protect it from the many. Finally, when all else fails, withdrawal of support or outright condemnation might be threatened or invoked.

In light of the issues, Roman Catholic women have some genuine strategic questions. Is the discussion about lay ministry and the "ministry of women in the church" really productive for women? Is women's ministry in the institutional church another way to sap women's strengths and divert them from their own concerns? Why should women fill in the gaps created by the current priest shortage when they will still receive low pay, no status, and little effective power? Because our consciousness has been raised about the clerical status of nuns, we need also ask about nuns in "quasi-clerical" positions, but I am not convinced that we need to demand a relinquishment of their power. Rather, they might be able to show other women how to obtain power and use it to subvert an oppressive system. It is not a question that can be decided easily, nor is it one that can be studied profitably from the vantage of sisterhood. If nuns have rank and privilege in the institutional church, they are also taking great risks to redefine themselves and their relationship to the institution.

Although Roman Catholic women have been beleaguered in the same way, inhibited from the full formation of an autonomous self, we are not sisters. Flannery O'Connor reminded us that "everything that rises must converge," and Catholic women have risen to claim their own interests and converged to find their collective strength; but sisterhood does not describe our reality, nor, I think, should it constitute a dream for the future. If we now know, from the women's movement and from our experience in the church, that we must resist the "protection" of the male mainstream, imagine ourselves as autonomous, and begin to form lasting bonds, then we should examine the kinds of bonds we are tempted to form. I believe that we need to conceptualize Womanchurch as allies in a working relationship rather than as sisters in a quasi-family unit. Whether we perceive the situation in the metaphor of conflict or in the more prosaic one of "having a job to do," we need to align ourselves with one another, despite personal feelings or differing political agendas, in order to reimagine the church in our own terms.

CONCLUSIONS

The women's movement, as we have seen, raises new questions in whatever context it arises. Usually, feminists demonstrate that the problems of an academic discipline or the parameters of an institution have been conceived too narrowly, and they work to extend the domain of their interests. The Womanchurch movement, grounded in the energy of the Women's Ordination Conference, has pointed to some fundamental inconsistencies in traditional Catholicism. A church that calls for social justice and makes itself vulnerable to the claims of justice is bound by logic to listen to the voices of oppressed women. Yet, as James Carroll says,

The church's rejection of women at this point reveals something fundamental about the dichotomizing mind of Catholicism; men here, women there; men initiate, women submit; men do, women feel; men preach the Word, women hear it. But the Word, as Paul says, cuts both ways. At bottom this is a question not only of justice, but of community. If the church is to survive as a community in a meaningful sense, then this dichotomy must be changed.[99]

Womanchurch cries out for this change. If women's ordination was its original issue, activism, social justice, the impetus of Vatican II, and the future of pluralistic, inclusive Catholicism are its bedrock.

Emerging as it has in the last part of the twentieth century, Womanchurch has many of the advantages of the larger women's movement. As Alison M. Jaggar has pointed out:

The very breadth of contemporary feminist concerns means that there is a "division of feminist labor," so that some feminists are preoccupied with some political struggles, some with others. Some feminists work in universities, some are active in left groups or in community organizing, some are black, some are lesbian. The variety of work and life experience of contemporary feminists results in a variety of perceptions of social reality and women's oppression. This variety is a source of strength for the women's liberation movement. Earlier waves of feminism sometimes have been charged with reflecting primarily the experience of white middle-class and upper-class women. While white middle-class women, at least, are still strongly represented in the contemporary women's movement, increasingly their perspective is challenged by perceptions that reflect the very different experiences of women of color, working class women, etc. The rich and varied experience of contemporary feminists contributes fresh insights into women's oppression and provides the women's liberation movement with new and valuable perspectives.[100]

Womanchurch is politically open to and welcoming of divergent perceptions and consciously aims to represent all those who wish to be part of it. As a self-critical and dialogical movement, Womanchurch is aware of potential antagonisms within itself and aware of its need for compassionate, responsive, efficient strategies for dealing with them. Alliances, task forces, coalitions, convergences, are all more suited to these tasks than sisterhood, and despite their less emotionally charged character, are all quite capable of allowing potentially opposed groups or individuals to "talk about the areas in their respective lives where each of them is loneliest, most frustrated, most afraid."[101]

Womanchurch thrives on diversity and needs a strong theological foundation. Unless Womanchurch can bond on the basis of a liberationist reading of the gospel, it will be tempted to find its strength purely in light of its feminist identity; but a feminist identity that is not grounded in something other than itself is left to the limits and divisiveness of sisterhood. Womanchurch, like historical Christianity, needs to stand on an exciting, gospel-inspired vision of the religious quest. Fortunately for the Womanchurch movement, Roman Catholic feminist theologians have built up a strong philosophical, exegetical, and practical foundation on which to build an inclusive, radical, prophetic, politically active, and spiritually alive community.

5. Enlarging the Discipline: Roman Catholic Feminist Theologians

What would have been the effect upon religion if it had come to us through the minds of women?

CHARLOTTE PERKINS GILMAN

Theology is experienced and expressed as an integrated imagery of wholeness, of head and body, heart and spirit. As women are doing theology out of their experience, they are tapping new sources of power within themselves, and this power is reflected through the written word.

BRIGALIA BAM

Never try to suppress the Spirit, or treat the gift of prophecy with contempt.

1 THESSALONIANS 5:19

Theology, formally defined, has the task of enlarging the borders of our language.

DOROTHY SÖLLE

In 1832 Elizabeth Cady Stanton led an exodus of women from her Presbyterian church as an eager young minister waxed eloquent on 1 Timothy 2:12.[1] One hundred thirty-nine years later, Mary Daly, preaching to the full chapel of the Harvard Divinity School, convinced a significant number of her hearers that the Moses story was paradigmatic: they followed her out of the building and out of the church.[2] These dramatic gestures are not meant to suggest a strategy so much as to convey a central tenet of feminist theology: it cannot be done within the confining atmosphere of patriarchal churches. From Charlotte Perkins Gilman in 1923[3] to Rosemary Radford Ruether sixty years later, feminists engaged in religious questions have been at pains to connect their vision to the realities of a wider world. It is not surprising, therefore, that feminist theology is rooted in theologies of hope and liberation or that Catholic feminist theologians owe a debt to the work of such profoundly humane and universalist writers as Karl Rahner. Roman Catholic feminist theology, begun by Americans and to some extent indebted to the profound insights of Paul Tillich, emerged in a context that had grown increasingly political, liberationist, and process-centered.

Without becoming enmeshed in details, this chapter will sketch the context and issues of feminist theology as it has grown in the Roman Catholic church. Since many of the creative insights of twentieth-century Roman Catholic theology rest philosophically on the work of Alfred North Whitehead and Karl Rahner, we will look first at Whiteheadian process thought and then at the "supernatural existential" as developed by Rahner to explain the intimate interplay between the divine and the human. Because contemporary theology is essentially ecumenical, the context will reflect the fruitful dialogue between Catholic and Protestant theologians, especially in terms of theologies of hope and liberation, specific applications of modern theology to agonizing world situations. Since this book concentrates on Roman Catholicism, however, the feminist theologians discussed here are all products of Catholic theological education and reflect specifically Roman Catholic backgrounds, concerns, and language. Although their theologies may have led them to an ecumenical perspective or even to the abandonment of historical Christianity altogether, their roots are Catholic, and they reflect many of the specific kinds of questions that have occurred in a Catholic context.

By way of context and general issues, and with attention to the work of Anne Carr, Elisabeth Schüssler Fiorenza, Rosemary Radford Ruether, and Mary Daly, we should be able to formulate a general description of Roman Catholic feminist theology and to demonstrate the broad range of questions it poses to traditional theology. Most of all, we should be able to see how it is that these theologians have laid the intellectual groundwork for a new Reformation. As Ralph Keifer noted in reviewing Edward Schillebeeckx's controversial book *Ministry,* "Reformation, then, requires a simultaneous crisis of liturgy, authority, spirituality and doctrine as its preconditions. It also requires the emergence of practical (and intellectually defensible) alternatives to the existing ecclesiastical structures."[4] By these criteria, Roman Catholicism is positioned for a new Reformation, and

Roman Catholic feminist theologians have begun to formulate "practical and intellectually defensible" alternatives to the church as we have known it.

FROM PROCESS THOUGHT TO POLITICAL THEOLOGY: THE CONTEXT

For over a hundred years, theologians and philosophers have wrestled with the "old God" mediated through Aristotelian or Scholastic categories. The attributes which we understood as divine made God the supreme exception to human experience: we grew and moved, whereas God was perfect and unchangeable, we anguished and changed, whereas God was sublime and complete. It was fairly easy to imagine God having no essential relationship with the world, incapable of being known through modes of human experience. "Process thought," an application of the general ideas of Alfred North Whitehead,[5] rests on the assumption that all existence, all reality, is continuous: the building blocks of the universe are analogous psychic energy-centers in process, undergoing incessant modification. If this assumption seems sensible when applied to human beings, it may seem senseless when talking about God; yet for Whitehead, God is the supreme exemplification of all metaphysical and human categories, not their exemption. God, therefore, is the ultimate explanation of process and, far from being unrelated to our world, is that being who is conditioned and affected by everything that happens here.

If all reality is process, and process is defined in terms of relationships, then perfection resides in movement, in a kind of ongoing creativity and relatedness. Since there is no such thing as an isolated process, it makes no sense in this system to speak of God in the abstract, *in se*: God can only be understood in terms of relationships, as the most perfectible, most related, and *therefore* most perfect being. God for Whitehead is full of possibilities, is the vision of what things might be. Yet divinity, dependent upon what human beings do with those possibilities, is affected by everything happening in the world. God is absolute, not in the traditional sense of final, total, unlimited, and unchangeable, but in the sense of encompassing in influence, related to, and suffering with all entities and being the ultimate and highest destiny of each. The divine experiencing is composed of the totality of all experience and is therefore larger and richer than any single actual experience. As single experiences enlarge and increase — as we respond to God's vision of what might be — God enlarges and increases. God's experiencing encompasses, urges, and directs all actual experiences by being at once their fuller context and their most compassionate witness. Since the primary category of existence in this system is experiencing in process, God is the ever more Becoming One, ever more related, ever more involved.

Clearly, in this view God's power lies in the lure of beauty, in the tenderness of compassionate persuasion, not in force. In the old system God was the total, efficient cause of all things, able to produce anything, to create out of nothing. But in this system, the process contains its own inner dynamic: God has the vision of all possibilities, and is the formal-structural source of all value, but has no power of coercion toward the actualization of this formal-structural value. God has only the power of what Whitehead calls *suasion*. God's vision of the best possible interrelationships, for example, presents the aim to process and functions as a lure to it, but cannot compel it.

In process thought, the novel emergence of the pulses of experience making up the world has the character of a divine revelation because it constitutes the concrete experience of God. Extolling human achievement, therefore, gives praise to God precisely because it recognizes God's envisioning made concrete in human and subhuman reality. If experience has claimed that human beings relate to God in strength, love, vulnerability, and weakness, process thought has made the same claim for God. God relates to us in strength because of the vision present in the divine primordial nature, in love because of a desire for more extensive and intensive relationship, in vulnerability because the divine destiny is tied to ours, and in weakness because God needs what we can give. Since the divine concrete experience depends on what we are able to give, God lures us on so that we will experience more and so have more to contribute to the process. Process thought, not unlike the Bible and the insights of the mystics, assumes that God is related, persuasive and involved with the world. If we integrate process thought, the partnership images of the Bible, and the insights of contemplative spirituality, it is possible to talk about a religiously lived life as a union that enriches both partners beyond their ability to achieve alone.

One major work of twentieth-century theologians has been to show that the supernatural is not disconnected from human life. As theologians wrestled with questions of divine self-communication (grace and revelation) in the light of human consciousness, they began to soften the antagonisms between traditional dualisms so that it became difficult to support the oppositions between nature and grace, the secular and the sacred, humanity and divinity.

Probably the most creative and prolific modern Catholic theologian has been Karl Rahner, a German Jesuit whose work encompasses the whole gamut of the theological enterprise.[6] Influenced indirectly by currents stirred by Pierre Teilhard de Chardin and Maurice Blondel, and more directly by Martin Heidegger and by Joseph Maréchal's reading of Thomas, Rahner became perhaps the most universally influential Catholic theologian since Aquinas. Since it is helpful to explain the general atmosphere in which he worked, we need to look briefly at the insights of some of those whose work moved Rahner.

Blondel, a French philosopher, argued in 1893 that belief is not a matter of accepting as true some unlikely story about God but more a matter of interpreting human experience in a particular way. For Blondel, "Human *action* shows a dynamism which moves us toward a goal lying beyond our power to achieve it."[7] A more familiar embodiment of that theory might be that of Teilhard de Chardin, who argued in the 1940s that the whole cosmic order is moving toward a goal (an "Omega point"), and that human life is moving toward increasingly higher states of consciousness.[8] For Teilhard, therefore, the kingdom of God is not disconnected from earth but draws the world along toward its fulfillment. Whether Blondel influenced Teilhard or not, he did have an impact on Joseph Maréchal, who then was able to interpret Aquinas to characterize human consciousness as a teleological dynamism toward "Being." Maréchal's "transcendental Thomism" opened the way for Rahner to integrate a teleological conception of consciousness into traditional Catholic categories.[9] With his great learning he persuasively argued that such a conception was already present, at least implicitly, in the tradition.

More important to Rahner than Maréchal, perhaps, was Martin Heidegger, one of the greatest philosophers of the twentieth century. Heidegger's argument that the "horizon of Being," or "world," as the context of experience encompasses any consideration, even that of the divine, enabled Rahner to formulate his own notion that the Spirit is a dynamism toward divine Being as the ultimate horizon or background of our experience. Thus the divine as "supernatural" is "existential," and is a constitutive ingredient of human experience.[10] Against the traditional dualism of nature and grace, Rahner argued that nature includes in itself the radical capacity for grace and that pure human nature does not exist apart from a "supernatural" destiny or context. The "supernatural existential" renders us restless for God, which means that human nature is self-transcending and therefore contains within itself the more, the power to go beyond present self definitions. The question of God, therefore, is a question of human existence, and the history of the world is, at the same time, a history of salvation.

If world history and salvation history are coextensive, and if world history necessarily involves novelty, then the meaning of revelation implies the possibility of saying something new. Traditionally revelation was thought of as a kind of inner light that makes belief (in God and sacred things) possible and/or the act by which God furnishes humanity with the necessary truths of salvation. Theologians had always distinguished between textual revelation and the ongoing work of the Spirit within the human community. Rahner, however, challenged that dichotomy by proposing that one cannot make a hierarchical separation between textual revelation and God's contextual work with/in the human community. What happens here and now is understood as revelation: the continuing communication of the divine through the life and work of the human community is not incidental to textual revelation. Human experience, therefore, is a fundamental datum of theology. Furthermore, the divine permeation of the human is so complete and intimate — God is so constitutive of our human existence — that almost everything we say about God can be translated into a declaration about facets of our own existence.[11]

Given the "new God" of process thought and the dynamic categories of a new revelation theology worked out by Rahner and others, a new generation of theologians — Catholic and Protestant — were prepared, in a sense, for the kinds of wrenching questions raised about the power of God in light of the Second World War. After the Holocaust and Hiroshima and Nagasaki, problems of theodicy and revelation demanded new answers, and theologians had to search through not only traditional theology but the rubble of the postwar world permeated by the image of an absent, powerless, or indifferent divinity. To some — later called "radical" theologians[12] — the whole question of God was beside the point: the celebration of "the death of God" left humanity free to get on with life without having to struggle with and eventually capitulate to capricious mystery. For others — later called secular theologians[13] — Christian or religious life was nothing more than responsible human life: Christians were religious insofar as they were politically responsible and gracious. Both of these theologies, cries from the heart, demanded that the old separations between this world and the next be declared irrelevant. If God were not involved with the world and religious life not capable of being expressed in political terms, then religion had no right to continue.

One political-religious response to the new situation was the theology of hope as expressed by Jürgen Moltmann, a Lutheran.[14] Inspired by the Marxist philosopher Ernst Bloch, who had argued that we cannot understand ourselves apart from our propensity to hope for the future, Moltmann made the future a central part of his theology: we bring the future kingdom into the present, he said, when we struggle to narrow the gap between justice and injustice. In this scheme, the church exists for the world, and the members of the church are to be at work in the political life of the world. Influenced later by critical theory and by process thought, Moltmann moved his focus on hope in Christ's future in a different direction, to a following of the historical Jesus. The crucifixion, for Moltmann, is bound up with justice and divine suffering leading to a political theology of the cross. In *The Crucified God*, Moltmann elaborated a theology of divine suffering that connects the Trinity with oppression and suffering in the world. God is not the one supremely above worldly pain but is inseparable from the godforsaken of the earth. The church, called to imitate God's love, is bound to identify with the outcasts of society and witness to the belief that "the glory of God does not shine on the crowns of the mighty but on the face of the crucified Christ."[15]

Moltmann's Catholic counterpart as a political theologian is Rahner's student Johannes Metz. Schooled in Scholastic theology and thoroughly conversant with Rahner's thought, Metz saw that the categories of Aquinas were inadequate to address the real problems of the world, especially that of oppression. Like Moltmann, Metz believes in the necessity for Christians to exert themselves in the political realm. Building on a deeply Catholic foundatoin, Metz argued that Christians ought to be prophetic witnesses not only to the world but to the church itself. For Metz, the gospel call for an uncompromising dedication to God and to the world is intimately bound up with the here and now.[16]

When these new political theologies were applied to the cultural realities of Latin America, another "new theology" inspired a variety of "liberation theologies" specific to the oppression of blacks, women, and the Third World poor. Since liberation theology arose most directly from the Latin American situation, we need to look there first for an understanding of its basic principles.

A central tenet of liberation theology is the belief that God is revealed in the historical praxis of liberation:[17] God's primary passion is to free humans from oppressed situations, and God's self-disclosure (revelation) occurs "when we recognize and accept God's summons to us to participate in the historical struggle for liberation."[18] Three important events or ideas influenced the development of liberation theology in Latin America: Paulo Friere's *Pedagogy of the Oppressed*[19] provided a method; the failure of the United Nations Decade of Development in the 1960s presented a concrete problem; and the ground-breaking documents from the Latin American bishops' conference at Medellín (1968) added God's blessing to a burgeoning movement.[20]

Friere devised a method to teach impoverished illiterates in Brazil (1959–64) that named and described the "culture of silence" of the dispossessed and so made education subversive. His literacy method "raised the consciousness" of the poor and persuaded them to see their connections with their own oppression: if they wanted freedom, Friere's method led them to believe, they had to assume the risks of freedom. His way of teaching reading and writing was based on action characteristic of the oppressed and subsequent reflection on that action (*praxis*), thereby disclosing its historical contingency. Thus there came also to light the "praxis" necessary for surmounting the oppression.

The failure of the UN Decade of Development effectively exposed the real aims of richer countries as they related to Latin American peoples. Hoping to increase the GNP of poor countries by 5 percent, rich nations cooperated to provide aid in the form of government loans and investments. They succeeded in their aim—the GNP increased—but by the end of the decade the United States was taking more money from these countries than it was giving to them.[21] The failure of the UN solution, therefore, made the enemy dramatically clear and opened new territory for the subversive methods of Friere.

When the bishops' conference at Medellín issued statements denouncing oppression in Latin America and condemning neocolonialism, Marxism, and capitalism in favor of a new socialism—a word beginning to find cautious use in official Roman Catholic church statements[22]—the documents blessed a burgeoning movement of social justice actions that had made it clear that the Roman Catholic church was squarely on the side of the oppressed. In effect, the bishops welcomed the work of the liberation theologians and politically active Catholics.

All these theologies—process thought, Rahner's work, political theology, the theology of hope, and liberation theology—were enormously influential, had a wide reception, and were filled with creative potential. When Vatican II opened new avenues of religious and liturgical experience for Catholics—especially Americans—it also tacitly encouraged them to study new theologians and to become aware of these new ideas. Postconciliar theology was critical and prophetic, not dogmatic, and it is no accident that two of the most powerful feminist theologians in the Roman Catholic tradition—Elisabeth Schüssler Fiorenza and Mary Daly—are both fully conversant with the range and depth of continental theology. In addition, Mary Daly was influenced by the thought of Paul Tillich. Nor is it coincidental that Rosemary Radford Ruether's work has been consistently informed by a biblical-prophetic interpretation or that Anne Carr's feminist methodology is deeply indebted to the thought of Karl Rahner.

The context is much richer and more complex than can be so briefly described: it includes the political realities of postwar Europe, the hopes of the Christian-Marxist dialogue, modern expressions of the women's movement in existential and political categories, the dividends of ecumenical cooperation, and the stimulus of critical theory. When we consider the Catholic Action strategy of Pius XI and the mystical body theology of Pius XII, we can begin to account for activism and excitement on the part of the laity; when we include the breakthrough of the Second Vatican Council, we can explain nonclerical interest in theology and philosophy. At the end of the 1960s it all seemed tremendously exciting. As Mary Daly said, "It appeared that a door had opened *within* patriarchy which could admit an endless variety of human possibilities."[23] Through that seemingly open door feminist theologians have gone into the tradition critically to understand new directions in theology, and they have come out again to articulate a feminist theology—widely interdisciplinary and cooperative—that begins with the experience of women and then claims the power of "solidarity with victims."[24]

FROM DE-CONSTRUCTION TO RE-CONSTRUCTION: THE CONTENT

Academic disciplines, as well as ecclesiastical life, have been shaped by a false consciousness that believes that female voices, thoughts, work, views, experiences, senses of value, and ways of approaching problems are unimportant and that one can somehow come to an understanding of the "humanities" from an androcentric perspective. The women's movement has challenged this *modus operandi* with a series of logical steps: (1) notice and point out that women have been ignored in the field; (2) notice and point out that what we do know about women, sparse though it is, is characterized by a high level of hostility, diminishment, frivolity or musty mystification; (3) search out and publicize the lost women in the discipline so that we can add as many figures as possible to an otherwise male pantheon; (4) begin a revisionary reading of the old texts and traditions so that they lose their power to terrorize and exclude women; (5) with new female characters and a revisionary reading, begin to challenge the discipline methodologically in order to redefine its borders, goals, and consequences; and (6) work toward a truly integrated field, which is not reduced by its prejudices against women, lower classes, variant sexual preferences, or anything else but represents the human in all its messy and rich diversity.

Feminist theology is not unlike other disciplines in the steps it has to take in order to find itself. We have to admit at the outset that the religious traditions of the West are relentlessly patriarchal in language, custom, practice, symbolism, memory, history, theological articulation, and ritual. Immersed in the realities of this litany, we have to ask, What we can do about it. Why should we stay within a tradition that gives us no vote and precious little voice, a tradition that is overwhelmingly negative about the female body, mind, and spirit? Understandably, there have been different answers to those questions. Feminist theologians have argued either to reject the tradition and search for new alternatives (usually focused on the Goddess and a revival of witchcraft) or to reinterpret the tradition in order to change its direction and open it to the influences and lives of women. The best representatives of the first alternative are probably Carol P. Christ and Starhawk, both of whom have written salient and engaging works attempting to show "why women need the Goddess."[25] Perceiving rightly that one cannot simply reject a symbol system without replacing it, Christ, Starhawk, and others have attempted to provide women with a new symbol system, new rituals, new stories, and a new body of durable metaphor for their religious lives. In so doing, feminists of the first alternative provide a strong and necessary dialectical partner for those whose perception of the problem has led them to a reinterpretation of the tradition, and a revisionary reading of the texts.[26]

The many and complicated tasks of Roman Catholic feminist theology can be traced here only in outline as they relate to the work of Anne Carr, Elisabeth Schüssler Fiorenza, Rosemary Radford Ruether, and Mary Daly. I have chosen the most well known and prolific representatives in order to sketch the extensiveness of the endeavor as it provides the intellectual basis for a number of possibilities, including the Womanchurch movement. In choosing these four theologians, I have omitted others — Margaret Farley's clear voice on ethical issues, Mary Hunt's articulation of a feminist theology of friendship, Joann Wolski Conn's work on female moral development and spirituality[27] — and have included one who would not even remotely identify herself as a Catholic feminist theologian. Whether they remain within or outside the tradition — Daly would not admit to being on the same planet with it — they have been shaped by its particular brand of clerical patriarchy, schooled in its theological methods, and rejected by its supremely devastating canons. Carr's contributions to a feminist theological method, Schüssler Fiorenza's liberationist hermeneutic, Ruether's prophetic perspective, and Daly's re-creation of the language give Roman Catholic feminist theology an exceedingly broad base on which to build the theology of the future.

RE-INTERPRETING THE SYMBOLS: ANNE CARR

Anne Carr (b. 1934), an active participant in the Women's Ordination Conference from its beginnings and a member of the WOC-Bishops' dialogue on the ordination of women,[28] wrote her dissertation on the theological method of Karl Rahner.[29] As one might expect, therefore, despite her articles on ordination and on the experience of women in historical Christianity,[30] she is primarily interested in questions of systematic theology. Beginning, as Rahner does, with the individual as a transcendent being with a capacity for relationship with God and nourished by the symbol-centered atmosphere of the University of Chicago Divinity School, Carr is mainly engaged in a reformulation of those Christian doctrines that are problematic from a feminist perspective. Essentially disagreeing with Carol Christ — that an investigation of Christian symbolism will either have to show that the core symbols "of Father and Son do not have the effect of reinforcing and legitimating male power and female submission, or it will have to transform Christian imagery at its very core"[31] — Carr perceives that Christian symbols offer more than this either/or interpretation.

Particularly interested in the doctrines of God, Christ, church, and revelation, Carr agrees with those feminist critics who see the church and its doctrines as patriarchal and unhealthy for women. She does not agree, however, that one must therefore either abrogate or re-create their symbols. For Carr, Christian symbols and doctrines suggest something more than the debasement or subordination of women. When they are interpreted as genuinely religious, Christian symbols drive toward a transcendence of their own culture-bound formulation, which means that they can move beyond the social and political patterns they have legitimated.[32]

In an article assessing the possibilities for a feminist theology, Carr admitted the alienating power of traditional Christian symbols but insisted that these same symbols — God, Christ, salvation history, for example — have been life-giving as well as destructive for women. As such, Christian symbols invite criticism from within themselves: "The task is to search for resources within the biblical, theological and intellectual tradition that enable Christian feminist theology to be understood as an urgent and intrinsic theological task."[33] Indebted to the work of twentieth-century philosophers and critics — Hans-Georg Gadamer, Jürgen Habermas, Paul Tillich, Paul Ricoeur, and David Tracy — Carr posited four requirements for a Christian feminist theology. One must, first of all, admit that it is possible to understand the past both critically and constructively: because the history of the Christian tradition is precisely the source of feminist questions, theologians must work from within it in order to de-construct and re-construct it. Secondly, feminist theologians must admit to and defend an openly "interested" scholarship of advocacy. Feminist theology is not neutral or "objective," but neither — were we to follow Habermas's arguments — is any other theology. Third, feminist theology must take into account the "mixed texture" of religious symbols, realizing that symbols remain under what Tillich called the "law of ambiguity," so that theologians can neither affirm nor deny them, only interpret them. A feminist interpretation engages in a dialectical process that is both suspicious and restorative. Finally, an adequate theological method must exhibit a double critique:

> On one side, the pluralism of feminist cultural and religious interpretations

must be related to the Christian symbols in their over-determined meaning, and their hidden, regressive or ideological dimensions exposed. On the other, the restored or purified meaning of the symbols, in their transformative possibilities, must be brought to bear on the culture and on religion itself. . . . The interpreted experience of women in society—economic, cultural, religious—is used to criticize those dimensions of the Christian tradition . . . which serve to legitimate the exclusion and subordination of women. . . . And the newly interpreted understanding of the gospel and of Christian symbols as authentically liberating for women is used to criticize a sexist culture in which women are systematically exploited.[34]

Carr's work, therefore, has been consciously interested in theological method and in the reinterpretation of Christian symbols. Typical of Catholic feminist theologians, she is active in the women's movement, has been a strong advocate for women's ordination, and has worked to make feminist questions more visible within the academy. Though her early feminist writing focused on various aspects of women's ordination, her writing since 1980 has been predominantly related to major systematic questions.[35] An article on Rahner's method[36]—"Starting with the Human"—explains Carr's own starting point: questions of the self are intimately related to questions about God, and human experience is a fundamental datum of theology. Accordingly, "women's recent reflection on their own experience in all its variety and their attempt to develop corresponding models of humanity is an important development in theological anthropology."[37] Grace, Christology, revelation, and God cannot be understood apart from the experience of women, nor can human experience be understood apart from "the God who is involved"[38] in our world.

When we recall Rahner's assessment of the future of the postconciliar church as essentially pluralistic, we can see that Carr is faithful to that hope. In her work on ordination as well as in her systematic theological reflection, she has consistently argued that practical and philosophical questions are open to diverse interpretations and enriched by pluralistic understandings. Describing her own work, she once said, "Feminist theology, as I envision it, finally joins Christian theology itself in its pluralism of voices. It is a genuine though somewhat feisty conversation partner in the give and take of Christian thinking."[39]

RE-CLAIMING THE CENTER: ELISABETH SCHÜSSLER FIORENZA

Elisabeth Schüssler Fiorenza (b. 1938), though following some of the same steps as other feminist theologians, has worked in a narrower framework (New Testament studies) and produced a more intense vision of feminist theology. Her background—German-born and - trained, first woman in her diocese to study theology and needing the bishop's permission to do so—immersed her for the first part of her scholarly life in ecclesiological questions. The conciliar atmosphere of the early 1960s supported her interest in the declericalization of the church, but it did not encourage research into women's issues. Her Licentiate thesis (1964) attempted to establish an inclusive ecclesiology by way of the de facto ministerial status of women in the German church.[40] Though she took women as an example of lay ministry, she was more interested in articulating a theological understanding of ministry that included both clergy and laity than in making a case for women's ordination, but the very process of research and writing raised her consciousness so that she discovered in her work a specifically feminist question. Although she adopted women's issues as her own in the early 1960s, she did so without much contextual support. By the time she participated in the Women Doing Theology workshop at Grailville (1972), however, women's studies programs and opportunities to become involved in the practical aspects of women's questions opened a much wider and more supportive context for her work.[41] Since then she has been extraordinarily active, writing, conducting workshops, lecturing, and otherwise spreading the new "good news" that women are *not* marginal in the Jesus movement.

If Schüssler Fiorenza could be reduced to a slogan, it would be an ecclesiological battle cry, "Reclaim the center!" Her feminist theology is grounded on a structural analysis of the church that follows a critical liberationist hermeneutic. In describing her own work she said:

> I would summarize my endeavors as attempts to articulate a feminist theology as a critical theology of liberation. Such a theology seeks to name theologically the alienation, anger, pain and oppression of women engendered by patriarchal sexism in society and church as well as to provide an alternative Christian vision of liberation. Such a theology is not based on the theological

anthropology of "complementarity of the sexes" nor on a metaphysical "female ascendency" principle. It does not advocate the co-optation of women's spiritual powers by ecclesiastical patriarchy nor the emigration of women from patriarchal society and church. Since it is based on the radical presupposition that gender is socially and politically constructed and that such a construction serves to perpetuate the patriarchal exploitation and oppression of women, it seeks to enable women theologically to explore the structural sin of patriarchal sexism, to reject its internalizations and ecclesial legitimizations, and to become in such a conversion the ecclesia of women, Womanchurch.[42]

Like other feminist theologians working from within the tradition, Schüssler Fiorenza names the oppressive structures of the church while, simultaneously working to rediscover the liberating elements of the tradition that will enable women to resist exclusion and marginalization.

Her most important articles have contributed to the middle steps of the feminist theological process, especially the revisionary reading of old texts and the creation of new paradigms. Foundational to an understanding of her later work is an appreciation of "Feminist Theology as a Critical Theology of Liberation," published in 1975.[43] Women, she says, are clearly discriminated against on the basis of sex and portrayed within the Christian tradition as either weak or mysterious. Official responses to feminist complaints usually include denial, co-optation, or condemnation and amount to a refusal to repent of the sin of sexism. In turn, feminists generally respond either by leaving the tradition—judging the patriarchalism of biblical tradition to be inexorable—or remaining within it only in order to transform it.

A first step in the transformation of our traditional perceptions is the unmasking of neutrality: when looking at the Bible, for example, we have to see that the formation and interpretation of the New Testament canon is culturally conditioned. Both the New Testament and its scholarship are androcentric. Schüssler Fiorenza, using the insights of critical theory,[44] argues that feminists do not try to "understand" the androcentricity of the New Testament but seek instead to criticize it. Inspired by liberation theology, she also argues that feminist critics have to "liberate" both the church and theology from their imprisonment in a white, middle-class, academic, and sexist system. A new theology and a new interpretive framework for the New Testament will be, she says, "rooted in community . . . expresse[d] not only in abstract analysis and intellectual discussion, but . . . [in] the whole range of human expression."[45] In order for such a new theology to emerge—one that includes the active involvement of "women and men, black and white, privileged and exploited persons" (p. 615)—structural change must occur both within the church and within the discipline of New Testament studies. Some elements of this change will respond to the need for new feminist myths by reappropriating lost women and reinterpreting traditional ones. Lastly, Schüssler Fiorenza believes, the "most pressing issue within the Catholic Church is . . . to create a 'new sisterhood' that is not based on sexual stratification" (p. 623).

She has followed the main themes of this article in much of her subsequent work. Her call for "a new sisterhood" was sounded at the first Women's Ordination Conference,[46] and in her critical response to the CARA study on women in ministry.[47] Because of her long-standing commitment to declericalization and structural change within Roman Catholicism, she is wary of women seeking ordination within the present system and has been at pains to warn against a "new clericalism" if ordination is sought without significant structural change. She has drawn the unspoken divisions between nuns and laywomen into open debate in order to expose the patriarchal strategy of dividing internally and to promote sisterhood.[48] My disagreement with her is over the word sisterhood, not over the concept of a powerful, united feminist collective within the church.

Her insistence on the need for new stories and new versions of old ones has emerged in articles on women apostles, on women in the early Christian movement, and on possibilities for a feminist spirituality. Her efforts to articulate a new interpretive paradigm for New Testament study and to urge a new hermeneutics that can prove that God is on the side of the oppressed, have led her to argue that an equalitarian interpretive framework is the only one that can do justice to the countercultural, pluriform, dynamics of the Jesus movement, and the only one that has the power to set free the egalitarian impulses of that movement both in the ancient traditions and in contemporary practice.[49] Her groundwork for a new church—ideally a community of coequal discipleship, but necessarily at the moment an ecclesia of women—has been laid in grass-roots gatherings of women,[50] as well as in scholarly forums in the academy.[51]

In all these directions—a new sisterhood, spirituality, reading of the tradition, hermeneutics, and church—Schüssler Fiorenza follows a liberationist and critical model. The insights of critical theory, that value-free interpretation is impossible and that texts and interpreters are politically motivated, forms a starting point for her evaluation. The tenets of liberation theology, especially the need for consciousness raising and the lives of the oppressed as a locus of divine activity, clarify for her the need to establish a feminist identity on the common historical experience of women's oppression. Our task is not to glorify or misremember the past, not to understand or excuse it, but to reclaim "the dangerous memory of former suffering" and seek the "subversive power of a critically remembered past."[52] Our ability to remember oppression allows us to ground our critique of the present. These themes achieve their fullest expression in her book on the feminist theological reconstruction of Christian origins.

In Memory of Her is titled to honor the anonymous woman in Mark 14:9 who anointed Jesus, "the faithful disciple who is forgotten because she was a woman."[53] Following the lead of Judy Chicago—"our heritage is our power"—Schüssler Fiorenza believes that rediscovering our heritage in the early Christian community will make it clear "that the Christian gospel cannot be proclaimed if the women disciples and what they have done are not remembered" (p. xiv). In the book she has two clear goals: a historical one, to reconstruct early Christian history as women's history; and a theological one, to make women's stories an integral part of the proclamation of the gospel so as to deny the sacred text its power to oppress women.

In Memory of Her is a risky book within the field of New Testament scholarship. New Testament scholars will undoubtedly argue with her interpretation of certain points—*sophia* theology, for example, or her exegesis of the deutero-Pauline material—but they may be most engaged with her use of a liberationist hermeneutic. One of the central tenets of liberation theology is the belief that God is revealed in the historical praxis of liberation: one looks for God's word today in the concrete experience of the oppressed. Applied to the New Testament,

a liberationist hermeneutic insists that oppressive texts be "demytholo-
gized as androcentric codifications of patriarchal power" that "cannot
claim to be the revelatory Word of God" (p. 32). Schüssler Fiorenza
is constrained to save the texts themselves from rejection by feminists
who see the Bible as hopelessly patriarchal. At the same time, she dis-
agrees with those biblical interpreters who argue either that misogynist texts do not say what they seem to say, or that they say it but do
not mean it. Finally, she will not accept what she characterizes as the
"neo-Orthodox" position of finding a "canon within the canon," ab-
stracting a quintessential theme in the Bible and then using it to ignore
other, more troublesome texts. For her, as for Elizabeth Cady Stanton
in the late nineteenth century, the Bible *is* androcentric and patriarchal: the theological task is not to ignore that fact or dilute it, but to
reclaim "such androcentric human and biblical history as women's own
history" (p. 28). She offers a critical reconstruction of women's historical oppression within patriarchal religion precisely to reclaim the
sufferings of our foresisters and to make them part of our own "subversive memory." Since this task calls for a paradigm shift, Schüssler
Fiorenza suggests, on the basis of her liberationist hermeneutic, that
we see the New Testament not as an archetype, but as a prototype, as
"critically open to the possibility of its own transformation" (p. 33).

Schüssler Fiorenza works within a creative tension that is both
feminist and Christian: as a feminist, she criticizes Christianity for being
guilty of the structural sin of sexism, while, as a Christian, she argues
that the tradition is not inherently or necessarily sexist. To sustain this
tension she focuses on the historical struggle of women and other
oppressed peoples, finding in their struggle the locus of God's liberating activity. She resists those outside the Christian tradition who
have — too easily, she thinks — relinquished women's biblical heritage,
and at the same time, resists those within the church who would judge
a feminist reconstruction to be eccentric or marginal.

When she opens the text to critical transformation from women's
experience — ancient and modern — she empowers women to reclaim
the center of their tradition while refusing to allow church pronouncements or ancient texts to marginalize us. Like other feminist
theologians, she refuses to accept the idea that God somehow wills

the subordination of women: the equalitarian ethics of Jesus, his behavior and words, were distorted by those who selected New Testament texts and by those who subsequently interpreted them. Schüssler Fiorenza attempts to unmask this distortion, to claim the revelatory value of the experience of oppressed women, and to bring contemporary women to see that those who wish to relegate us to the fringes of the tradition stand themselves on its very edges.

Who stands in the authentic stream of the tradition of Jesus? Those who understand the equalitarian, antiestablishment, politically subversive, radical, prophetic, God-driven words and life of Jesus. If an alternative patriarchal tradition has won out over time, "this 'success' can not be justified theologically, since it cannot claim the authority of Jesus for its own Christian praxis."[54]

Schüssler Fiorenza establishes theoretically the task of feminist theology, and she connects theory with practice by following the liberationist insight that "only active commitment to the oppressed and active involvement in their struggle for liberation enable us to see our society and the world differently and give us a new perspective."[55] In order to have a specific, advocacy stance — a feminist hermeneutics — theology must become the theory of practice. Combining insights from the Frankfurt School and liberation theology, Schüssler Fiorenza argues that theology is partisan and rooted in emancipatory praxis. Her reconstruction of Christian origins — including the epilogue describing the ecclesia of women — can strengthen the women's movement (traditionally hostile to religion and to the Bible) by connecting our heritage to our power and showing how that heritage, *because* it is linked with oppression, can be subversive in the present situation.

RE-APPROPRIATING THE PROPHETIC: ROSEMARY RADFORD RUETHER

Rosemary Radford Ruether (b. 1936) has worked through most of the steps of the process and is the most prolific writer in the Roman Catholic feminist community. Because her work has been directed by her own existential interests —"I have never taken up an intellectual issue which did not have direct connections with clarifying and resolving questions about my own existence"[56] — and because "social sin" has been a catalyst for her thinking and writing,[57] Ruether's work is wide-

ranging. One finds her equally at home in her area of academic spe-
cialization—the classics and early Christian writers[58]—and in the
ecclesiastical and social issues of the times: she has written articles on
birth control, divorce, the council and its aftermath, civil rights, the
Vietnam war, political and historical Christianity, the Jewish–Christian
dialogue, Zionism, ecology, nuclear arms, and base communities.[59] She
has published more than two hundred articles and close to twenty
books. Far from being a misty-minded academic, she is remarkably
activist, not only as a lecturer, but as a seasoned political demonstra-
tor.[60] When asked about the many different causes she has espoused
she says, "These issues were experienced by me not as a series of alter-
nating commitments, but as an expanding consciousness of the present human social dilemma."[61]

Much of her early work was done in the context of the post–Vatican II church, where, she believed, a revolution in consciousness had
occurred.[62] When she speculated about future communities, they
were invariably self-gathered, ecumenical, prophetic, and supportive
of the full personhood of all members. In her perspective, the church
of the future was committed to this world, not the next, able and willing
to repent of its sins against blacks, Jews, women, Third World peoples, and Native Americans: it was made up of small communities,
essentially declericalized, and opposed to the dualisms that separate
human beings from themselves and others. All these characteristics have
appeared in her articles and books on women. Refusing consistently
to hierarchicalize oppressions, she sees "sexism, racism, classism and
other kinds of oppression as interconnected in an overall pattern of
human alienation and sinfulness."[63]

Ruether (along with Daly) did pioneering work in the first two steps
of the feminist theological task. Her "Male Chauvinist Theology and
the Anger of Women" (1971) was a perceptive and challenging summary of the issues at a time when very few people understood the
dimensions of the problem of women in the church.[64] *Religion and
Sexism: Images of Women in the Jewish and Christian Traditions* (1974)[65] can
be taken as a companion book to Daly's *The Church and the Second Sex*
(1968). Daly's work shows that the Catholic church both idealizes and
humiliates women, whereas Ruether's thought demonstrates precisely

how Judaism and Christianity have functioned to project denigrating views of women and then to use them in service of a "divinely willed" oppression.

Besides pointing to the absence of women in the tradition, and exposing the devastating hostility toward those few who can be found within Christianity, Ruether has also done some of the first work on the third step: her *Women of Spirit: Female Leadership in the Jewish and Christian Traditions* (1979), edited with Eleanor McLaughlin, is a solid forerunner to the important new series she has edited with Rosemary Skinner Keller, *Women and Religion in America*.[66] Since the availability of previously neglected sources is crucial to the feminist project, *Women and Religion in America* is especially important both to an understanding of American religious history and to women's history: this three-volume series reproduces primary documents and pictures, describes the work of women in important American religious movements, and offers a view of female strength and greatness that has never been glimpsed until now.

The revisionary reading of the texts and the methodological challenge to the discipline appears, for the most part, in Ruether's later work. Because Ruether's critical vision is essentially social, it usually incorporates analyses of several different struggles into a general prophetic viewpoint. Furthermore, her belief that the "woman's story must encompass the entire scope of the human dilemma, . . . must presuppose a comprehensive setting of the issue,"[67] leads her to explore a multitude of topics with the hope of connecting the logic and power of various liberation movements. *New Woman, New Earth,* for example, contains essays on sexism, ministry, Mariology, anti-Semitism, witchcraft, racism and sexism, the psychoanalytic revolution, socialism, and an argument for the ecological dimensions of the women's movement.[68] These essays draw their cohesive strength from the passion of her involvement and the depth of her understanding of religious responsibility. "Reconciliation with God means the revolutionizing of human social, political relations, over-throwing unjust, oppressive relationships. The sociopolitical dimension is never lost in Hebrew messianism, but always remains the central expression of what it means to obey God."[69] In this sense, her feminist critique is never "pure" but is always connected with other social realities.[70] Further-more, by being practical as well as constructive, an activist as well as an intellectual, she shows that she does not respect the old prejudicial barriers that once separated the systematic theologians from the pastoral.

The biblical basis of Ruether's social critique is her understanding of the prophetic impulse. Perceiving in the Hebrew prophets "an ecological theology" that "transforms the Canaanite year cycle of natural-social renewal into the prophetic dialectic of judgment and promise," she notices a clear shift in emphasis from "season cycles to historical crisis."[71] Prophecy is a decisive break with the status quo, an essentially self-critical understanding of God's intentions that posits God "as [an] advocate of the oppressed, overturner of an unjust order, whose action in history points forward to a reconstructed commu-nity" (p. 33). When we pray that God's will be done on earth as in heaven, we often think of heaven as another world, apart from the perils and confusion of our normal lives. For Ruether, however, heaven "is neither the confirming halo of existing creation, nor is it another world into which we can escape from this world. Rather it is the mandate of that rectified world that stands as judgment and hope over against things as they are" (p. 33).

As process theologians can talk about a God who is involved, Ruether can envision a Christian community involved in the tasks of liberation in this world. Her theology, therefore, is essentially libera-tionist and includes the belief that there is no such thing as an apoliti-cal theology, that God has shown a preferential option for the oppressed and calls on us to respond to calls for liberation. As a liber-ationist she extols praxis and understands that human experience (the experience of women in particular) is a fundamental datum of theology.

Sexism and God-Talk,[72] Ruether's systematic theology, is at once a deconstruction of traditional categories and a reconstructive vision of theology from a feminist perspective. In an interview published after the book appeared, she said that she works on the assumption that the primary task of feminist theology is to free the church from patriar-chy: feminist theology exposes the sexist structures of the church challenging it to recognize the distortions of the Christian message created by its patriarchal heritage.[73] In positive terms, feminist theology challenges the church to "reconstruct its social patterns, language and theology to affirm the full humanity of both women and men."[74] *Sexism and God-Talk* confronts traditional theology on all levels. Ruether begins from a new starting point: women's experience, rather than God (philosophically understood) or the teachings of the magisterium (dogmatically defined), provide the matter with which she will form a new theology. There is nothing novel in her assertion that theology is based on experience, or in her insistence that theology ought to be situated in a dialectical relationship with culture, constantly subject to criticism and reinterpretation. Startling, however, is the foundational weight of *women's* experience and female cultural paradigms.

Ruether's presuppositions, far from narrowly confessional, absorb and transform insights from nontraditional sources—heretical or marginal groups within the Christian movement, primary theological themes newly read, non-Christian philosophy and post-Christian worldviews—in a search for a more genuinely inclusive theological perspective. The critical principle of this feminist theology is simple: "whatever denies, diminishes, or distorts the full humanity of women is . . . appraised as not redemptive. Theologically speaking, whatever diminishes or denies the full humanity of women must be presumed not to reflect the divine or an authentic relation to the divine, nor to reflect the authentic nature of things, nor to be the message or work of an authentic redeemer or a community of redemption."[75] The positive corollary states that whatever promotes the full humanity of women is "of the Holy." Feminist theology, as Ruether points out, is not unique in claiming this principle, but it is perhaps shocking that women are now claiming this principle for themselves.

Like Ruether's other work, this book incorporates many themes and issues. Like any good theology that undertakes to define a whole range of concepts and yet stands modestly before the task; her book claims no more for itself than its place as "*a* theology," but does not pretend to be the last word on the subject. Unlike many systematic theologies, *Sexism and God-Talk* is witty and useful in the practical exigencies of life. In labeling patriarchal ideology as blasphemous, Ruether calls women to claim the liberation/exodus motif for themselves. She suggests a new, unpronounceable name for the deity — God/ess — and argues that our task in religious language is not to add the Goddess to our currently male-defined God, but to reject the crippling dualisms that accrue when God is imagined in exclusively masculine terms. The dualisms that operate in language are carried over into the practical order in terms of a rejection of nature, the body, and women as impure, tempestuous, unclean, and uncontrollable.

Ruether rejects the dualistic anthropology that identifies female nature with fallen nature and suggests instead a new appropriation of androgyny as "integrated wholeness" with a large capacity for relationality. In rejecting earlier attempts at egalitarian anthropologies — eschatological, liberal feminist, and romantic — she formulates the question under her liberationist-prophetic argument for an integrated social order. As in her earlier work, she advances feminist issues within the framework of ecology, ecumenism, socialism, and a liberated world order.

In reevaluating Christology she asks if a male savior can save women and then argues that the most important characteristic of Jesus is *kenosis*, self-emptying, which she interprets as the relinquishment of the claims and powers of patriarchy. The fact that churchmen have raised the maleness of Jesus to some kind of ontological status and used it to marginalize women does not erase the fact that in Christ we are called to relate to the fullness of humanity, not the perfection of masculinity, nor does it obliterate the fact that Jesus' "vision of the kingdom is one of radical social iconoclasm."[76] In a chapter on Mariology, Ruether suggests a "liberation Mariology" in which Mary heralds economic liberation, but the implications of this reading are not clear since it is increasingly accepted by scholars that we know virtually nothing about the historical Mary. Ruether is more persuasive historically in her reappropriation of Mary Magdalene, though as a religious symbol, her liberationist Mariology is provocative and self-transcending.[77]

The second half of *Sexism and God-Talk* is more practical. Her discussion of evil is social rather than philosophical and concludes with models of male and female conversions from sexism. Her work on community and ecology is resonant with a lifetime of concern for building community and participating in a renewed social order. Eschatology, far from diverting our attention from the tasks at hand, is used here to draw attention away from the things of heaven and clarify our "responsibility to use our temporal life span to create a just and good community."[78] For Ruether, "feminism is not a new principle, but rather an extension of the fundamental principle that the word of God comes in judgment upon all social structures of injustice."[79]

Ruether's liberationist theology, like biblical prophecy, is based on a concept of conversion and repentance. The identification of the Latin American church with the poor in the late sixties is, for Ruether, the embodied power of liberation theology, because it comes from "a church that knows that it came as part of a system of exploitation and acted for much of its history as a tool of domination of the poor by the rich."[80] For her, prophecy is valid only as a form of self-criticism, not as a means of castigating communities and systems other than one's own. Her criticism of Catholicism and of aspects of American economic and political practice is, she believes, the legitimate task of an American Catholic. Feminism incorporates everything else. "For me the commitment to feminism is fundamental to the commitment to justice, to authentic human life itself."[81]

RE-INVENTING THE LANGUAGE: MARY DALY

Mary Daly (b. 1928) is Roman Catholic by background and education but has abandoned the church and what she calls "American sadosociety" because she finds them both to be unredeemably sexist and essentially necrophilic. Still, because her first book, *The Church and the Second Sex* (1968), was a ground-breaking event for American Catholic feminists and because her latest book, *Pure Lust* (1984),[82] undertakes to redefine some traditional Catholic doctrines—the Immaculate Conception, for example—and reclaim the power of traditional Catholic systems like "the four cardinal virtues," she must be considered in any discussion of Roman Catholic feminist theology. Even beyond her interest in and her clear contributions to feminist theology, however, Daly exhibits some peculiarly Roman Catholic dynamics: her later work, especially, is marked by dogmatic authoritarianism, a flight from and denigration of the world, a strong desire for transcendence, and an elitist understanding of the intellectual life, all hallmarks of preconciliar Catholicism.

The academic facts of Daly's life—B.A. (St. Rose College, 1950), M.A. (The Catholic University of America, 1952), four years of teaching in a small Catholic college (Cardinal Cushing, 1954–59), Licentiate and doctoral degrees in theology (University of Fribourg, 1961, 1963), and Ph.D. in philosophy (same university, 1965), teaching at Boston College since 1966, promoted and tenured there in 1969—appear to be straightforward, but contain within them the story of her radicalization. If studying in Europe in the 1960s caught Daly up in the renewal dreams of the Second Vatican Council, teaching at a Jesuit university in postconciliar Boston introduced her to the reality reserved for reforming smart women: almost simultaneously with the publication of *The Church and the Second Sex*, Daly was fired. Her publications up to 1968 had been suffused with clear analysis, impatient anger, and hopefulness,[83] but her writing after a nationally publicized tenure case—save for two spirited displays of resilience[84]—took on a new tone, and her interests shifted away from Catholicism and toward feminism.[85] At the same time, she withdrew her energy from equal rights and put her talents in the service of revolution.

Her second book, *Beyond God the Father* (1973), was a transitional one: it connected to the past by way of being a theological argument for a process God, dynamic revelation, and a realized eschatology; it mirrored the present because it was a feminist manifesto; and it augured for the future by being, at a fundamental level, a book about language. Most of Daly's subsequent work has aimed at a radical transmogrification of the language: she inverts and invents words in order to describe a new world of "radical feminist friendship and sisterhood." In this new space, old language is so many "double binding words that block our breakthrough."[86] Listening to women—footnoting the "free-floating creativity" of their conversations—is an important and specifically feminist part of *Beyond God the Father*.[87] Since, as women, we "have had the power of naming stolen from us" and "have not been free to use our power to name ourselves, the world, or God" (p. 8), we are called to a new consciousness: in "hearing and naming ourselves out of the depths, women are naming *toward* God, which is what theology always should have been about" (p. 33). Our own liberation, therefore, is rooted in the liberation of language — and in the use of a new method. "Under patriarchy," Daly says, "method has wiped out women's questions so totally that even women have not been able to hear and formulate" them (p.11). A new method involves "a *castrating* of language and images that reflect and perpetuate the structures of a sexist world" (p. 9). Constructively the new method involves a new creation, a "countercultural phenomenon *par excellence* which can indicate the future course of human spiritual evolution" (p. 11).

Her new naming began with God. The spiritual revolution of women lies not in the rejection of God, but in the rejection of God *the Father*. Since Daly believed that a new feminism ought to be cosmic and religious, but that traditional understandings of God were universally bad for women, she suggested a process God, "God the Verb," a deity for the active, communal, revolutionary consciousness of women. Moving to a revisionary reading of the myth of Eden, Daly argued that women have to rename themselves by refusing to believe the story of the Fall: for her, the real "original sin," is the credulity of women, the fact that they have believed this damning story and so have internalized blame for the guilt and evil in the world. Renaming Christ by way of a dynamic concept of revelation—"the creative presence of the Verb can be revealed at every historical moment, in every person and culture" (p. 71)—she revised traditional Marian doctrines by linking Mary with the powers of the ancient Goddess, and so ended the first, and overtly theological, speculative part of the book.

The second part of *Beyond God the Father* is neither as dazzling nor as persuasive as the first. My impression is that Daly began with an idea that the women's movement was the means to a profound spiritual revolution for humanity and grew noticeably less sanguine toward the masculine half of humanity as she developed her ideas. Perhaps Carter Heyward was right in suggesting that Daly's genius is with words and concepts and that she shows a relative discomfort with problems of the practical order.[88] More than that, however, as she reflected on stories of the mutilation, abuse, harassment, and murder of women by men, she began to name things — ethics, for example, became "phallic morality"— in such a way that male/female cooperation grew increas-

ingly problematic. Furthermore, inverted usage of religious terms —
as in "the most unholy trinity of rape, genocide and war"— served to
distance her from religious language. However much she talked about
"exodus community" or "cosmic covenant and male liberation," her
heart was not in it. By the final chapter she argued that life on this planet
depends on women breaking free from destructive myths, naming
themselves, feeling the enabling power of God the Verb, and opposing the male madness that is leading us all toward extinction. One of
the epigraphs for the last chapter quotes Robin Morgan, "I am a mon-
ster. And I am proud." Monstrous or not, by the end of *Beyond God
the Father* Daly had prepared herself to take "the qualitative leap beyond
patriarchal religion."[89] From this point forward, her work became
clearly post-Christian, utterly nonreformist and geared toward leaving this world of patriarchy behind.

Radical feminism, for Daly, is "very much an Otherworld Journey."[90] One travels in stages, first by exorcising any and all Fathers —
internalized demons that inhibit women from Be-ing — and then by
remythologizing. The religion of radical feminism is centered around
the Goddess, and the prehistoric myth is not the story of Eve, but the
prelapsarian paradise of primal matriarchy. Old symbols, however
revised, will not do for Daly's vision: new symbols and new language
are clear requirements for her kind of radical feminism. Her reading
of history leads her to call the world "the land of the Fathers," an
essentially "rapist society" in a constant "state of siege."[91] In this place,
women are always marginal, and men use "mindbinding" the way the
Chinese used footbinding, to keep women seductively crippled. History, then, a series of stories from the land of the fathers, is a horrific
parade of denigrations, mutilations, and holocausts. Her reading of history is not altogether unusual, but her analysis of that reading is shocking: others read the record and blame concepts — dualism, ignorance,
class structures, for example — Daly reads it and blames men. It is this
vision that she carries forward in her third book.

Gyn/Ecology (1978) is a drama of salvation with women, not Christ,
at the center. The suffering servant of Christianity is not mentioned
in this book, but he is clearly replaced: the second section of the book
can be interpreted as a radical feminist *via dolorosa*. We are taken from

station to station, from Indian suttee to Chinese footbinding, to European witch burning, to African genital mutilation, to American gynecology and are invited to see "whose sorrow is like unto her sorrow?" Given the "deep and universal intent to destroy the divine spark in women,"[92] Daly offers flight from this world as the only alternative. Having led her readers, like Dante, on a hellish journey that is an enlightening if ghoulish prerequisite for admission into paradise, Daly calls upon us to adopt "Spooking, Sparking and Spinning."[93] Spooking is refusing to be seduced "into a State of Animated Death." Sparking is female friendship, the community support system for Spinning, the creation of a new world. Her vision, not unlike that of ancient Christian hermits who fled into deserts so as not to be corrupted and destroyed by the world, asks women to become conscious that the world is in grave danger of destruction and so is inherently death-dealing, especially to women. Her solution—again, not unlike that of a monastic Christianity that argued that only those living on the edges of the sacred could experience God—rests on a belief that only those living on the boundaries of patriarchy have the freedom to create a new world.

Gyn/Ecology, like her latest book, *Pure Lust* (1984), results from what Daly calls "gynocentric writing." Since words have been used to deceive us, we must "dis-spell" them, create new ones, change normal rules of capitalization, and derive new meanings. Describing her task, Daly says (p. 24):

Gynocentric writing means risking. Since the language and style of patriarchal writing simply cannot contain or carry the energy of women's exorcism and ecstasy, in this book I invent, dis-cover, re-member. At times I make up words. . . . Often I unmask deceptive words by dividing them . . . when I play with words I do this attentively, deeply, paying attention to etymology, to varied dimensions. . . . At times I have been conscious of breaking almost into incantations, chants, alliterative lyrics. At such moments the words themselves seem to have a life of their own.

As a philosopher, she knows the power of words and so presumes to wrench them away from patriarchal usage in order to discover their power for women. If this task appears to be out of the mainstream, it is only because the times require it: "This is an extremist book," she says about *Gyn/Ecology*, "written in a situation of extremity, written on the edge of a culture that is killing itself and all sentient life" (p. 17). In searching for alternatives, Daly looks at both the church and the world and finds both deadly. Those feminists who have left the church for "the secular world" fool themselves if they think they find any safety there. Daly also castigates the "post-Christian extensions of the Christian myth" in a merciless parody of religious language and finally argues that feminists must develop attitudes of positive or creative paranoia in order to perceive the world as it is, a dangerous environment bent on the destruction of women.[94]

In *Beyond God the Father* Daly realized that she would not get very far by being nice. "The beginning of liberation," she said, "comes when women refuse to be 'good' and/or 'healthy' according to prevailing standards . . . [and assume] the role of witch and madwoman."[95] In a determined and logical way, Daly has assumed that role in her last two books: her descriptions of the structures and functions of both church and state are usually outrageous and often wickedly funny. In a technical sense of the word, she is blasphemous. As such, she frightens many people and intends, I think, to disrupt our perceptions and engage our feelings.[96] Her books, though they may be flawed on an etymological level, work very well on a visceral level. Her anthropological presupposition—that men are necrophilic and women are biophilic—is clearly inadequate as a theological starting point, but as a piece of guerrilla theater, played out against the background of positive paranoia, it makes the discussion so shrill that we may begin to appreciate the futility of attempting to be reasonable in an unreasonable situation.[97]

In this way, Daly functions as a prophet: she has an urgency of vision and brings an unwelcome message to an uncomprehending audience. She is bold, full of courage and rage, and her terrifying message is meant to show us that our own survival is at stake. When Elijah presented the Israelites with the stark choice between Baal and Yahweh he was dramatic, and his theatrical sense had just been affirmed by a heaven-sent conflagration.[98] A successor to Elijah, Daly's props come from a different source. Although she is dramatic and offers a similar stark choice—between radical feminism and Christianity, between being a co-opted "fembot" or a madwoman[99]—played out against the backdrop of a theatrical holocaust, the differences lie in her scenario. God does not set things on fire, but the patriarchy does; the sacrifice is not the swift slaying of oxen, but the torturous sacrifice of women; and the event is not a one-time incident but a policy.

If Daly is going to function as a prophet of feminism, however, the specifics of her vision may not be as compelling as her determination "to risk defying any attempt to make us minimize women as our focus, our passion, our lifetime commitment."[100] Indeed, though we may want to build on her power and implement her rage to energize our own action, we need to weigh critically the alternatives she presents. Unlike Carr, Schüssler Fiorenza, and Ruether, Daly sees no possibilities within the community. Her choices are clear and dogmatic: "there is [such] a profound contradiction between the inherent logic of radical feminism and the inherent logic of the Christian symbol system,"[101] that one must choose between them. Her "absolute distinction between 'strong, woman-identified women' and women who are too weak or too damaged to join them . . . leaves us little hope for change,"[102] and sets up an elitist appropriation of "the Truth" that is "catholic in the worst sense."[103] She projects an image of an all-female Utopia, ecologically sane, agricultural, and populated by self-affirming, women-identified, intellectual women, and she clearly loves the earth and feels in tune with it,[104] but the identification of this place as "Otherworld" reinstates the divisive dualisms Catholicism has been attempting to soften.

Beneath the dogmatism, the flight from the world, and the deliberate blasphemies, however, one finds a consistent search for transcendence or for what preconciliar theologians called Being, a word Daly appropriates for herself by hyphenating it (Be-ing). From her first published article (1965)[105] to her latest book (1984) she has called on readers to strive "toward a higher level of human existence."[106] In feminist terms, she calls on women to say "I Am" in the face of an official denial of their being. In her linguistic metier, she says that writing is a transcending experience, "for our Words having been stolen, are coming home to us. The Cosmic Writer is any Lusty woman who speaks the Words of her own being."[107] Because transcendence is a spiritual concept, Daly's aim toward it gives her work a religious character.

The location of the source of transcendence has changed for her, however, though she is still indebted to process thought and models of continuous growth. In *Beyond God the Father* she argued that it is impossible to leave God behind and therefore necessary to destroy the "myth of God the Father" in order to be empowered by God the Verb. In *Pure Lust*, feminism, not God, is the Verb, a process that continues and draws us along with it. The Verb has the same function, to encourage belief in the self, community, and a new age; but it is no longer perceived as outside women or alien to their experience. The spirit of transcendence rests within women, yearning for activation.

CONCLUSIONS

Feminist theology is rooted in a complex theological reawakening that took place in the last part of the nineteenth century and continues today. It is indebted to many different theological streams and to liberationist models of political theology. Earliest feminist attention to religion — Matilda Joslyn Gage's *Woman, Church and State* (1893),[108] for example — was written by those who worked without benefit of professional training. Theology and philosophy were not disciplines open to women — Harvard did not admit women to its Divinity School until 1955 — and the "languages of divinity," Latin and Greek, were thought to be either too difficult or too sacred to share with women. When Elizabeth Cady Stanton attempted to draw the interest of female scholars to her *Woman's Bible* project in the 1890s, she had only minimal success and so produced an exegetical work whose significance lies more in its commonsense insights and clear courage than its scholarly brilliance.[109]

Since the 1960s, however, theologically trained feminists have systematically awakened consciousness about the oppressiveness and inadequacy of Christian symbols, traditions, and texts.[110] As a special issue of the *National Catholic Reporter* editorialized, the work of feminist theologians — in all religious traditions but focused in this issue primarily on Catholics — will finally benefit everyone, not just women.[111] The variety of perspectives makes it clear that Catholic feminist theology is much more extensive and its practitioners much more numerous than can be evidenced here.

Since a key to feminist theology is the experience of women, and since women's experience even within a single religious tradition like Roman Catholicism is extraordinarily diverse, there is no monolithic Roman Catholic feminist theology. As we have seen in the four theologians mentioned in this chapter, approaches to and understandings of feminist theology vary with each theologian. Though the differences might be used by hostile critics to argue that women are incapable of formulating a definitive theological perspective, the very diversity points to a primary value of feminism in any field: Roman Catholic feminist theologians do not seek an absolute statement, but prize interconnectedness, the unity in difference, the respect for variety in female experience, and the strength found in the expression of many voices.

Whatever their differences, however, Roman Catholic feminist theologians agree that their work cannot be done or understood within narrowly defined traditional categories. Like feminists in other disciplines, these theologians seek to change the limits of the discipline so that Catholic theology is more truly reflective of the universal differences it purports to represent. Similarly, they agree that the present language about God—linguistically and conceptually—is not only inadequate, but oppressive, to more than half the members of the believing community. The apparent inexorability of Catholic patriarchalism has moved Daly to leave the tradition behind in search of the transcendence offered by separatist feminism, but the radical reappropriation of some traditional Roman Catholic doctrines in her latest book may argue for the difficulty of abandoning one's heritage. Whatever the particularities of Daly's struggle, she can neither find life within the Catholic tradition nor divorce herself entirely from its influence. Carr, Schüssler Fiorenza, and Ruether have a similar problem, but from a different perspective: they refuse to be squeezed out of their tradition and so define themselves consciously as Roman Catholics, yet at the same time they resist the proponents of that tradition who would quiet them, relegate them to secondary status, or refuse to admit the validity of their theological investigations. They stand within Catholicism, therefore, to challenge its language, symbol system, and biblical interpretation. At the same time they are active respondents to the imperiled situation of women in the parish, women seeking ordination, and women searching for alternative communities of celebration and practice.

The Womanchurch movement, like early Christianity, is struggling for an identity within a tradition it finds both to be life-giving and oppressive. Like the young Jesus community, it is countercultural, at least in the ecclesiastical sense, and threatening to patriarchal structures. Attempting to be inclusive and to honor the experience of women, it embodies a wide range of "causes" and encourages its members to follow the voice of the spirit wherever it is heard. Like the early Christian movement, Womanchurch is found thoughout a wide geographical region and sometimes takes on the characteristics and proclivities of its local environment. It is loosely coordinated and not hierarchically organized, and so may well have many more adherents than can be counted using present tallying methods.

If, however, Womanchurch is to grow into a living and life-giving alternative or into the kind of energetic movement within Roman Catholicism that will indeed transform it, then Womanchurch, like the early Christian movement, will have to have theologians, intellectuals who can find the clarifying and redemptive qualities in feminism as the ancient "Fathers" found those same things in Hellenism. We know from early Christian history that the best of the "Fathers" were men involved in the day-to-day life of the church: they were often pastors, preachers, missionaries, or administrators as well as thinkers, and were characterized by a passion for God newly understood in the incarnate Christ. The Roman Catholic feminist theologians discussed in this chapter for the most part, are immersed in the vicissitudes of daily life, possess intellectual gifts that they bring to bear on the serious conflicts women have with traditional Catholicism, and are characterized by a passion for God. That passion is newly understood in the lives of the marginalized, especially in the oppressed realities of women's experience.

The Womanchurch movement has vision, organization, and an important and growing body of theological reflection. It needs also a revisionary sense of prayer as a means to celebrate its life liturgically and understand its journey transformatively. And so, finally, we turn to Roman Catholic feminist spirituality.

6. Affirming the Connections: Roman Catholic Feminist Spirituality

All the wild witches, those most noble ladies,
For all their broomsticks and their tears,
Their angry tears, are gone.

W. B. YEATS

We need meditations to help us discover, trust and express our inner wisdom, love our bodies, and use the full power of our inner strength and emotions to guide and inspire us in our personal/social/political lives.

HALLIE INGLEHART

I am not ready to surrender Mary to our opponents.

DOROTHY SÖLLE

Spirituality is faith made explicit in life: one's deepest convictions with respect to the ultimate are embodied in the relationships one has with others, with the created order, and with the divine. In traditional Roman Catholic teaching, spirituality is often described as an ascent motivated by a desire for union with God. Because Roman Catholic spirituality has its roots in the ascetic traditions of the ancients, it has too often been the call of a few heroic souls aiming at perfection. The Second Vatican Council, however, reaffirmed the more orthodox view that sanctity is for everyone: "all the faithful, whatever their condition or state, are called by the Lord . . . to perfect holiness."[1] Spirituality is predicated on the belief that it is possible and desirable to have a deeply intimate relationship with the divine. In the early and medieval church, such a relationship often seemed to require the obliteration of the self: one left the world, disciplined the body, and mastered the ego in order to be ready for union with God. Traditional Catholic spirituality had a decidedly masculine character to it, for just as the transcendent God mastered the chaos in order to create the world, so the spirit must master the flesh, the will master desire, in order to become obedient to the patriarchal God. In contemporary Catholicism, however, spirituality can be characterized as an openness both to the self and to God. As Karl Rahner says, "The experience of self *and* the experience of God . . . constitute a unity; the experience of self is the condition which makes it possible to experience God."[2] These two spiritualities — obliteration of self and affirmation of self — reflect different understandings of God. In the first, God is utterly transcendent, unknowable, and unapproachable; in the second God is more clearly involved with the world, evident in the events of one's life, and accessible. An ancient Christian writer trying to summarize a similar opposition said, "This neither is Thou, this also is Thou,"[3] meaning that no experience really manifests the divine since God is beyond all expression, yet each image of goodness or charity encountered in one's daily life is, in fact, an epiphany of God in the created order. Roman Catholic spirituality has resonated between these two insights. The first finds its classical expression in the *via negativa*, represented by Dionysius the pseudo-Areopagite (sixth century) or the *Cloud of Unknowing* (fourteenth century);[4] the second, the way of affirmation, is found in the creation-centered spirituality of Meister Eckhart[5] (1260–1337) or in the poetic mysticism of Dante[6] (1265–1321). Significantly, the way of affirmation has been deeply related to women. Eckhart's sermons, replete with references to the feminine dimensions of the divine, were preached to the Beguines, a late medieval independent sisterhood persecuted and suppressed for their refusal to capitulate to the cloister model of religious life. Dante's entire salvific vision in the *Divine Comedy* was centered on the woman, Beatrice, his perfect grace-bearing image.

Feminist spirituality, inside and outside the Roman Catholic church has been characterized by connectedness, a modern expression of the way of affirmation that seeks to explore and experience the supportive, nurturing, involved God/ess[7] who desires union through relationship. Just as feminists have found the Christian tradition inadequate in its language, symbols, and theology, feminist spiritual writers decry the inability of traditional spirituality to reflect women's experience and to provide women with a compelling inducement for their spiritual lives. Alternatives to classical expressions of spirituality include

Goddess worship and witchcraft, supported by those who believe that women need new religious symbols, and political spirituality, espoused by those whose religious vision is rooted in liberation theology and in the "inescapable political dimensions" of prayer and justice.[8] Along with those alternatives, and in dialogue with them, Catholic feminists can review their own mystical tradition — especially as it has been articulated by women — and they can reclaim Mary from those repressive forces who have used her to keep women "humble and in their place."[9]

THE ALTERNATIVES: GODDESS WORSHIP AND POLITICAL SPIRITUALITY

"The essence of feminism," Dorothy Sölle has said, "is the creation of something new."[10] Throughout this book we have seen that the feminist critique of Roman Catholicism has challenged old models and demanded new understandings of history, ecclesiology, and theology. A sense of enabling newness within historical Christianity has, in large part, motivated the work of the many different Roman Catholic women represented here. An equally strong sense of hopelessness about revising Christian symbols, however, has led a group of contemporary feminists to eschew Christianity in search of the Goddess.[11] For Carol P. Christ, "'God' is a symbol that may have outlived its usefulness as an exclusive mediator between humans and the ultimate reality which grounds and sustains their lives." According to her, "we are living in a revolutionary time when new religious symbols are being formed by a process of syncretism and creativity."[12] Furthermore, since the absence of the Goddess in biblical religion is no accident, feminists cannot attempt to reappropriate those traditions but must seek a religious expression that has the Goddess in its center. As Starhawk has argued, since "the decline of the Goddess religions, women have lacked religious models and spiritual systems that speak to female needs and experience." In the absence of female deities, women "are taught to submit to male authority, to identify masculine perceptions as their spiritual ideals . . . [and] to fit their insights into a male mold."[13]

Building on the insights of Jung and Tillich, Christ believes that human beings need symbols in order to have some access to the mysterious dimensions of life. Since symbols are ultimately richer than words used to describe them, and since they point to a reality beyond themselves, they have the power to draw people into participation with transcendent reality. Symbols, in other words, mediate the religious dimension of life and provide a source of meaning for people, like myths that attempt to answer the great questions of existence. Following the work of Clifford Geertz, a cultural anthropologist, Christ realizes that symbols have political ramifications, they "affect behavior and social attitudes and politics."[14] If all these things are true, and if the symbols of traditional Christianity are overwhelmingly male, then feminists "might well conclude that the demise of religion would be the best thing that could happen in Western society" (p. 234). But Christ, as a theologian, is interested in the revitalization of religion, not its death, and so argues that feminists must resist the notion that symbols are eternal or ineluctably unconscious. In the face of those who insist that religious symbols cannot be created, Christ calls on feminists to reclaim their power to create a new symbol system that will move people to change their understanding of divinity. When she argues that women need the Goddess, she is not merely hoping that traditional religion will recapture the "feminine dimension of the divine"[15] but that feminists will work toward an entirely different religious consciousness that affirms the female body and the energy of the female will and the revaluation of female bonding.

In its ritualistic form, the Goddess movement is related to a reappropriation of witchcraft, but its principle function is to empower women. As Starhawk says in *The Spiral Dance*:

The importance of the Goddess symbol for women cannot be overstressed. The image of the Goddess inspires women to see ourselves as divine, our bodies as sacred, the changing phases of our lives as holy, our aggression as healthy, our anger as purifying, and our power to nurture and create, but also to limit and destroy when necessary, as the very force that sustains all life. Through the Goddess we can discover our strength, enlighten our minds, own our bodies and celebrate our emotions. We can move beyond narrow, constricting roles and become whole.[16]

Witchcraft and the Goddess have sometimes appeared to be the logical outcome of a feminist theological critique. *Womanspirit Rising,* an anthology edited by Carol P. Christ and Judith Plaskow, moves directly from a questioning of old theological categories, through the restructuring of the tradition, to the creation of new rituals.[17] Since the search for and celebration of the Goddess and the reaffirmation of women's power in witchcraft are serious attempts to nurture a new religious consciousness, they are religiously conservative responses to those feminists whose negative experiences within traditional religion have led them to reject religion altogether.

At the same time, because of its relationship to a number of theological and anthropological questions, the Goddess movement is at the heart of some major conflicts within feminist circles. Insofar as Goddess feminists argue for the primacy of Goddess religion — stating that biblical religion and Christianity both actively suppressed and tried to destroy the more ancient Goddess religion — the debate is confined to scholars of the ancient Near East and is relatively esoteric, since the evidence in either direction usually requires highly developed linguistic, archaeological, and textual skills. Insofar as the argument moves toward establishing the existence of ancient matriarchal societies, it is joined by anthropologists who question the evidence and its interpretation.[18] Pertinent to the *theological* debate are the positions drawn by some matriarchal feminists about the differences between male and female nature. In their most truculent form — found, for example in Daly's *Gyn/Ecology* — these arguments conclude that female nature is peaceful and biophilic, whereas male nature is warlike and necrophilic. While these arguments are serious and undoubtedly will continue, it may be enough for some feminists to allow the possibilities of matriarchies and a primal Goddess religion to function symbolically, their reality being less important than the power released when women imagine them.

The Goddess alternative is, after all, the conscious re-creation of a religious symbol. For Christ and others, it is not sufficient to neutralize masculine symbols and language so that men can continue to imagine their religious tradition androcentrically while women make their own silent imaginative shifts. The use of the term *Goddess* and a deliberate use of God-She constructions in religious speech and writing "will help to bring the attitudes and feelings of the deep mind into harmony with feminist social and political goals, *and* reciprocally, . . . will express and bring to articulation the feminist intuition that the struggle for equal rights is supported by the nature of reality."[19]

The work of Christ and others, though it has not persuaded Roman Catholic feminists to abandon biblical religion in search of the Goddess, has made an impact on Catholic feminism and is a significant dialectical partner for its theologians. Rosemary Radford Ruether has had serious disagreements with Goddess feminism, especially with what she takes to be its naïve historical and anthropological standpoints, yet her own term for a "fuller divinity . . . that yet unnameable understanding of the divine that would transcend patriarchal limitations and signal redemptive experience for women as well as men,"[20] is God/ess. God/ess is different from Goddess, for it intends to combine the masculine and feminine forms of divinity while still affirming the divine unity, yet, even though Ruether says it is "unpronounceable," it reads and sounds like Goddess and so insinuates the feminine divine principle into one's consciousness, which is one of the points Christ insists upon. Elisabeth Schüssler Fiorenza, in developing her critical feminist hermeneutics, praised Christ's work and agreed with its fundamental point, that "at the heart of the spiritual feminist quest is the quest for women's power, freedom and independence."[21]

More interesting, perhaps, is the willingness of female Catholic liturgists to invoke the Goddess in their search for new ways to express their personal and collective experience of the divine. In 1983, two midwestern Catholic women led an Isis ceremony in their hometown to celebrate the harvest. Whatever the religious intentions of the ritual—it was held at City Hall in the context of a civic festival—both leaders were in serious pursuit of the Goddess within themselves, another key aspect of Goddess feminism.[22] One can find similar development in women's groups. The Grail workshop in 1978 that led to *Image-Breaking, Image-Building* was designed to "generate alternative images of God and forms of worship," and worked, ecumenically, within the Christian tradition.[23] The 1984 Grail workshop Sophia and the Future of Feminist Spirituality, however, while still consciously centered within "the Christian tradition," focused on Sophia as "a goddess-like figure in the Hebrew and Christian traditions" and was more obviously designed to move beyond traditional frameworks.[24]

Whether Roman Catholic feminists will be attracted to witchcraft is not clear, but the attempt to find God in themselves is leading some of them to the same insight Christ often cites when talking about the Goddess:

At the close of Ntosake Shange's stupendously successful Broadway play *For Colored Girls Who Have Considered Suicide When the Rainbow Is Enuf*, a tall beautiful black woman rises from despair to cry out, "I found God in myself and I loved her [I loved her] fiercely." Her discovery is echoed by women around the country who meet spontaneously in small groups on full moons, solstices, and equinoxes to celebrate the Goddess as symbol of life and death powers and waxing and waning energies in the universe and in themselves.[25]

In its political form, "feminist spirituality" often goes beyond the Goddess to a holistic conception of the universe. *The Politics of Women's Spirituality*, an apologia for feminist spirituality edited by a partisan of the Goddess movement who calls herself "a retired Catholic," is an extensive collection of writings by those committed to finding a postpatriarchal spirituality.[26] The presence of (usually former) Catholics in Goddess feminism is probably predictable on the basis of their liturgical formation. But the effects of the Goddess on Roman Catholic feminism are not yet clear. If feminist theology begins with women's experience, and if more women articulate their experience in terms of the Goddess, this alternative, once almost unthinkable in Catholic circles, might emerge as a barometer of women's frustration with institutional religion.

Though the Goddess movement is not without its political sensibilities, I mean to differentiate it from political spirituality which focuses on social justice commitments rather than on a particular religious vision. Political spirituality encompasses a variety of religious beliefs, though it has been most clearly articulated as an expression of liberationist-based Christianity. Political spirituality might be considered a modern embodiment of what Catholics used to call "the active life," as opposed to the contemplative one. Contemplative life, centered on prayer and mysticism, was usually predicated on a flight from the world to allow one sufficient time and space for prayer. Active spirituality, on the other hand, directed at good works, was based on the belief that one finds God in the needs of the poor and the sick and the dying. Though it is not really possible to make neat separations between contemplative and active goals—one searching for direct union with God, the other attempting to follow Jesus' commands to love one's neighbor—the mentality that has felt comfortable with a division between the secular and the sacred is often likely to resist the mixing of religion and politics as inappropriate and antithetical to the divine design.

As we have already seen, American Catholic feminists are increasingly political and have come to read the gospel primarily as a mandate for social justice. Roman Catholic feminist theologians, coalitions of nuns and laywomen, and the Womanchurch movement have all understood our task in political terms and have called upon Catholic women to join centers that educate, lobby, research, and struggle for systemic justice. Whether they gather locally for a feminist worship service or nationally for the Women's Ordination Conference, Catholic women, with a heightened consciousness of global injustices, are prepared to engage in boycotts, demonstrations, and other justice actions. Invariably adherents speak of both religion and politics.

Political spirituality is being used by Roman Catholic feminists to criticize both the church (for its oppressive and fundamentally unjust sexist structures) and the state (for its exploitation of the poor, military involvement in Latin America, and other things). Not only is politics not a dirty word, it is now understood to be a spiritual word: according to these women, contemporary spirituality must be politically conscious. To quote Maureen Fiedler's keynote address at the first Womanchurch convention, "Authentic spirituality today calls us to work toward a world and a Church where power is shared, not oppressive. That is *political and spiritual* work: these are not and cannot be separate spheres of life for Womanchurch."[27] After giving a political science analysis of the institutional church and the politics of Jesus, Fiedler summarized the politics of Womanchurch: no one, she argued, can read us out of *our* Catholic tradition, we refuse to be marginalized or to accept that the present hierarchical church is truly reflective of the Jesus traditions; we will not let the institutional church go unchallenged; and we will resolve to place the cries of suffering people ahead of the law.

Her view is shared by other Catholic feminists. Central to understanding Schüssler Fiorenza's gathering of the ecclesia of women is her subscription to the Redstockings' manifesto, "until all women are free, no woman is free," a statement that not only reflects her understanding of the women's movement but helps to set the agenda for what she understands to be the work of the church.[28] Ruether's chapter "Ministry and Community" recommends base community models that are not only intentionally declericalized and that reclaim the sacraments but that also spread "this vision and struggle to others."[29] Part of being church is to engage in political activity. As Ruether argued in another context, "The church has always played a political role, from the first moment of its existence."[30] As a determined opponent of dualisms, Ruether will not separate the secular from the sacred and so cannot imagine a spirituality without political dimensions.

If spirituality is faith made explicit in life, then modern Catholic faith ought to provide a clue for the strength of political spirituality. One modern American Catholic whose life evidenced an integrated faith and who deeply influenced both political action and spirituality in this country was Dorothy Day.[31] Day, the founder of the Catholic Worker movement (1934), was noted for her untiring work for the poor in the slums of major American cities: her radical poverty, persistent pacifism, and steady support of the downtrodden have had a major impact on radical Catholicism in the United States. In some ways she embodies the epitome of modern Catholic spirituality: deeply rooted in the traditions, committed to care for the poor, and profoundly prayerful, Day was never "just an activist" but struggled to maintain a balance between active Christianity and searching prayerfulness. Modern Catholic spirituality, therefore, is a blend of ancient asceticism, medieval expressions of religious experience, and modern social and ecumenical consciousness. Holiness, no longer the call to a few but now a responsibility for everyone, is expressed in an enormous range of spiritual options. Modern responses to the call of Jesus, rather than being enacted in cloisters, might well resemble the lives of the four American women killed in El Salvador in 1981: by all accounts they were prayerful, idealistic, and determined to seek God by serving the poor in a desperate situation.

In embracing the political dimensions of spirituality, the Womanchurch movement, and Catholic feminists in general, show an enthusiastic response to the spirit of Vatican II as well as a commitment to the principles of liberation theology. They also reflect the profound integration of "active" and "contemplative" spirituality that has been going on in the twentieth century. While it is usually clear what kinds of politics engage these women, and though one can predict that their social justice interests will probably embrace most of the major problems in the world, it is not always clear where their spiritual directions take them in terms of prayer.

The relative difficulty of characterizing Catholic feminist prayer life lies in its newness. Influenced by the ecumenical movement, eager to be attentive to profoundly moving prayer forms long ignored in the institutional church—Native American, Hispanic, and black Catholic senses of the divine and modalities of celebration—and increasingly alienated from the structures of the tradition by sexist language, Catholic feminists are in the process of creating new liturgies and reclaiming the sacraments for themselves. In this way, just as their politics are spiritual, their spirituality is political: the celebration of the Eucharist by women is a consciously political action as well as a sacramental one; it responds to what many women feel is the movement of the Spirit in their lives and at the same time constitutes a clear act of ecclesiastical disobedience.[32]

Both of these alternatives—Goddess feminism and political spirituality—enrich Roman Catholic spirituality. The first addresses fundamental discontinuities between women's experience and the overwhelmingly masculine symbols and language used by the institutional church to articulate it. The second gives Catholic women an integrated vision of the universal call to holiness sounded at the Second Vatican Council and, at the same time, provides opportunities for the kinds of collective action that the women's movement extols. It is hard to imagine Roman Catholic feminists without political awareness. Even contemplative nuns, who probably tended to conceptualize their vocation as praying for "the world," now take more responsibility for knowing what is going on in the world and are as likely to undertake writing weekly letters for Amnesty International as they are to indulge in acts of mortification. It is also unlikely that Roman Catholic feminists will overlook the importance of the feminine dimensions of the divine; many appear to be in active pursuit of the Goddess linguistically or liturgically. Both these alternatives, therefore, are useful mirrors as we look at the tradition.

THE MYSTICAL TRADITION: EMPOWERING DIMENSIONS OF SPIRITUALITY

The Roman Catholic tradition has a long list of female saints, most of whom were canonized for the same reasons men were, for holiness, heroic practice of virtue, martyrdom, spiritual wisdom, and service to the church. Though the old Roman Canon of the Mass consigned women to the list of martyrs, it was, nevertheless, symbolically important to hear a list of women read aloud each day during liturgy: "Felicitas, Perpetua, Agatha, Lucy, Agnes, Cecilia, Anastasia, and all your saints." The confinement of women to roles of virgin and martyr was undoubtedly debilitating for future generations of women,[33] but the *fact* of female saints and the encouragement of sanctity in women were probably stimulating. It is difficult to weigh the relative advantages and disadvantages of a skewed tradition against the absence of one. Still, if Catholic feminists had only the women in the old calendar as models, and if they were confined to the traditional interpretation of their virtues, one can easily see why they would be tempted to abandon their history, even though it has many "holy women" in it. Worse than that women were described sexually—by way of their virginity—and typically upheld for martyrdom, is the debasement that forms a leitmotiv in the hagiographical tradition. Female saints are said to have a predilection for kissing lepers, defiling themselves with the excrement of paupers (as a penance), allowing themselves to be disciplined (whipped and confined) by male spiritual directors, and being persuaded that the choice for God meant the abandonment of their children.[34] It is true that one can find male saints with the same grotesque routes to sanctity—interestingly, it is the black man, Martin de Porres, who opts for the masochistic expedient—but there are fewer of them, and there are many other options: males can become canonized for being abbots, intellectuals, hymn writers, soldiers, kings, preachers, teachers, hermits, wisdom figures, crusaders, and popes. And they can do so without having to go down in history for their virginity.

If the tradition of female sanctity is sullied with debasement, submission, and powerlessness, it obviously needs to be countered or revised. On the one hand, we can argue against the *hagiography* as we have against American Catholic history: its boundaries must change to include wider and deeper understandings of female holiness, and new interpretive categories must be employed to criticize restrictive old ones. On the other hand, we can begin a revisionary reading of the tradition by focusing on some medieval mystics and using modern interpretive tools to uncover the liberating dimensions of their lives. We have models of strong women—nuns and laywomen—and an obscure but instructive insight into the "motherhood of God" that can tell us something about the ways feminine characteristics have been used to describe and understand the deity.

Although it is true that one can find examples of masochistic or sickening "sanctity" in predominantly male interpretations and accounts of the mystical tradition, one can also discover women whose lives or visions may have meaning in contemporary struggles. Dorothy Sölle believes that the mystical tradition is especially empowering for feminists because it values experience, supports a continuing process of liberation, and demands an openness to new understandings of the divine nature and attributes. Mysticism, she believes, leads to clarification of language and commitment and to a yielding of the self that enhances solidarity.[35] Teresa of Avila, Catherine of Siena and Julian of Norwich—albeit in quite different ways—all provide the kind of support which can lead to liberation.

Ecclesiastical authorities have finally proclaimed Teresa of Avila and Catherine of Siena to be "Doctors of the Church," but that designation is not enough to counteract the selective memory of their power. Teresa may have been a conventual reformer and mystic—qualities elusive to most women—but she is much more interesting as a woman coming to terms with her own power and autonomy in a male-dominated culture. What she did is important, but that she did it in her own way in sixteenth-century Spain is even more impressive. Catherine has been romanticized as a virgin caught up in a spousal relationship with Christ—again, qualities that do not serve as enticements for most ordinary women—but her social and political consciousness and her determination to pursue a spiritual vocation outside the confines of organized religious institutions are perhaps more immediately relevant to feminist interpreters. Though she sometimes spoke disparagingly of feminine softness, she was able to "use theological and social stereotypes of female weakness without being personally touched" by them, an impressive ability in fourteenth-century Italy.[36] In a time when some feminist theologians are searching for feminine dimensions of the divine and maternal aspects of God, it is instructive to first look at Dame Julian of Norwich's experience and then examine the strong tradition of the "motherhood of Jesus" in twelfth-century Cistercian monks to see if the motherhood of God was primarily developed by men or by women. One may then ask if it can be used effectively by feminists.

Teresa of Avila (1515–1582), a Spanish Carmelite nun generally remembered as a religious reformer and mystic, was declared a "Doctor of the Church" in 1970, thereby ascending into the exclusive ranks of distinguished and saintly theologians. No longer "just a saint," Teresa now stands with a select company headed by Augustine, Ambrose, Jerome, and Gregory the Great: her spiritual writings are recognized as theologically profound. On those grounds alone she is important for Catholic feminists, having attained a status previously reserved for men only. Too, her character—shrewd, determined, intelligent, feisty— makes her attractive to Catholic women, though it would be inaccurate to describe her as a feminist. Still, when placed in her complex historical context and interpreted psychologically, Teresa may be more relevant to Catholic feminists than is apparent at first glance. Her "mysterious illness" and her subsequent dialogues with Christ gave her a path to power in a culture decidedly closed to feminine autonomy.

As Teofanes Egido has convincingly argued, the failure of Teresian biographers and Carmelite historians to place Teresa within the historical conditions of sixteenth-century Spain obscured the risks she took with her spiritual reforms and falsify her background.[37] Teresa's Jewish heritage, for example, was deliberately ignored and obfuscated by subsequent generations of Carmelites obsessed with "blood purity" as a requirement for entry into religious life.[38] Teresa's paternal grandfather was a Jew forced into Christianity by the Inquisition and then disqualified from holding municipal office or engaging in a variety of business ventures. The response of the Inquisition to Jews was malevolently simple: they were publicly disgraced, forced to choose between death and apostasy, nicknamed "marranos" (little pigs) and "set in an antagonistic social milieu . . . of not always silent hostilities, of polite opposition, and of social isolation."[39] In many cases the (desired) result was financial ruin, which removed the "contaminating" family from further social intercourse with the pure-blooded aristocrats. Teresa's opposition to discrimination of this kind was radical, but can only be so understood in the setting of her culture rather then in the shadow of her mystical life.

When one thinks of Teresa of Avila as a spiritual reformer, one thinks of her insights into prayer.[40] For her, God existed, not outside the self, but deeply within, constantly beckoning and enticing individuals into relationships of quiet union. But this desire for a personal, experiential encounter with God was daring and dangerous in sixteenth-century Castile, "closed to Europe, open to heaven, with its iron-fisted police system to intercept every outside ideological intrusion which might smell of heresy, with the Holy Office of the Inquisition (as popular as it was feared) to smother possible internal outbreaks."[41] The climate of suspicion in which Teresa worked identified mysticism with Lutheranism and was basically hostile to the desire for personal, experiential encounters with God such as Teresa advocated. "Moreover, given the combination of 'orantes' [pray-ers], women, and Jewish ancestry, we can understand the real battle which Madre Teresa — with these three counts against her — had to wage so that her 'spiritual' orientation not be denounced by the zealous watchdogs of the faith, and so that she might transmit a reform made up of communities of pray-ers [orantes]."[42] Even more important than the kind of prayer advocated by Teresa were the odds against which she had to struggle for a woman's right to such a prayer experience. Her efforts cannot be appreciated apart from this context, and her revolutionary understandings and struggles for women's right to direct experiential encounters with God cannot be properly understood when her life and work are wrapped up in pious generalities.

Along with an awareness of her courage and iconoclasm, we might find some resonances with feminism if we approach Teresa's life from a psychological perspective. Psycho-histories need to be used with caution, but they can sometimes provide suggestive interpretations and encourage new understandings. Catherine Romano's "Psycho-Spiritual History of Teresa of Avila" attempts to "utilize Freudian insights, but not without critical additions and modifications of orthodox analysis."[43] For Romano, Teresa was incapable of integrating early adolescent experiences of competence and leadership ability with female roles permitted in her culture. Her early assertive personality gave way to twenty years of emotional confusion and sickness, a defense used all too often by women today when their talents and ambitions are thwarted by stunted social roles or expectations. Her conversion experience — in which she accepted Christ's love for her — empowered her to create a new self, to become an assertive religious leader with a high degree of autonomy and self-affirmation. Prevented by her culture from assuming this identity on her own, she "project[ed] her wishes onto her Divine Lord and [had] him command her to do what she ha[d] long yearned to do" (p. 284). For the rest of her life, therefore, she received and obeyed spiritual commands, receiving from her Lord even the permission to disobey her superiors. Teresa's development, so interpreted, has heroic proportions: "neurotic patterns, once established, are difficult to change and, yet, through intense work, she changed her own . . . she found her own way of allowing her unconscious to surface to serve her needs" (p. 293). Romano concludes that Teresa was, finally, "remarkably healthy" and well-integrated.

For Joann Wolski Conn, Romano's interpretation confirms that women's spiritual quest "concerns women's awakening to forces of energy larger than the self . . . for women, conversion is not so much giving up egocentric notions of power as passing through an experience of nothingness finally to gain power over their own lives."[44] Conn's work on feminist interpretations of traditional spirituality led her to challenge basic assumptions about women's natural passivity or innate possession of religious virtue. As Catholic feminists examine their tradition, therefore, it must be with a more genuinely feminist and deeply historical awareness. Without such awareness, Teresa remains an impressive reformer, mystic and *doctore ecclesiae*, labels which are not to be discounted. On the other hand, when those designations are combined with her power to affirm her own unique spirituality, her successful self-discovery and integration process, and her determination to defy narrow cultural and religious norms in pursuit of her own vision, then in addition to being a "doctor of the church," she is a midwife to Womanchurch.

Catherine of Siena (1333?–1380), until declared a "Doctor of the Church" in 1970, was known in the calendar of saints as a "Virgin." Since her letters—full of social consciousness, political involvement, and institutional criticism—have not been readily available in English, American Catholic women know her mostly through her mystical *Dialogues.* The stunning or nauseating (and possibly apocryphal) details of her vowed virginity include her having received a wedding ring from Christ, her spouse, kissing lepers and ingesting the pus from their suppurating sores.[45] Her youthful vow of virginity can be interpreted as a sign of heroic sanctity and dedication to God's work; it can also be seen as her way of avoiding the traditional choice offered to women of her time—either a husband or a cloister—in order to pursue a spiritual vocation as a laywoman.

According to Carola Parks, Catherine's understanding of humility as self-knowledge was tied necessarily to action. "Far from advocating a spiritual masochism or a put-down of self and of one's gifts, Catherine urges a discovery and development of one's talents"[46] and a coming to grips with the image of God within us that leads to love and service of neighbor. As an advocate for the poor and vociferous critic of the institutional church, and as one whose faith deepened, not in spite of her involvements in social-political affairs, but in the midst of them, Catherine's values are not dissimilar from the basic principles of a liberationist perspective.

As C. H. Lawrence noted in a centenary essay, Catherine's "social assumptions would not . . . qualify her to be patroness of the modern feminist movement; but it is of the greatest interest that she succeeded in fulfilling her individual vocation as a mystical teacher and prophet in an ecclesiastical and secular world ruled by men, in which all female initiative was discouraged."[47] One of twenty-five children, unable to write but able to read, Catherine's attraction for the mystical life was not altogether unusual in the fourteenth century, but the "paradox of Catherine's career was that she lived the contemplative life outside the framework of any religious institution, first in a family household and later in the full glare of public activity" (p. 393). Contemplation might have been encouraged at the time, but not female leadership, and Catherine was a leader and an activist. Her failure to join an existing religious order may well be due to the fact that none of them would have given her the same freedom of movement and activity she claimed for herself as a third-order laywoman. Most of all, Catherine of Siena was a critic: her mysticism and her criticism of a scandalous eccelsiastical situation were two aspects of the same vocation. "Hagiographers exaggerated the practical effectiveness of Catherine's interventions in ecclesiastical politics,"[48] but she nevertheless remains important as a voice of loving protest. She was in some ways limited by the cultural and ecclesiastical boundaries of her own time and one should not look to her for structural analysis and criticism of either church or society. But she did manage to find a space for herself as an independent woman, where she operated, for the most part, above suspicion and with the clear support of the Dominican friars.

Teresa of Avila and Catherine of Siena, a nun and a laywoman, both doctors of the church — the only two women so designated — both mystics, acted on an authority received directly from Christ in visions and mystical conversations. Both were able to participate in important religious reformations, to impress and influence those around them, and to do what they wanted to do with their lives. That their authority was "from Christ" and not claimed as their own does not detract from the power of their lives or the influence of their religious vision. Nor does their inability to claim their own authority support theories of female passivity: it probably says more for their realistic assessment of their own cultural situation and their ability to get what they wanted in spite of it. These women can be remembered for having and sustaining an independent position in a church that, even more than today, discouraged and often punished female initiative. Neither saint is a feminist by any modern definition of that word, but both are what Alice Walker calls "womanists" in the sense that their behavior can be described as "outrageous, audacious, courageous or *willful*."[49]

Although it is necessary to have models of strong women in the spiritual tradition, feminists also insist on a fuller conceptualization of divinity, because a God understood in exclusively male terms and language is inadequate and stultifying. As we have seen, some feminists have abandoned historical Christianity altogether in order to reconstruct and participate in the religion of the Goddess. Others have not abandoned the tradition but try to minimize or ignore the masculine characteristics and attributes of the deity and prefer to imagine divinity in feminine terms. For them, Julian of Norwich (c. 1342–after 1413) is an important herald, because of her well-developed understanding of the "motherhood of God." An English anchoress who had a series of sixteen visions in 1373, Julian is virtually unique in the mystical tradition for her joy and sweetness. In her visions Christ never scolds or warns but is eager to show her that divine love is the key to all mysteries. God is full of mercy and forgiveness and aims "to make us glad and merry."[50] Christ continually assures Julian that "all shall be well and all shall be well and all manner of thing shall be well" (p. 91). Typical of other mystics, Julian understands God as our Father and spouse, but in contrast to the normative tradition, she also sees God (and Christ) as Mother: "As truly as God is our Father, so truly is God our Mother," she says (p. 161). In reporting on God's words to her, she records this passage (p. 161):

I it am: the might and the goodness of the Fatherhood. I it am: the wisdom and the kindness of Motherhood. I it am: the light and the grace that is all blessed love. I it am, the Trinity. I it am, the Unity. I it am, the high sovereign Goodness of all manner of thing. I it am that maketh thee to love. I it am that maketh thee to long. I it am, the endless fulfilling of all true desires.

Because Julian's God does away with blame and is full of mercy, she is Mother as well as Father: mercy, Julian notes, "belongs to the Motherhood of God" (p. 128). In an intensely lyrical chapter, she compares the properties of motherhood — kindness, nurturance, the ability to feed a child, tenderness, and sweetness—to the characteristics of Christ, who is even more kind and tender and able "to feed us with himself" (p. 164).

When assessing the impact of Julian's understanding of God it is important to remember two things: first, maternal and feminine aspects of God can be found in the Bible and in early Christian literature, so Julian is not original;[51] second, the most coherent development of "the motherhood of God" and the nurturing qualities of Christ occurred in the writings of twelfth-century Cistercian monks, so that as a concept it has had more importance historically for men than for women. As Caroline Walker Bynum has shown in her brilliant book, the sweeping religious changes in the twelfth century, coupled with specific needs of Cistercian life, led a series of monks—most of them abbots—to develop a concept of the "motherhood of Jesus" based on female stereotypes and used in response to problems they encountered with their own experience of religious authority.[52]

According to Bynum, the idealization of the mothering role and its use by cloistered males does not mean that women were held in any higher esteem: on the contrary, simultaneous with the use of female religious imagery were institutional moves to curb female power and influence. In fact, religious "writing by cloistered males in the twelfth and thirteenth centuries shows at least as much hostility toward actual mothers and actual women as it does romanticizing of them" (p. 145). Though it is true that there was a rise of affective spirituality and a feminization of religious language in the twelfth century, women were still conceptualized in stereotypical ways and understood to be inferior. In a positive sense, but no less stereotypically, women were seen to be generative and sacrificial, loving and tender, accessible and nurturing, the very qualities God possessed and exhibited in Christ: God was creative, loving and present in the Eucharist. God's love for creatures was therefore understood to be maternal in the sense that it was instinctive and accessible.

In a time when piety was becoming more lyrical and emotional, when there was an emphasis on the humanity of Christ, feminine images and female saints increased. Mystical union, understood erotically, was difficult for men to imagine unless they either understood themselves or Christ as feminine, and given their contempt for real women, it was easier to imagine Christ in mothering ways than to conceptualize themselves as females. Interestingly, in the early Middle Ages, when women seeking spiritual life were advised to "become men" through the sacrifice of their sexuality, it was not unusual to find pictures of the Virgin Mary with a beard: in the twelfth century, however, when the soul was described in feminine terms and men related to Christ as mother, one can find pictures of Christ with breasts.[53]

Contrary to the theory that the motherhood of God was invented or used by women, Bynum shows that Cistercian abbots, when called to respond to monastery problems with what they considered to be feminine characteristics — gentleness, nurturance, tenderness, accessibility — projected those qualities onto Christ and then imitated them. Their need to supplement authority with love led them to develop a concept of God that was particularly loving. In doing so they romanticized motherhood, used female stereotypes, and imagined Christ as a nursing mother even while they maintained their distance from and contempt for actual women.

In contrast to the motherhood concepts used by Cistercian monks in the twelfth century, Bynum shows that the understanding of motherhood by nuns was much more integrated. For the female mystics at Helfta a mother was stern as well as comforting, charged with discipline as well as nurturance.[54] Similarly, if Christ was a tender mother, he was also a tender father: female "writers do not use the idea of God as mother to complement judgment with nurture" (p. 158). Bynum suggests that the differences reflect different cultural expectations about male roles (p. 158):

The male role as delineated in the twelfth-century romance was certainly no less military than the male role in the somewhat earlier epic; but the knight of the romance was required to supplement leadership and prowess with good manners, affection and social graces. All this suggests a general ambivalence about authority and about male roles in twelfth-century society.

Women's relative lack of ambivalence about authority was not so much a function of not having any, but rather a result of their authority being based on a mystical relationship with Christ. Male authority, based on office, was subject to the demands of the institutional and cultural context, whereas female authority, "based directly on divine inspiration" (p. 159), was more certain and less anxiety-producing. Bynum's contrasting group of women—the thirteenth-century mystics at Helfta—appear to have a much stronger self image, are able to conceptualize women in positive and powerful terms, and do not make stereotypical associations: for them, male and female are both strong, both tender.

Roman Catholic feminists, in contrast to many of those in other branches of the Christian tradition, have a list of female saints and a tradition of female mysticism. Insofar as those saints have nothing to recommend them but martyrdom and some variation of enslaved religiosity, they can be ignored; but on the chance that their lives might contain hidden embodiments of power or assertiveness, they deserve some attention. Any woman, especially a strong one, can be buried in piety or given insufficient credit for her independence. An exclusive focus on Teresa of Avila as a mystic without corresponding attention to her uphill struggle for personal integration and power obscures an important part of her value for feminist interpreters. Similarly, it would be easy to emphasize Catherine of Siena's obedience to the pope or disparagement of female weakness to the neglect of her independence and personal power, but by so doing, we would lose a potentially important model for a self-styled dedicated life. Since it would be easy to romanticize God's "motherhood" we must take some care to be critical in assessing the importance of that concept either in terms of Julian of Norwich or the Cistercian monks. The fact that the concept itself embarrasses modern scholars and "makes theologians wince" (p. 110) is probably a good sign in terms of the power of the image, but it does not support a general view that the motherhood of God was a concept devised by and for women. In an attempt to utilize the motherhood of God as a feminist insight, we need to avoid the sex-role stereotyping that accompanied much of its use in former times and aim for the more balanced concept that understands both masculine and feminine as tender and both as strong. One of Bynum's points about the powerful maternal imagery used by the nuns at Helfta is that women who grew up (from childhood) in female monasteries were less likely to be influenced by the contemporary stereotypes of women as morally and intellectually inferior (p. 185). Our ability to use non-stereotypical feminine images of the divine, therefore, might correlate with our opportunity to experience women as independent, strong, lively, and holy, to see in women a fullness of human capability and responsiveness to the divine.

A GARLAND OF MARYS: RECLAIMING THE POWER

Who is Mary for the feminist theologian? Does she constitute "yet another Christian symbol which must be examined and ultimately rejected as limiting the human potential of women?"[55] Or is she a model of liberation, "the One who has first given birth to herself, and thus brings God forth among us?"[56] Historically we know virtually nothing about her—no words or deeds or actual attitudes survive—and textually she is mentioned by name only once in the New Testament.

One approaches her, therefore, not as a historical person, but as a religious symbol. Though I do not deny that there is a theology of Mary in the New Testament, I do not believe it has played a primary role in Catholicism. Most Roman Catholic women have experienced Mary's symbolic power as a traditional reflection of hierarchical values: Mariology has generally been used to preserve pure femininity, support complementarity, and justify male domination. As a symbol of perfect motherhood *and* spotless virginity, Mary embodies an impossible combination of attributes that makes her, as Marina Warner has said, "alone of all her sex."[57] Women who attempt to relate to a virgin-mother are doomed from the outset.

In the Catholic tradition, certain qualities of Mary chosen to keep women in their place have been set up for conscious edification and imitation. In patriarchal religion Mary has been first and foremost an image of passive humility: male theologians have taken one phrase of the annunciation story—"let it be done to me according to thy word"—and absolutized it, so that Mary becomes a reification of male power over women. When Mary takes her place in the heavenly pantheon—as Queen of Heaven, crowned by the same popes who crowned (and canonized) Charlemagne and gloried in "Christ the King"—she presides over the hierarchy and supports their system. She can then become a heavenly spokeswoman for their causes — anticommunism, antiabortion, women as the heart of the home — and a model to divert Catholics from the political consequences of Vatican II.[58]

Before rejecting the submissive Mary as hopelessly inadequate for feminist needs, it helps to remember that even in religious history she has another side. Depicted in more sensual and human terms in the Middle Ages, Mary carried many of the attributes and powers of the ancient goddesses. Ruether noted when assessing the parallel streams of the tradition that

there is the Mary of the monks, who venerate her primarily as a virgin and shape her doctrines in an antisexual mold. But there is the Mary of the people who is still the earth mother and who is venerated for her power over the secret of natural fecundity. It is she who helps the woman through her birthpangs, who assures the farmer of her new crops, new rains, new lambs. She is the maternal image of the divine who understands ordinary people in their wretchedness.[59]

As a champion of the poor she was known in some quarters as "the madonna of rogues," the one who could be counted on to help rebels, or even to serve as a midwife for a "fallen abbess." Mary, in other words, can also be a model of subversive activity, "very much alive in the history of all who are oppressed."[60] She is, therefore, as are all good religious symbols, ambiguous, even though she has been experienced by many Catholic women predominantly in terms of complementarity.

As a symbol of passivity Mary has been "a stick to beat smart girls," as Mary Gordon says, an enemy of intellectuality.[61] As an image of purity, Mary stands in contrast to real women, who, not having been immaculately conceived, are inherently impure. John Chrysostom (c. 347–407), the eloquent, "golden-mouthed" archbishop of Constantinople, described woman thus: "the whole of her bodily beauty is nothing less than phlegm, blood, bile, rheum and the fluid of digested food . . . if you consider what is stored up behind those lovely eyes, the angle of the nose, the mouth and cheeks you will agree that her well-proportioned body is merely a whited sepulcher."[62] What are women to do with this disgust-filled view of real women as it measures up against the purity of Mary? "What hope is there for the rest of us, who eat, breathe, menstruate, make love, bear children? How do we bridge the gap between ordinary women, the repository of phlegm, bile, rheum and the fluid of digested food and the Tower of Ivory, House of Gold, Queen of Heaven?"[63]

What would it mean to read the symbol of Mary differently? In the first place, all the texts would have to be used, not just the "humble" ones; but, in addition to that, we might consider using all the Marys in the New Testament. Though a literal analysis demands that we discriminate between Mary the mother of Jesus and other Marys, a symbolic interpretation allows unconventional moves. There are "Marys a-plenty" says H. D. in her long poem, *Trilogy*,[64] and if we conflate the texts so that the different Marys and Mary traditions become aspects of a single self, "Mary" might be able to function as a powerful icon for feminists.

When we examine all the texts about Mary the mother of Jesus we already have a stronger picture. The angelic greeting "the Lord is with you" is not only a fundamental religious affirmation of human–divine partnership, it recalls one of the primary tenets of Goddess feminism, the discovery of the divine within oneself. If one really believes that God/ess is within, it is possible to believe that things are more than they seem to be, and it is probable that one experiences some form of empowerment.

Yet if we have been encouraged to think of Mary as powerful, it is only to see spiritual strength predicated on human passivity. Carlo Caretto, focusing on the annunciation pericope in the Gospel of Luke says:

It is really my misery which attracts His power, my wounds which shout after Him, my nothingness that makes Him throw Himself open to me . . . "He has regarded the lowliness of His handmaiden," said Mary when she saw, accepting her nothingness, the essential love of God and felt her flesh become the dwelling place and nourishment of the Word Incarnate. . . . How wonderful that Mary's nothingness should attract God's all.[65]

Interpreted in the light of divine power and human weakness, this text is often put in male/female terms: the dominant male God overshadowing the subordinate female soul. As such, texts like this become paradigms for male headship and female acquiescence. What would it mean, however, to read the annunciation story less androcentrically? We must ask, first of all, what God finds attractive about nothingness. Given that most women in the world are already "lowly" and reduced to some form of nothingness, it is hard to use even the mystical insights of someone like Eckhart to redeem this concept.[66] A more fruitful interpretive approach, therefore, is probably a liberationist one.[67]

Throughout the Old Testament it is clear that God honors the lowly. The canticle of Hannah (1 Samuel 2:1–10), which is the source for the Magnificat, is a testament of God's raising up the lowly, that is, showering them with positive attention. In Exodus 2:23–5, when the humiliated, enslaved people of God cry out, "God hears the cries of the poor." Furthermore, there are many instances in the Bible of God empowering a "weak" person. In Judges 6:15, for example, Gideon is told, bluntly, "Go save Israel." His logical disclaimer, that he is too *weak* to save Israel, is met with God's promise, "I shall be with you." One can read the annunciation story, therefore, not as an example of a humble, self-effacing woman, but as a symbol of divine empowerment vis-à-vis the poor and the weak. The annunciation and nativity are not celebrations of motherhood but stories of God's saving actions. Mary, then, every bit as much as Gideon, Hannah, or Sarah, is the recipient of a mission from the Lord. As such, she is, as Schillebeeckx says, "a type of the redeemed community," one who is willing to go to the limits, as the church should be willing to do.[68]

God's attraction to the lowliness of Mary, therefore, says more about God than it does about her: God has a preference for the poor that is clear throughout the Bible, and "God's opting for the poor makes the poor the preferential locus for understanding who the church is. The church *is* the poor and oppressed whom God is vindicating. The non-poor join the church by joining God in that preferential option for the poor and identifying themselves with the cause of the oppressed."[69] It is now possible to see the angelic greeting —"Hail, full of grace"— in its full biblical context as an expression of God's continued raising up of the lowly. As a poor woman and a virgin, Mary represents those classes of the subjugated who will be lifted up and filled with good things when the Messiah comes.

Mary's role as the "first theologian" is perhaps clearest in this context. The evangelist Luke could have made Joseph the hero of the infancy narratives (as Matthew did), or he could have ignored Mary and Joseph altogether (as Mark did), or he could have abstracted Jesus' birth into the philosophical realm (as in the Gospel of John); but he features Mary and has her interpret the tradition (represented here by the canticle of Hannah) in the light of this new, empowering experience. Furthermore, in Luke's Gospel Mary represents Israel. Inspired, perhaps, by the references to the "daughter of Zion" in Zephaniah 3, Luke uses Mary's impending sorrow—the prophecies of Simeon—as a symbol of the division in Israel caused by the prophet Jesus.

Why, then, when many of us remember the annunciation story, do we remember most often the words "Be it done unto me according to thy word?" The overwhelming message of the story for women is not acquiescence, but empowerment: "the Lord is with you . . . you are full of grace . . . have found favor with God . . . will bear the Son of the Most High . . . whose kingdom will have no end." Surrounded by this divine favor, Mary makes no demur, but simply asks a logical question: "How can this be since I have no husband?" When the angel explains and supports the story with a sign (her cousin Elizabeth's pregnancy), only then does Mary utter the word, "Be it done unto me according to thy word," an acknowledgment of her willingness to enter into a profoundly different kind of divine-human partnership. When she travels to her cousin and is greeted with the words "Blessed are you among women," Mary makes no neurotic disclaimer but responds with power: she knows she is favored by God and she rejoices in it; she recognizes her "low estate," but says, as well, "All generations shall call me blessed." The annunciation story need not be read as if it is about a passively perfect young woman overwhelmed by divine duty, but can be interpreted as a story of a rather self-possessed poor woman who "finds favor with God" and is willing to cooperate with a wild plan of salvation, a woman strong enough to risk believing something incredible about herself.

Other stories of Mary can be read in more powerful ways as well. The story of Jesus getting lost in the temple is not necessarily a tale of a hassled mother or one about children's natural capacity to produce anxiety in parents. And it need not end with her silenced by her son's cryptic response. We might notice that though both parents look for Jesus and find him, it is Mary who speaks, not Joseph. Luke's focus is on the woman: the parallel story about Jacob being troubled by his son but keeping his own counsel (Genesis 37:9–11) could have been used by Luke to draw Jesus' father into the story, but it was not. Mary is featured, and she has the last word: Jesus "went down with them . . . and was obedient to them." To take another example: the crucifixion story often encourages us to imagine a subdued, quiet woman at the foot of the cross, but it has more power than that. Mary Gordon contrasts Mary's grief at the crucifixion with Clytemnestra's madness over the death of Iphigenia and says that Mary is remarkable for her profound grief without madness.[70]

The Mary who emerges from a reading of all the texts, therefore, is a much stronger woman. For many feminists, Mary is the image of creativity without male intervention, who responded to God, not as a woman, but as a free person, "not bound by physical dependence upon man's cooperation, nor by social constraint to seek a man's approval."[71] In the Magnificat she is, by all exegetical accounts, a spokeswoman for the anawim ("little people"). The poor who had remained faithful to God throughout Jewish history are represented by the poorest of the poor, a Jewish woman, and in the representation she is elevated and recognized as a necessary partner for an extraordinary divine act in history.

Part of Mary's power lies in her responsiveness to divine initiative, but much of it rests with her humanity. Whether or not her heavenly power and attributes are similar to those of the Goddess, "She is one of us,"[72] inescapably human. Her predicament as an unwed mother has been used by missionaries trying to appeal to poor women and prostitutes in Mexican slums,[73] and just as liberationist Maryknolls see the face of the crucified Christ in the lives of the poor, so they see Mary in

simple, poorly clad young girl[s] . . . many young girls like that. They trod the roads of Bolivia, Peru and Guatemala carrying incredible loads over even more incredible mountains. They have little or no education and they have been working since they learned to walk.[74]

Mary's oneness with humanity makes her an appealing and natural subject of pattern theology: it is she, not Jesus, who gives hope by way
of her connectedness. Jesus' place in heaven, predicated on his divinity, is comforting, but not reassuring in the same way as Mary's
heavenly presence. The combination of Mary's humanity and divinity can tell us something about ourselves: the belief in the divine presence within us and our willing response to it opens up the possibility
of apotheosis.[75]

In order to gather the fullness of Mary symbolism, we need to turn
to *all* the Marys, perhaps even to all the (usually nameless) women in
the New Testament. Their persistence, shrewdness, insight, and daring are parables for us as women even while their stories were used
by Jesus as parables for religious readiness and response. Jesus says
nothing negative about women—perhaps he is the only major religious figure or founder for whom this is true—and, in fact, he treats
them in extraordinary ways. Furthermore, Luke's sensitivity to women
as members of the poor and despised classes, vindicated by the messianic prophet, adds a social justice dimension to Mary's symbolic
power in the Magnificat. In order to gather this womanly strength and
to find the power of the composite symbol of Mary, the texts have to
be read symbolically as an aggregate even though they are not presented
that way in the New Testament. If spirituality functions through mul-
tivalent religious symbols, then it may be argued that by gathering all
the Mary texts together as facets of a single self, I am attempting to
appreciate the depth of the symbol.

As we have seen, patriarchy thrives on division. Women are weak-
ened by those who divide women in two, pitting them against one
another or finding in individual women two disparate, antagonistic
parts. The Eve/Mary typology used by ancient Christian writers has
succeeded in convincing some women that they contain within themselves both virgin and whore and so must choose to live either as angel-
in-the-house or strumpet-in-the-street. Since solidarity is impossible when we internalize the invidious suggestion that different parts
of ourselves are at war with other parts, an integrated, positive view,
first of the self and then of women in general is a step toward strength-
ening those bonds that help us to resist domination and schizophrenia.

Since the symbolic use of Mary as virgin-mother has contributed to divisiveness, and since a revisionary reading of the Mary symbol might help to reduce those antagonisms, I am using what Elisabeth Moltmann-Wendel calls the "courage to be subjective" when I conflate the texts to see what possibilities for self-discovery present themselves in the composite picture.[76]

The most important of the other Marys is Magdalene. Some interpreters have suggested that she is the woman from whom Jesus cast out seven devils, that is to say, a woman who was either a great sinner or quite crazy. She has been dismissed as a hysteric and used by hostile interpreters to deny the resurrection as a figment of her hallucinated imagination. On the other hand, Elizabeth Cady Stanton chose to look at the resurrection story and see Mary's discernment in the face of male blindness:

> Though the disciples, in visiting the tomb, saw nothing but cast off clothes, yet Mary sees and talks with angels and with Jesus. As usual, the woman is always most ready to believe in miracles and fables, however extravagant and though beyond all human comprehension . . . the women saw Jesus and the angels, though the men, who went to the tomb twice, saw Nothing.[77]

I do not think it matters for my purposes whether Magdalene had seven devils cast from her or not, though incredulous male commentators might want to use lunacy as an alternative explanation for her subsequent courageous and iconoclastic deeds. She sat at the feet of Jesus — a role unheard of for women at that time — and, far from being dismissed by him, was invited to learn the good news and to participate in ministry. She was present at the trial and crucifixion of Jesus while male disciples fled, and she was, by all accounts, the first witness to the resurrection. One interpreter says that "there is a certain irony in that Jesus appeared first not to his chosen disciples but to a woman."[78] Irony for whom? Jesus' first postresurrection appearance to a woman — to this woman in particular — is consistent with his behavior toward women all his life, a steady breaking of precedents. It is, additionally, consistent with God's attraction to the poor and so connects Jesus's friendship with Mary Magdalene to God's favoring of the virgin Mary. The only problem with Jesus' first appearance to Magdalene is Peter's refusal to believe her and Paul's ignoring the report altogether. Magdalene is, if one follows the tradition, a leader, preacher, healer, and close friend to Jesus.

Mary the sister of Martha, or Mary of Bethany, is the woman who anointed the feet of Jesus — an act of devotion, extravagance, and, as a preparation for burial, of prescience — and who, in choosing to listen to Jesus rather than to work in the kitchen with her sister, is said to have chosen the better role. Mary the mother of James and Mary the wife of Clophas are mentioned in conjunction with Jesus' burial and anointing, traditional "woman's work" heroically performed. In another place and time, a woman's burial ministrations for an outlaw was the stuff of great drama: Antigone's heroic burial of Polynices has lived through the centuries as the tortured decision of a passionate woman. We could, therefore, admire the strength and passion of these burying women rather than taking their work for granted and consigning it to a place of little importance.

The other Marys, therefore, expand the symbol of Mary the virgin-mother. Taken together, all the Marys constitute a rich Mary symbol. We have now a woman who finds the divine within herself and so can participate in an extraordinary partnership with the heavenly powers; a woman whose poverty is attractive to God and whose voice is used to herald the messianic age; a woman who can command obedience from "a divine son," and yet, breaking the cultural limitations of her times, can dare to be a disciple; a woman who may have been crazy at one time, but who thrives with affirmation and attention, whose experience of Jesus' power transforms her into the most faithful of disciples. She is — to use some of the nameless women — no longer stooped, no longer bleeding, not at all shy about pressing her own claims. Poor herself, she still shares what she can with the poor, both bound and exalted by her solidarity with them. This symbolic Mary listens to Jesus, studies with him, knowing that her "natural place" (in the kitchen) is not so natural in the face of her new experience; she can set aside traditional roles to follow this person.   She understands his mission, foresees and accepts his death as the apostles never could (or did), and makes an extravagant gesture of compassion in her acceptance of it. When, finally, he is buried, she does not remain quivering in some isolated upper room but goes forth "the next day" to see to the body, to bring spices to it (as the Magi had brought spices to the child), and she is granted the favor of Jesus' first appearance. The connections between this final act of anointing, the anointing of the feet, and the gifts of frankincense and myrrh brought to the child Jesus give us a way to connect Mary with rich symbols in mythology and with other biblical events and women (Mara/bitterness, Mary/myrrh). This is done in a most astounding way in H. D.'s poem *Trilogy*:

I am Mary, she said, of a tower-town,
or it once must have been towered

for Magdala is a tower;
Magdala stands on the shore;

I am Mary, she said, of Magdala,
I am Mary, a great tower;

through my will and my power,
Mary shall be myrrh;

I am Mary—O there are Marys a-plenty,
(though I am Mara bitter) I shall be Mary-myrrh;

I am that myrrh-tree of the gentiles,
the heathen; there are idolaters,

even in Phrygia and Cappadocia
who kneel before mutilated images

and burn incense to the Mother of Mutilations,
to Attis-Adonis-Tammuz and his mother who was myrrh;

she was a stricken woman,
having borne a son in unhallowed fashion;

she wept bitterly till some heathen god
changed her into a myrrh-tree;

I am Mary, I will weep bitterly,
bitterly . . . bitterly.[79]

H. D. obviously connects Magdalene with Mary the mother of God and with the ancient Goddess, Queen of Heaven. In doing this, she anticipates one line of contemporary feminist thought and reflects an ancient identification. She also gives us a way to reclaim Mary and resist her misuse by patriarchal interpreters.

In drawing all the Marys together, we obliterate the division between the inimitable Mary mother of God, "alone of all her sex," and us. We gather this garland of Marys in an act of symbolic integration and identity, choosing to find ourselves sketched in the full picture rather than to suffer the psychic division perpetrated by those who would have us meekly accept our lot in life under the patronage of the "Queen of Heaven." All the Marys, taken together, connect us in time and space with the Goddess, with mythical and biblical women, with the dark side of ourselves (the seven devils), with discipleship and with confidence that though everything is the same, everything is somehow different. "A house divided against itself cannot stand," said Jesus. Neither can women, divided against themselves or set in opposition to the unreachable "mother of God."

CONCLUSIONS

Feminist spirituality is both old and new, alive to ancient rhythms of the Goddess while willing to experiment with spontaneous feminist rituals. It is rooted in the tradition—sometimes eager to claim connections with the eucharistic celebration of the Christian church—and yet opposed to its expression of exclusive male power. Roman Catholic feminist spirituality is clearly political, in the sense that it is predicated on a worldview that finds the sacred in what used to be called the secular, and yet may have something much in common with mystical prayer: perhaps God/ess can only be experienced in a combination of active service on behalf of the marginalized and lively, daring participation in moments of divine disclosure deep within the soul.

Assessing some of the currents and possibilities of Roman Catholic feminist spirituality is the most appropriate way to end this book. It recapitulates the questions of feminist historians by interrogating—if only briefly—the tradition of female sanctity in Roman Catholicism. At the same time, by choosing to look differently at Teresa of Avila and Catherine of Siena, it reminds us that nuns and laywomen have always encountered opposition in the Catholic church when they embodied visions that were at odds with the option of complementarity or cloister presented to them by patriarchal males allegedly speaking for God. In looking at Julian of Norwich, we are reminded of how much we need feminist theologians and critical interpreters of the tradition in addition to visionaries. Most of all, in gathering the many Marys together to intuit the possibilities of a composite symbol, we gain some sense of the need for solidarity and the power of collective action.

In times of increasing repression against women in the American Catholic church, we need new "holy cards." If we tend to see Martha as a model of service, a woman in the kitchen, we have to reimagine her—as the hidden tradition did—as a dragon-slayer, as a "tenacious, wise, combative, competent, emancipated woman with many practical responsibilities in the community."[80] If we picture Mary Magdalene, in our mind's eye, sitting attentively at the feet of Jesus, then we need now to look at sixteenth century paintings which show her in the pulpit preaching, a woman who was "eloquent and persuasive. She could speak and did not find it difficult to exert her authority."[81] If we remember the mother of Jesus sitting calmly with the disciples or standing sorrowfully at the foot of the cross, we might revisualize her as they do in Latin America as "the *madonna leone* [who] rides naked on the back of a lion and—at least for our tamed and corrupted sense of religion—appears to be more witch than saint."[82] If we have always been told that there is a dark side in us, a seething black power inherited from Eve, then we must look at Denise Levertov's brilliant reappropriation of this "inimical power" as budding wings, the "power of flight."[83]

Since this book has been organized around the need to change structures and to resist patriarchal patterns of authority, it has focused very much on women's work—pratical, political, intellectual—and action. In traditional Catholicism, prayer and work were often separated: the old Benedictine motto, *ora et labora*, helped to set the tasks of the body apart from those of the heart and to give spirituality a space, shape, and meaning of its own. In the solitary center of the Catholic spiritual tradition we find the mystics, those heroic explorers of the borders between human and divine life. Mystics sought union with God/ess without much guidance or reassurance, but with an intuitive under-standing that in confronting themselves they were enabled to move beyond themselves. In their own way, they could stay within the tra-dition as rebels, or at least as pioneers, testing the limits, finding a para-doxical empowerment in weakness, and learning to trust their own experience. New Catholic women, indebted to the theology of Vati-can II and supported by the courage and questions of the women's movement, are in the process of reimaging the church in our own terms. In that creative and partly subversive task we can clearly find support in collective action and what we have seen as political spirituality; but we also have a power in our own tradition—which is a gift as well as a burden.

Notes

INTRODUCTION

1. *New York Times* (15 Feb. 1985).
2. *National Catholic Reporter*, vol. 21 (15 Feb. 1985), p. 5.
3. See, e.g., "Discord in the Church," *Newsweek*, vol. 125 (4 Feb. 1985), pp. 50–63; and Penny Lernoux, " 'Debate's Less on Theology Than on Who Runs Church' " *National Catholic Reporter*, vol. 20 (14 Sept. 1984), pp. 1, 21.
4. On October 7, 1984, "A Catholic Statement on Pluralism and Abortion" appeared in the *New York Times* accompanied by the signatures of ninety-six lay and religious Catholics, including some theologians. The statement pointed to the fact that there is a diversity of opinion among committed Catholics and theologians as to whether abortion is morally wrong in all instances and whether in certain circumstances "direct abortion, though tragic, can sometimes be a moral choice." The group also suggested that there is more than one legitimate Catholic position and said, "It is necessary that the Catholic community encourage candid and respectful discussion on this diversity of opinion within the Church." The Sacred Congregation for Religion at the Vatican responded by sending form letters to the superiors of the twenty-four religious women who signed the statement. The Vatican letter demanded a public retraction from the signers under threat of dismissal from their religious communities.
5. Langdon Gilkey, *Catholicism Confronts Modernity* (New York: Seabury Press, 1975), p. 202.
6. See, e.g., Eva Catafygiotou-Topping, "Women Hymnographers in Byzantium," *AOHNAI* (1982–83), pp. 98–111, and "Belittling Eve," *Greek Accent,* vol. 5 (Nov./Dec. 1984), pp. 25–27, 49f.
7. Teresa of Avila, *Interior Castles*, intro., sec. 4.
8. See, e.g., Antonio M. Stevens Arroyo, *Prophets Denied Honor: An Anthology on the Hispanic Church in the United States* (Maryknoll, N.Y.: Orbis Books, 1980), esp. pp. 5–7, 99, 153.

CHAPTER 1: WHO *CAN* FIND A VALIANT WOMAN?

Epigraphs: Adrienne Rich, "Natural Resources," in *The Dream of a Common Language* (New York: W. W. Norton, 1978), p. 67; John Boyle O'Reilly, *Watchwords from John Boyle O'Reilly*, ed. Katherine E. Conway (Boston: Joseph George Cuppels, 1891), p. 20; Mother Jones, quoted in Judith Nies, *Seven Women: Portraits from the American Radical Tradition* (New York: Viking Press, 1977), p. 123.

1. Usually they can name Catherine Tekakwitha (1656–1680), Elizabeth Bayley Seton (1774–1821), Frances Xavier Cabrini (1850–1917), and Dorothy Day (1897–1980).
2. James Hennesey, *American Catholics: A History of the Roman Catholic Community in the United States* (New York: Oxford Univ. Press, 1981).

3. Edwin Ardener, "The 'Problem' Revisited," in *Perceiving Women*, ed. Shirley Ardener (London: J. M. Dent & Sons, 1975), pp. 19-27, quotation from p. 25. Ardener published an earlier essay on which this one is based: "Belief and the Problem of Women," ibid., pp. 1-17.

4. Gerda Lerner, "Placing Women in History: A 1975 Perspective," originally appeared in *Feminist Studies*, vol. 3 (1975), pp. 5-15, revised and published in *Liberating Women's History: Theoretical and Critical Essays*, ed. Berenice A. Carroll, (Urbana, Ill.: Univ. of Illinois Press, 1976), pp. 357-67, quotation from p. 365, emphasis mine.

5. Robert Trisco, ed., *Catholics in America 1776-1976* (Washington, D.C.: U.S. Catholic Conference, 1976). In this volume there are 6 essays about women out of 60, and 41 index items out of 431.

6. Delores Barracano Schmidt and Earl Robert Schmidt, "The Invisible Woman: The Historian as Professional Magician," in Carroll, *Liberating Women's History*, pp. 42-54, quotation from p. 44. American history books, they say, depict "a world without women," p. 54. For more on this issue, see Eleanor Flexner, *A Century of Struggle* (New York: Atheneum, 1973), pp. vii, xii, xiii.

7. Mary Kay Tetreault, "Notable American Women: The Case of United States History Textbooks," unpublished paper, 1984. Tetreault examined a dozen textbooks published between 1979 and 1982 and found that the "extent to which these textbooks have included the contributions of notable American women is nothing short of remarkable." Still, the books can be faulted precisely because they "have incorporated notable women who contributed in areas or movements that were traditionally dominated by men . . . [and] fail to present the efforts of notable women who worked for change in areas critical to the majority of women — childbearing and childrearing, housework and paid work. By failing to present notable women who worked for change in those areas most central to women's lives, the idea is reinforced that housework and reproduction, for instance, are ahistorical and static. Students are taught to devalue women's concerns."

8. Elaine Showalter, "Women and the Literary Curriculum," in *College English*, vol. 32 (1971), pp. 855-62, quotations from pp. 855, 856. It cannot be argued that there *are* no women authors. See Sandra M. Gilbert and Susan Gubar, eds., *The Norton Anthology of Literature by Women* (New York: W. W. Norton and Company, 1985) which publishes the work of over one hundred literary women.

9. Anne Wilson Schaef, *Women's Reality: An Emerging Female System in the White Male Society* (Minneapolis: Winston Press, 1981). The characteristics of the "White Male System" as defined by Schaef are reminiscent of medieval Catholicism's understanding of itself. The White Male System, according to Schaef, sees itself as the *only* one (other systems are aberrant phenomena, to be discounted or destroyed), as *knowing everything* (being able, even called, to sit in judgment on everything), as *innately superior* (able to be judged by no one), and as *capable of being perfectly logical, rational, and objective*. If we applied those characteristics to the Roman Catholic church today we might squirm in embarrassment. Yet many of us used to define the Roman Catholic church in precisely those terms and have had to work hard to be disabused of triumphant Catholicism by postconciliar theology. Just as Vatican II redefined church, the women's movement encourages a radical widening of horizons in our culture to include women's experience.

10. Judith Fetterley, *The Resisting Reader: A Feminist Approach to American Fiction* (Bloomington, Ind.: Indiana Univ. Press, 1978).

11. As cited in *Mary Ritter Beard: A Sourcebook*, ed. Ann J. Lane (New York: Schocken Books, 1977), p. 172.

12. Simone de Beauvoir, *The Second Sex* (New York: Alfred A. Knopf, 1952; Vintage Books ed., 1974), pp. xxii, xxiii.

13. Elizabeth Cady Stanton, Susan B. Anthony, and Matilda Joslyn Gage, eds., *History of Woman Suffrage* (originally published, New York: Fowler & Wells, 1881; republished, New York: Arno Press & The New York Times, 1969). Vol. 1, p. 81, cites a Congregationalist minister who said, "The power of woman is her dependence . . . when she assumes the place and tone of man as a public reformer . . . her character becomes unnatural, . . . [she] will fall in shame and dishonor."

14. Sarah Grimké, *Letters on the Equality of the Sexes and the Condition of Woman* (Boston: Isaac Knapp, 1838; reprinted, New York: Source Book Press, 1970), pp. 10 f.

15. Berenice A. Carroll, "Mary Beard's *Woman as Force in History:* A Critique," in Carroll, *Liberating Women's History* (see n. 4), pp. 26–41, quotation from p. 27.

16. Stanton et al., *History of Woman Suffrage*, vol. 1, p. 70.

17. Lane, *Mary Ritter Beard*, p. 1.

18. Beard, for example, accused feminists of being blind to class issues, but she herself was apparently blind to the fact that the "significant women" whose contributions she valued so highly were almost always women of rank or property.

19. De Beauvoir, *Second Sex*, pp. xxxiv, xviii–xix. De Beauvoir was influenced by Sartre's work on Hegel's "master/slave" relationship. For a feminist analysis of Hegel's master/slave relationship, see Mitchell Aboulafia, "From Domination to Recognition," in *Beyond Domination: New Perspectives on Women and Philosophy*, ed. Carol C. Gould (Totowa, N.J.: Rowman & Allanheld, 1984), pp. 175–85.

20. Joan Kelly-Gadol, "The Social Relation of the Sexes: Methodological Implications of Women's History," in *Signs*, vol. 1 (1976), pp. 809–23, quotation from p. 814.

21. See Carroll "Beard's *Woman as Force*"; also see Lane's commentary throughout her book *Mary Ritter Beard*.

22. Virginia Woolf, *A Room of One's Own* (New York: Harcourt, Brace & World, 1929), pp. 48–52. Woolf speculated that if Shakespeare *had* had a gifted sister she would have been sufficiently discouraged, obstructed, and ignored that she probably would have ended up an anonymous suicide. The feminist critics Sandra M. Gilbert and Susan Gubar, attempting to redress the all-too-common perception that there simply have never been female poets of great stature, published *Shakespeare's Sisters: Feminist Essays on Women Poets* (Bloomington, Ind.: Indiana Univ. Press, 1979).

23. Lerner, "Placing Women in History" (see n. 4), and "New Approaches to the Study of Women in American History," in *Journal of Social History*, vol. 4 (Fall 1969), pp. 333–56; reprinted in Carroll, *Liberating Women's History* (see n. 4), pp. 349–56.

24. Lerner, "Placing Women in History," p. 366

25. Kelly-Gadol, "Social Relation of the Sexes," p. 810.

26. Lerner, "Placing Women in History," pp. 360, 365.

27. Mary Daly, *The Church and the Second Sex* (New York: Harper & Row, 1968) makes a case against the Roman Catholic church from its inception to the present day. Daly's research is meticulously detailed and depressing; nevertheless, she ends on a more or less hopeful note about the future. In a subsequent edition of the book, however, she added a "Post-Christian Introduction" that repudiates her naïveté in the earlier work and sounds a radical call for rejection of a hopelessly misogynist tradition (Harper Colophon ed., 1975).

28. One interesting example of the anti-Catholic bias of early feminist historians can be found in Inez Haynes Irwin, *Angels and Amazons: A Hundred Years of American Women* (New York: Doubleday, Doran, 1933). In this 499-page book, with a 2300-item index, only nine Roman Catholics are mentioned (mostly in passing):

Margaret Brent (colonial history); Mother Angela Gillespie (for nursing work during the Civil War); Joan of Arc; five Catholic women associated with the labor movement (Mother Jones, Agnes Nestor, Leonora Barry, Mary Kenny O'Sullivan, and Leonora O'Reilly); and Dorothy Day, whose heroism during the Suffrage March in Washington (1917) is here recognized and praised.

29. John Gilmary Shea, *The History of the Catholic Church in the United States* (New York: John G. Shea, 1886–92; reprint, New York: Arno Press, 1978). Shea was a layman with a strongly clerical view of church history.

30. John Tracy Ellis, Professorial Lecturer in Church History at the Catholic University of America, published what quickly became *the* textbook in the field, *American Catholicism*, 2d rev. ed. (Chicago: Univ. of Chicago Press, 1969). It devotes no more than 2 pages to women out of 254, and of approximately 480 items in the index, only 12 refer to women, mostly to anonymous nuns. Thomas McAvoy, a historian at the University of Notre Dame, published his major work in 1969: *A History of the Catholic Church in the United States* (Univ. of Notre Dame Press). In 468 pages of text, the material on women amounts to less than a page, and only 5 index items out of 375. In his work, even Elizabeth Seton, the first American Catholic canonized saint, merits no more than eight lines.

31. John Tracy Ellis, *Documents of American Catholic History*, 2d ed. (Milwaukee: Bruce, 1962).

32. In the popular, flawed but interesting, work of Theodore Maynard, 110 women are mentioned in an index of 1,400 items, but that is about all that happens to them. Maynard, unlike Shea, thought that American Catholicism was more than bishops and priests, and he tried to assess the cultural contribution of American Catholics, their educational efforts, corporate vision, etc. He was, therefore, more inclusive of women than most American Catholic historians. See *The Story of American Catholicism* (New York: Macmillan, 1942). Later popular histories do not do as well for women. The Commonweal volume *Catholicism in America* (New York: Harcourt, Brace, 1953) has essays by seventeen male contributors, and women are not mentioned at all save for one passing reference to Dorothy Day. John Cogley's *Catholic America* (New York: Dial Press, paperback ed., 1973) has 34 index citations to women out of approximately 700 items. Though scholarly works do not do much better, Philip Gleason's *Contemporary Catholicism in the United States* (Notre Dame, Ind.: Univ. of Notre Dame Press, 1969) does include one essay by a female historian, and his *Catholicism in America* (New York: Harper & Row, 1970) has an article about women, James Kenneally's fine essay on woman suffrage in Massachusetts. First published in *The Catholic Historical Review*, vol. 53 (Apr. 1967), pp. 43–57 as "Catholicism and Woman Suffrage in Massachusetts," Kenneally's article was reprinted in Gleason's book as "Catholicism and Woman Suffrage."

33. Hennesey, *American Catholics* (see n. 2). In this book, women, orders of sisters, and women's organizations are mostly mentioned in passing, though there are three pages about Dorothy Day, two paragraphs on woman suffrage, and an excellent one-page summary of the life and work of the labor leader Mother Jones. It is not clear, however, that Jones was a practicing Catholic even though she did plan her own funeral and it is true she was buried from the Catholic church. Several of the women mentioned in the text are *not* in the index, so my count (fewer than 50 women out of a 1,300-item index) may be somewhat inaccurate.

34. See Jeanne Madeline Weimann, *The Fair Women: The Story of the Women's Building, World's Columbian Exposition, Chicago, 1893* (Chicago: Academy Chicago, 1981),

pp. 29, 39, 58, 64–66, 370. See also Archibald J. Byrne, "Starr, Eliza Allen," in *Notable American Women 1607–1950: A Biographical Dictionary*, ed. Edward T. James et al. (Cambridge: Harvard Univ. Press, 1971), vol 1, pp. 350–351. *Notable American Women* will hereinafter be abbreviated *NAW*. Ellis's set of documents is enormously useful to teachers and students of American Catholicism, but it is not helpful for women's issues. Of the 163 primary documents he published, only 11 refer in some way to women, and some of those do so only tangentially (e.g., the letter of Thomas Jefferson *to* the New Orleans Ursuline Sisters); in approximately 664 pages of text, only 38 deal with women.

35. Lerner, "Placing Women in History" (see n. 4), argues against oppression and struggle as a methodological assessment tool. When historians ask how women have been oppressed, they ask a useful question, she says, but they make it appear as if women are largely passive or reactionary. Further, she argues, women's rights struggles like suffrage are not really as *central* a concern as male historians make them out to be.

36. Barbara Misner, "Historiography of Women's Religious Communities in the 19th Century"; and Elizabeth Kolmer, "Historiography of Women's Religious Communities in the Recent Past"; both papers presented at the Perspectives on American Catholicism conference at the University of Notre Dame, Nov. 19–20, 1982, sponsored by the Cushwa Center for the Study of American Catholicism; Evangeline Thomas, *Women Religious History Sources: A Guide to Repositories in the United States* (New York: R. R. Bowker, 1983).

37. John Paul Cadden, *Historiography of the American Catholic Church, 1785–1943* (Washington, D.C.: Catholic Univ. Press, 1944; reprint by New York: Arno Press, 1978). Of the 117 pages of text, women occupy about one page as authors, subjects, wives, and daughters.

38. Esther Pariseau (later Sister Joseph of the Sacred Heart) was a French-Canadian who went as a missionary to the Oregon territory in 1856. She was an accomplished carpenter and actually designed and built major structures herself. As her Mother General said when she died, "She excelled not only in feminine arts . . . but she was also skilled in works considered the domain of men." She built what the *Vancouver* (Washington) *Independent* called "a gigantic structure . . . probably the largest brick building in the State of Washington, being three stories high and covering about two acres of ground." She not only built, she begged the funds, by going to mining towns, traveling down rivers, camping out in the wilds between one goldfield and another. A remarkable woman, yet when a male Visitor came to check up on her and her sisters, he accused her of not relying sufficiently on divine providence. See Mary of the Blessed Sacrament McCrossan, *The Bell and the River* (Palo Alto, Calif.: Pacific Books, 1957).

39. The rules for women religious in the pre-Vatican II church may have something to do with this insofar as few of them were permitted to travel for research purposes. I suspect that most of the female historians listed in Cadden's historiography wrote their dissertations at Catholic University and did not travel to archival collections. I am indebted to Barbara Misner for sparking this suspicion.

40. Barbara Misner's "Historiography" (see n. 36). See also Misner's dissertation, "A Social Comparative History of the First Eight Permanent Communities of Women Religious Within the Original Boundaries of the United States, 1790–1850." (Washington, D.C.: Catholic Univ. Press, 1981).

41. John Tracy Ellis and Robert Trisco, eds., *A Guide to American Catholic History* (Santa Barbara, Calif.: ABC-Clio, 1982), p. xii. They do not have complete coverage

on nuns, something I discovered quite by accident. Indiana University Library, marvelous as it is for many things, is not where one would normally expect to find books on American Catholic sisterhoods, yet even here I found several books on the shelf that were not included in the Ellis and Trisco bibliography; all were published by university presses or by religious community presses. I would have to conclude that finding these books was not a priority of their search.

42. James Hennesey "American Catholic Bibliography 1970–1982," Working Paper Series 12, No. 1, Fall 1982 (Univ. of Notre Dame: Charles and Margaret Hall Cushwa Center for the Study of American Catholicism), p. 22.

43. Ibid., p. 19.

44. Kelly-Gadol "Social Relation of the Sexes" (see n. 20), p. 810. Also see the work of Daniel O'Neill, which is *comparative*, e.g., "Women in the Church: An Analysis of the Origins of St. Paul's Nuns, 1851–1930," in which O'Neill compares the work of the sisters with that of priests in the same place at the same time. His paper was presented at the Notre Dame conference Perspectives on American Catholicism (see n. 36).

45. One place to test some historical theories about women's history as a separate culture might be the Grail Movement. It began in the Netherlands in 1921 as an international movement for single Catholic women and has grown into an ecumenical women's movement with decidedly feminist priorities. Its members now include married women and women religious as well as single women. For a historical study of the Grail see Alden V. Brown, "The Grail Movement in the United States, 1940–1972: Evolution of an American Roman Catholic Laywoman's Community" (Ph.D. diss., Union Theological Seminary, 1982).

46. Abigail McCarthy, interviewed for television by Edwin Newman, remembered that, when she was in school, Day was not permitted to speak on college campuses (Program on NBC, "Women in the Catholic Church," 27 Feb. 1983). Some places in the United States were apparently less congenial than others: Southern California, e.g., was off limits for her, according to Mel Piehl, *Breaking Bread: The Catholic Worker and the Origins of Catholic Radicalism in the United States* (Philadelphia: Temple Univ. Press, 1982). Julian Pleasants, founder of the South Bend Catholic Worker House in 1941, told me that Notre Dame would not let Peter Maurin speak there in the 1930s and that, when Day came to visit the Worker house in South Bend in 1941, university officials let her come to the campus to speak but would not permit any publicity about the speech. In searching through Catholic college libraries for back issues of the *Catholic Worker*, one often finds a gap in the collection for the early 1940s, indicating that Catholic colleges did not subscribe to pacifist, antiwar publications, Catholic or not. Day was also an active suffragist, imprisoned and beaten with other radicals; see Judith Nies, *Seven Women: Portraits from the American Radical Tradition* (New York: Viking Press, 1977), pp. 179–206. Day's contribution to woman suffrage also earned her one of the few Catholic places in Irwins *Angels and Amazons*, (see n. 28.).

47. One important new source is Hasia Diner, *Erin's Daughters: Irish Immigrant Women in the Nineteenth Century* (Baltimore: Johns Hopkins Univ. Press, 1983). Diner shows that Irish women immigrated in larger numbers than men, had a high degree of independence both before and after passage, and headed a disproportionate number of households. In the old conception of American Catholic history we find an unqualified success story, but if we take a book like Diner's into account, as well as the work of some feminist historians, we can begin to ask whether that success was won at too high a price.

48. Helen Haines, "Catholic Womanhood and the Suffrage," *Catholic World*, vol. 102 (Oct. 1915), p. 55–67, quotation from p. 67.
49. A phrase associated with Catharine Beecher (1800–1878), who did *not* approve of the suffrage movement, it reflects the way in which upper-class American women in the nineteenth century were enshrined on a pedestal whose base was formed out of ladylike virtues of piety, purity, submissiveness, and domesticity. See Katherine Kish Sklar, *Catherine Beecher: A Study in American Domesticity* (New York: W. W. Norton, 1973).
50. James Kenneally, "Eve, Mary and the Historians: American Catholicism and Women," in *Horizons*, vol. 3/2 (1976), p. 187–202, quotation from p. 187.
51. Sidney R. Bland, "Lucy Burns," in *NAW*, vol. 1, pp. 124–25, quotation from p. 125.
52. Ibid., p. 124.
53. We have a description from Lucy Burns herself of being force-fed in an American jail: the incident she describes took place in 1917.

> Wednesday, 12 P.M. Yesterday afternoon at about four or five, Mrs. Lewis and I were asked to go to the operating room. Went there and found our clothes. Told we were to go to Washington. No reason, as usual. When we dressed Dr. Gannon appeared, said he wished to examine us. Both refused. Were dragged through halls by force, our clothing being partly removed by force, and we were examined, heart tested, blood pressure and pulse taken. Of course such data was of no value after such a struggle. Dr. Gannon told me that I must be fed. Was stretched on bed, two doctors, matron, four colored prisoners present, Whittaker in hall. I was held down by five people at legs, arms and head. I refused to open mouth, Gannon pushed the tube up left nostril. I turned and twisted my head all I could, but he managed to push it up. It hurts nose and throat very much and makes nose bleed freely. Tube drawn out covered with blood. Operation leaves one very sick. Food dumped directly into stomach feels like a ball of lead. Left nostril, throat, and muscles of neck very sore all night.

Irwin, *Angels and Amazons*, (see n. 28), p. 387.
54. When the Democrats did not support national woman suffrage, the Woman's Party worked to mobilize women in Western states (twelve of them allowed women to vote) against Wilson and the Democrats. Paul and Burns put up billboards saying "Women of Colorado, You Have the Vote. Get It for Women of the Nation by Voting Against Woodrow Wilson. Their Party Opposes National Woman Suffage." A photograph of a woman pasting up this billboard advertisement can be found in the Women's History Collection, Division of Political History, Smithsonian Institution; it has been reproduced as a postcard by Helaine Victoria Press, Martinsville, Ind. 46151.
55. *NAW*, vol. 1, p. 125.
56. Ibid.
57. Kenneally, "Eve, Mary, and the Historians" (see n. 50), p. 201.
58. *NAW*, vol. 1, p. 125.
59. Gibbons said, "I regard 'woman's rights' as the worst enemies of the female sex," and believed that in those states where women could vote their lives had not improved much. See Allen Sinclair Will, *The Life of Cardinal Gibbons, Archbishop of Baltimore* (New York: E. P. Dutton, 1922), pp. 783–84. See also John Tracy Ellis, *The Life of Cardinal James Gibbons, Archbishop of Baltimore, 1834–1921*, vol.2 (Milwaukee: Bruce, 1952), p. 541. For a summary of the counterarguments, see Helen Haines, "Catholic Womanhood and the Suffrage," in *Catholic World*, vol. 102 (Oct. 1915): pp. 55–67. For a summary of Gibbons's views, see "Cardinal Gibbons on

Woman's Suffrage" in *America*, vol. 16 (16 Dec. 1916), p. 242. For an example of pious argumentation gone wild, see Henry O'Keefe CSP, "Suffragettes and Cloistered Nuns" in *America*, vol. 19 (5 Apr. 1919), pp. 662–63.

60. "Either a husband or an enclosure wall" (quoted in Leon Joseph Suenens, *The Nun in the World* [Westminster, Md.: Newman Press, 1963], p. 46).

61. See, e.g., J. N. Moody, "The Dechristianization of the French Working Class," *The Review of Politics*, vol. 20 (1958), pp. 46–69.

62. Philip Foner, *Women and the American Labor Movement*, 2 vols. (New York: Free Press, 1979–1980). See also James J. Kenneally, *Women and American Trade Unions* (Montreal: Eden Press Women's Publications, 1981).

63. Kenneally, p. 1.

64. Kenneally, p. 2; Foner, vol. 1.

65. Kenneally, p. 3; Foner, vol. 1, pp. 120–21.

66. Kenneally, p. 11; Foner, vol. 1, pp. 185–213.

67. For information about Leonora M. Barry, see Eleanor Flexner, "Leonora Marie Kearney Barry," in *NAW*, vol. 1, pp. 101–2; Foner, vol. 1, pp. 198–207; Kenneally, pp. 13–17; and Barbara Mayer Wertheimer, *We Were There: The Story of Working Women in America* (New York: Pantheon Books, 1977), pp. 184–91. Irwin, *Angels and Amazons* (see n. 28) is correct about her accomplishments, but mistakenly says that she was the mother of Leonora O'Reilly and gives her married name as Leonora Barry O'Reilly instead of Leonora Barry Lake.

68. The average weekly wage for industrial workers around 1880 was about $8.00, based on computations from the U.S. Bureau of the Census, *Historical Statistics of the United States: Colonial Times to 1957* (Washington, D.C.: Government Printing Office, 1960), pp. 90–91. Toward the end of the nineteenth century, women wage earners received about three fifths the wages of men (see Clarence Long, *Wages and Earnings in the United States, 1860–1890* [Princeton, N.J.: Princeton Univ. Press, 1960] p. 104). She should have been earning at least $4.80 per week, but in fact took home $.65. I thank Joan Huber for these calculations.

69. See Foner, *Women and the American Labor Movement*, vol. 1, p. 203; she not only compiled these statistics, she saw the need to change them through trade unionism; when she turned them over to the Labor Department, however, they cited them but refused to recommend any action.

70. Ibid., p. 200.

71. *NAW*, vol 1, p. 102.

72. "Yet, she had brought to public attention a full picture of the abysmal conditions of workingwomen and had collected a body of statistics and descriptions that were to prove useful in future struggles," Foner, *Women and the American Labor Movement*, vol. 1, p. 207.

73. Kenneally, *Women and American Trade Unions*, p. i.

74. Irving Dillard and Mary Sue Dillard Schusky, "Mary Harris Jones," in *NAW*, vol. 2, pp.286–88; Foner, vol. 1, pp. 280–93, vol. 2, pp. 36–39, 276–77; Wertheimer, *We Were There*, pp. 342–51.

75. Nies, *Seven Women* (see n. 46), p. 97. See also Irwin, *Angels and Amazons* (see n. 28), p. 323.

76. Hennesey, *American Catholics*, (see n. 2), p. 215. See also Archie Green, "The Death of Mother Jones," *Labor History*, vol. 1 (Winter 1960), pp. 78–80, for the words to the song sung at her funeral.

77. I am indebted to James Kenneally for this information.

78. Hennesey, *American Catholics*, p. 215.

79. Arthur M. Schlesinger, Jr., introduction to Joanna L. Stratton, *Pioneer Women: Voices from the Kansas Frontier* (New York: Simon & Schuster, 1981), p. 12.
80. See Hennesey, "Bibliography" (see n. 42).
81. See Evangeline Thomas, *Sources* (see n. 36). Besides giving the archival holdings of sisterhoods, this important reference work also lists published sources about the group.
82. For a look at the independent character of American nuns in the nineteenth century and their subsequent curtailment see Mary Ewens, "Removing the Veil: The Liberated American Nun," in *Women of Spirit*, ed. Rosemary Ruether and Eleanor McLaughlin (New York: Simon & Schuster, 1979), pp. 256–78.
83. John Tracy Ellis, "Mother Mary Baptist Russell," *NAW*, vol. 3, pp. 213–14.
84. Katherine Burton, "Mother Marie Joseph Butler," *NAW*, vol. 1, pp. 272–73; Mother M. Williams, "Mother Mary Aloysia Hardey," *NAW*, vol. 2, pp. 130–32; Sr. Joan Bland SND, "Sister Julia McGroarty," *NAW*, vol. 2, pp. 466–68 (see also Angela Elizabeth Keenan, *Three Against the Wind: The Founding of Trinity College, Washington, D.C.* [Westminster, Md: Christian Classics, 1973]); Sr. Josephine Morgan and Sr. Catherine Carroll, "Sr. Georgia Lydia Stevens," *NAW*, vol. 3, pp. 369–70; Karen Kennelly CSJ, "Sister M. Madeleva Wolff," *NAW*, vol 4, pp 741–72.
85. Lois Green Carr, "Margaret Brent," *NAW*, vol. 1, pp. 236–67; see also E. R. Richardson, "Margaret Brent, Gentleman," *Thought*, vol. 7 (1933), pp. 533–47; and J. Herman Schauinger, *Profiles in Action: American Catholicism in Public Life* (Milwaukee: Bruce, 1966), p. 9. Schauinger sketches thirty-three American Catholics, from Christopher Columbus to John F. Kennedy: Margaret Brent is the only woman and she gets 2 pages (out of 247 pages of text). Theodore Maynard, choosing the diminutive form, calls her "the first American suffragette," but that is probably anachronistic (*Story of American Catholicism* [see n. 32], p. 76).

John B. Blake, "Mary Sargent Neal Gove Nichols," *NAW*, vol. 2, pp. 627–29. Ellis, as noted, included Eliza Allen Starr in his *Documents* collection partially because she was a convert. In his article on famous converts in the Trisco bicentennial volume he does not mention Nichols.
86. John P. Clum, "Nellie Cashman," in Mary G. Boyer, *Arizona in Literature* (Glendale, Calif.: Arthur H. Clark, 1934), pp. 365–80, quotation from p. 380.
87. It is not clear what Clum meant by his reference to the Cassiar gold rush; gold was discovered in the Cassiar district in 1871, but I have no reference to a gold *rush* there, and no mention of Cashman; see William R. Hunt, *North of 53°: The Wild Days of the Alaska-Yukon Mining Frontier, 1870–1914* (New York: Macmillan, 1974); and William S. Greever, *The Bonanza West: The Story of the Western Mining Rushes, 1848–1900* (Norman, Okla.: Univ. of Oklahoma Press, 1963). Neither book mentions Cashman, but both give a good idea of what life was like in frontier mining towns, especially in Dawson, where Cashman spent the last days of her life.
88. Avery (1851–1929) converted to Catholicism in 1904 after many years as an activist in the Socialist Labor Party. After her conversion, she became an effective *anti*-socialist and a pioneer supporter of the Roman Catholic social justice ideas of *Rerum Novarum*; she was a staunch supporter of trade unions and collective bargaining. She may be most famous for launching the Catholic Truth Guild, an organization of laypeople trained to preach Catholicism on street corners. As such, she forms part of the story of American Catholicism as it was affected by various American and English lay preaching experiments. See James P. Shenton, "Martha Gallison Moore Avery," *NAW*, vol. 1, pp. 69–71; and Debra Campbell, " 'I Can't Imagine Our Lady on an Outdoor Platform': Women in the Catholic Street

Propaganda Movement" *U.S. Catholic Historian*, vol. 3 (Spring/Summer 1983), pp. 103–14.

89. Mary Ewens, *The Role of the Nun in Nineteenth Century America* (New York: Arno Press, 1978), originally a doctoral dissertation for the University of Minnesota. See also Mary Ewens, "The Leadership of Nuns in Immigrant Catholicism," in *Women and Religion in America*, vol. 1, *The Nineteenth Century*, ed. Rosemary Radford Ruether and Rosemary Skinner Keller (New York: Harper & Row, 1981), pp. 101–49. In this article Ewens recounts some of the magnificent work of nuns in the nineteenth century, mentioning the likes of Blandina Segale, a Cincinnati Sister of Charity "who travelled alone to Colorado in 1878 at the age of twenty-two and spent eighteen years working in Colorado and New Mexico. During this period she put up a school and a hospital without prior resources, ended the lynch law in New Mexico, tamed Billy the Kid, built the tallest building in the territory, and proved herself more than the equal of the forces of greed and violence around her," p. 141. See also Segale's own account, *At the End of the Sante Fe Trail* (Milwaukee: Bruce, 1948).

90. See Sister Mary Laurence Hanley, "Mother Marianne of Molokai," in Trisco, *Catholics in America*, (see n. 5) pp. 171–73; and Leo Vincent Jacks, *Mother Marianne of Molokai* (New York: Macmillan, 1935).

91. Olga Hartley, *Women and the Catholic Church* (London: Burns, Oates & Washbourne, 1935), pp. 222, 223.

92. Irwin, *Angels and Amazons* (see n. 28), p. 147.

93. Sister M. Madeleva CSC, "Mother Angela Gillespie," *NAW*, vol. 2, pp. 34–35.

94. Irwin, *Angels and Amazons*, p. 150.

95. See Ellen Ryan Jolly, *Nuns of the Battlefield* (Providence, R.I.: Providence Visitor Press, 1927), which discusses the work of twenty-one different communities. Jolly lists the names of the sisters from each community who worked as nurses during the Civil War and presents overwhelming evidence of their importance. In order to have a monument erected, the committee had to persuade the War Department of the value of the sisters; this book was written from the evidence gathered for that purpose. See also Irwin, *Angels and Amazons*. Not a volume that is fair to *Catholic* women in American history, *Angels and Amazons* is clear about the important role of nursing nuns during the Civil War: "In the emergency both the Federal and Confederate governments had turned to the only organized nurses we had—the Roman Catholic sisterhoods. They responded promptly," p. 150.

96. Irwin, *Angels and Amazons*, p. 149.

97. Mary Ewens, "Leadership of Nuns," (see n. 89), p. 101.

98. See Katherine Burton, *According to the Pattern: The Story of Dr. Agnes McLaren and the Society of Catholic Medical Missionaries* (New York: Longmans, Green, 1946), which recounts the lives of both McLaren and Dengel.

99. Ibid., p. 179.

100. Ibid., p. 187.

101. Mary Louise Lynch, Medical Mission sister in Washington, D.C., telephone conversation with author, March 1983.

102. Ewens, "Leadership of Nuns," p. 102.

103. Sister Albertus Magnus McGrath, *What a Modern Catholic Believes About Women* (Chicago: Thomas More Press, 1972), p. 90.

104. A source like Diner's *Erin's Daughters* (see n. 47) might lead us to examine the high alcoholism rate among Irish men and the disproportionate number of female-

headed households in Irish-American families and to begin to develop categories to analyze such data.

105. Aaron Abell, *American Catholicism and Social Action: A Search for Social Justice, 1865–1950* (Notre Dame, Ind.: Univ. of Notre Dame Press, 1963), p. 223.

CHAPTER 2: FROM IMMIGRANTS TO EMIGRANTS

Epigraphs: Olga Hartley, *Women and the Catholic Church* (London: Burns & Oates, 1935), p. 242; Sara Maitland, *A Map of the New Country* (London: Routledge & Kegan Paul, 1983), p. 200.

1. Florence R. Rosenberg and Edward M. Sullivan, *Women and Ministry: A Survey of the Experience of Roman Catholic Women in the United States* (Washington, D.C.: Center for Applied Research in the Apostolate, 1980), p. 175.

2. Margaret Ellen Traxler, "Women in the Church Speak Out: Call in the Clowns," *Probe*, vol. 12 (Dec. 1983/Jan. 1984), p. 2. She says, "A million and a half Catholic women no longer attend church." Traxler presented her figures to a cardinal in a large American diocese and received a "flip reply" from his chancellor, to wit: "And so, perhaps two million men, too." In fact, women are leaving the church in numbers far disproportionate to those of men, and the American Catholic bishops recognize that "the alienation of women from the Church is a serious pastoral problem that has many ecclesiological implications" (*Origins* [25 June 1982], p. 90).

3. Many labor unions began as offshoots of so-called secret societies. Because these societies had often been anti-Catholic — the Freemasons, for example — Catholics were forbidden to join them. In 1887, fearing that the Vatican might condemn the fledgling Knights of Labor (they had been condemned in Canada in 1884), progressive bishops — led by Cardinal Gibbons and including John Ireland and John J. Keane — prevented a Roman condemnation of the Knights. They did this against vociferous criticism from conservative bishops. Hennesey, *American Catholics* (see chap. 1, n. 2), p. 188.

4. J. N. Moody, "The Dechristianization of the French Working Class," *The Review of Politics*, vol. 20 (1958), pp. 46–69.

5. In November 1983, the American bishops announced that they were going to write a pastoral letter on issues surrounding women in the church. Part of the initial process was a dialogue between a committee of bishops and some Catholic feminists in which the women asked the bishops to write about patriarchy rather than about women. For more on the history and process of this work, see Ruth McDonough Fitzpatrick and Mary Frohlich, "Update: The Bishops' Pastoral on Women," *New Women, New Church*, vol. 7 (Sept. 1984), pp. 6–7. For information on the closed official hearings (held in Washington in March 1985) see *Origins* vol. 14 (21 March 1985), pp. 651–66. (*Origins* is the official publication of the National Conference of Catholic Bishops.) For a report on the set of open "counter-hearings," see Joan Turner Beifuss and Mary Fay Bourgoin, "Catholic women voice divergent views, concerns at D.C. hearings," *National Catholic Reporter* vol. 21 (15 March 1985), pp. 35–36. The pastoral has stimulated a number of local conferences designed to allow women to voice their concerns about the bishop's project. A conference at Rosemont College (Rosemont, Pa.) 6 October 1985 is one good example of such a meeting.

6. Julia O'Faolain and Laura Martines, eds., *Not in God's Image: Women in History from the Greeks to the Victorians* (New York: Harper Torchbooks, 1973).

7. Barbara Ehrenreich and Deirdre English, *For Her Own Good: 150 Years of the Experts' Advice to Women* (New York: Doubleday Anchor, 1979), pp. 125–31.

8. Rosemary Radford Ruether, ed. *Religion and Sexism: Images of Woman in the Jewish and Christian Traditions* (New York: Simon & Schuster, 1974). See also "The Angel in the House," in *Victorian Women: A Documentary Account of Women's Lives in Nineteenth-Century England, France and the United States*, ed. Erna Olafson Hellerstein, Leslie Parker Hune, and Karen M. Offen (Stanford, Calif.: Stanford Univ. Press, 1981), pp. 134–40.

9. O'Faolain and Martines, *Not in God's Image*, pp. 284–331.

10. Augustine Rössler, "Woman," *The Catholic Encyclopedia* (New York: Robert Appleton, 1912) vol. 15, p. 687. Rössler published a book earlier that won the approval of Pope Benedict XV as having "the Roman Catholic position on women" (see *Acta Apostolica Sedis*, vol. 6 (1915), p. 7). Rössler argued against woman suffrage on the basis that woman's nature was essentially unchangeable and that female nature was designed for and only fit for work in the home or elementary schools; see *Die Frauenfrage vom Standpunkte der Natür der Geschichte und der Offenbärung* (Freiburg: Herder, 1907).

11. Patricia Martin Doyle, "Women and Religion: Psychological and Cultural Implications," in Ruether, *Religion and Sexism,*, pp. 15–40.

12. Talcott Parsons, *The Social System* (New York: Free Press, 1951).

13. Elizabeth Janeway, *Man's World, Woman's Place: A Study in Social Mythology* (New York: Dell, Delta Book ed., 1971).

14. Kate Millett, *Sexual Politics* (New York: Avon Books, 1969). According to Millett, "There is no remedy for sexual politics in marriage" (p. 147) since heterosexuality itself functions to control women. Many early feminists, in an attempt to demythologize sex, challenged the view that "real sex" required a penis or that "true orgasms" were only possible by way of penetration with a penis. See e.g., Anne Koedt, "The Myth of the Vaginal Orgasm" in *Radical Feminism*, ed. Anne Koedt, Ellen Levine, and Anita Rapone (New York: Quadrangle Books, 1973), p. 198–207. In Millett's view, in any case, men use their sexual power to control and dominate women.

15. The ancient embodiment of this split was that found in ancient Greece where the public life of the *polis* was totally separate from the private sphere of the household. See Katherine Tillman, "Women and Public Virtue," *Listening*, vol. 14 (Spring, 1979), pp. 111–21. The eighteenth-century separation, accomplished in the context of a rising bourgeoisie, was quite different: *private* was associated with private property and meant to free an owner from any state control or interference. Furthermore, though the private sphere was not the same as the family, it was in the eighteenth century that *private* attained its intensified meaning of intimate. See Hannah Arendt, *The Human Condition* (Chicago: Univ. of Chicago Press, 1958), chap. 2. See also Mechthild Hart, "Toward a Theory of Collective Learning," (Ph.D. diss., Indiana University, 1984), pp. 57–69.

16. O'Faolain and Martines, *Not in God's Image*, pp. 284–331.

17. Mary P. Burke, *Reaching for Justice: The Women's Movement* (Washington, D.C.: Center of Concern, 1980). I am also indebted to Mary Burke's insights as presented for a seminar, Women and Power, funded by the Lilly Endowment and held in Indianapolis in 1983.

18. Hart, "Toward a Theory," (see n. 15), p. 96. For an analysis of the early stages of the contemporary women's movement by an activist participant, see Leah Fritz,

Dreamers & Dealers: An Intimate Appraisal of the Women's Movement (Boston: Beacon Press, 1979).

19. Linda Gordon as quoted in Hester Eisenstein, *Contemporary Feminist Thought* (Boston: G. K. Hall, 1983), p. xii.

20. Iris Young, as quoted in Eisenstein, *Contemporary Feminist Thought*, p. xiii.

21. Eisenstein, *Contemporary Feminist Thought*, p. xiii. Eisenstein's book, which has been enormously helpful to me as I prepared this section of the chapter, is an excellent summary and analysis of the issues. I am indebted to her for the critique of radical feminism that suggests that it must now turn to universalism, structural change, and social justice, and I marvel at and have followed her placement and chronology of contemporary feminist authors.

22. This problem is a complex and unresolved one, and the two books that probably do most to further the debate are Michelle Zimbalist Rosaldo and Louise Lamphere, eds., *Woman Culture & Society* (Stanford, Calif.: Stanford Univ. Press, 1974), esp. the essay by Sherry Ortner, "Is Female to Male as Nature Is to Culture?" pp. 67-89; and Peggy Reeves Sanday, *Female Power and Male Dominance: On the Origins of Sexual Inequality* (Cambridge: Cambridge Univ. Press, 1983).

23. Adrienne Rich, *Of Woman Born: Motherhood as an Experience and Institution* (New York: W. W. Norton, 1976).

24. Adrienne Rich, "Compulsory Heterosexuality and Lesbian Existence," *Signs* vol. 5 (Summer 1980), pp. 631-60.

25. Phyllis Chesler, *Women and Madness* (New York: Doubleday, 1972). See also Walter R. Gove and Jeannette F. Tudor, "Adult Sex Roles and Mental Illness," in *Changing Woman in a Changing Society*, ed. Joan Huber (Chicago: Univ. of Chicago Press, 1973), pp. 50-74.

26. Susan Brownmiller, *Against Our Will: Men, Women and Rape* (New York: Simon & Schuster, 1975).

27. "That the scientific world view had its dangers was not a new idea. But what a feminist perspective contributed was the realization that this stance was linked to male psychology and male dominance," says Hester Eisenstein, *Contemporary Feminist Thought*, p. 101.

28. Mary Daly, *Gyn/Ecology* (Boston: Beacon Press, 1978).

29. Walter M. Abbott, ed., *Documents of Vatican II* (New York: Guild Press, 1966), pp. 710-19, contains Pope John's opening address to the council, delivered October 11, 1962. Betty Friedan published her book *The Feminine Mystique* in 1963 (New York: Dell).

30. The history of Roman Catholic theology from the nineteenth century onward moved toward the council in the sense that the momentous changes effected there were the fruition of decades of work, thought, and experimentation. The liturgical movement is a good example: the conciliar changes seemed to come quickly, but the work of liturgical reform had been going on in Europe throughout the nineteenth century (beginning with Prosper Gueranger [1805-1875], a Benedictine monk, and given impetus by Pope Pius X [1835-1914]). In America, liturgical experimentation (at St. John's Abbey, Collegeville, Minnesota) occurred throughout the twentieth century. For more information on the "preparation" for the contemporary revival of the women's movement, see Judith Hole and Ellen Levine, eds., *Rebirth of Feminism* (New York: Quadrangle Books, 1971). For a look at the "women's movement" before its 1960s flare-up, see Dale Spender, *There's Always Been a Women's Movement This Century* (London: Routledge & Kegan Paul, Pandora Press, 1983).

31. NOW "can be traced to a series of interrelated and overlapping events that occurred between 1965 and 1966." See Hole and Levine, *Rebirth of Feminism*, pp. 81-95, who give a summary of its origins and goals.

32. Documents from the National Council of Catholic Bishops consistently address problems associated with poverty, old age, war, exploitation of the weak, and related issues. See, e.g., *Concerns of Poor Women* (Washington, D.C.: USCC, 1979), which is a study/action guide on the questions prepared to bring the problems to the attention of American Catholics. *Origins* contains a record of American Catholic episcopal concern with social justice.

33. Eisenstein, *Contemporary Feminist Thought*, p. 143.

34. Jean Baker Miller, *Toward a New Psychology of Women* (Boston: Beacon Press, 1976), p. 128.

35. Betty Friedan, *The Second Stage* (New York: Summit Books, 1981).

36. Karl Rahner, "Towards a Fundamental Theological Interpretation of Vatican II," *Theological Studies*, vol. 40 (1979), pp. 716-27. See also Karl Rahner, "Dream of the Church" *The Tablet* (17 June 1981), pp. 52-55.

37. Hester Eisenstein, *Contemporary Feminist Thought*, p. 144.

38. Daly, *The Church and the Second Sex* (see chap. 1, n. 27), was the first book to make "the case against the church" from a feminist perspective and with such meticulous research. Daly was inspired by and followed some of the leads of Simone de Beauvoir, *The Second Sex* (see chap. 1, n. 12.).

39. Fritz, *Dreamers & Dealers* (see n. 18), pp. 22-82. See also Sara Evans, *Personal Politics* (New York: Vintage Books, 1980).

40. Frederick B. Tolles, "Mott, Lucretia Coffin," in *NAW*, vol. 2, pp. 593.

41. Fritz, *Dreamers & Dealers*, p. 25.

42. William B. Faherty, *The Destiny of Modern Woman in the Light of Papal Teaching* (Westminster, Md.: Newman Press, 1950).

43. Anne Carr, in *Research Report: Women in Church and Society* ed. Sara Butler (New York, Catholic Theological Society of America, 1978), p. 37.

44. Michael Novak, "Man and Woman He Made Them," in *Communio*, vol. 8 (1981): pp 229-49, quotation from p. 244.

45. Faherty, *Destiny*, commenting on Pius XI's teaching about women, says: "Not only was this subjection to her husband's authority not derogatory of her human rights, it actually had to be maintained, Pope Pius XI insisted, if she were to preserve her dignity. Should woman become completely emancipated from the home as the radical feminists demanded, the respect traditionally accorded her in the Western world, centered as it was around her great prerogative of motherhood, would disappear. If she allowed herself to be enticed away from the family, the home would collapse, and she be merely a competitor of man in a rugged, materialistic world" (p. 108).

46. Modern papal teaching usually begins by stressing that men and women share equally in redemption, that their common human nature gives them a common eternal destiny, but supporters of complementarity do not believe that men and women have an equality of gifts or roles.

47. Ortner, "Is Female to Male?" (see n. 22), p. 69.

48. Laity Commission, *Why Can't a Woman Be More Like a Man?* (London: Catholic Information Services, n.d.), p. 6.

49. Sally Cunneen, *Sex: Female, Religion: Catholic* (New York: Holt, Rinehart & Winston, 1968), p. 29.

50. Pius XII, *Guiding Christ's Little Ones* (Washington D.C.: National Catholic Wel-

fare Conference pamphlet, n.d.), addressed mothers and teachers in 1941 to instruct them about educating children. To nuns, the pope said, "Yes, you too are mothers; you work side by side with Christian mothers in the work of education; for you have a mother's heart, burning with charity. . . . You are truly a sisterhood of spiritual mothers whose offspring is the pure flower of youth" (p. 15).

51. Suenens, *Nun in the World* (see chap. 1, n. 60) p. 13.
52. Daly's *The Church and the Second Sex* (see chap. 1, n. 27) was a groundbreaking book in this area. Rosemary Radford Ruether's *Religion and Sexism* (see n. 9), though not devoted exclusively to Roman Catholicism, nevertheless provided a critical collection of misogynist texts from Scripture and tradition.
53. A composite picture of women gathered from some of the "Fathers," esp. Augustine, Jerome, and Ambrose. It is Ambrose (339–397) who describes women as seductive in youth and garrulous in old age. See *Expositionis in Evangelium secundum Lucam libri X* in *Patrologia Latina*, ed. J. P. Minge, (Paris: Garnier Fratres, 1887), vol. 15, col. 1938.
54. I am indebted for this summary to Phyllis Bird, "Images of Women in the Old Testament," in Ruether, *Religion and Sexism*, pp. 41–88.
55. The liberationist theme has been the quintessence of Rosemary Radford Ruether's interpretation; the equalitarian structures of the early Jesus movement have been the focus of Elisabeth Schüssler Fiorenza's exegetical work.
56. Bernard Prusak, "Woman: Seductive Siren and Source of Sin?" in Ruether's *Religion and Sexism*, pp. 89–116, quotation from p. 107.
57. *Circles of Community*, British Council of Churches Study Guide, 1982, as cited in *Why Can't a Woman Be More Like a Man?*, p. 17.
58. John L. McKenzie, *Source: What the Bible Says About the Problems of Contemporary Life*, Basics of Christian Thought Series, vol. 1 (Chicago: Thomas More Press, 1984), p. 199.
59. Daly, *The Church and the Second Sex* (see chap. 1, n. 27), p. 41.
60. McKenzie, *Source*, p. 202, says that the Congregation of the Faith is *not* interested in preserving a cultural structure of male domination, but feminist interpreters would disagree with his assessment.
61. Schüssler Fiorenza, "'You Are Not to Be Called Father': Early Christian History in a Feminist Perspective," *Cross Currents*, vol. 29 (Fall 1979), pp. 301–23.
62. Rosemary Ruether, "Entering the Sanctuary: The Catholic Story," in Ruether and McLaughlin, *Women of Spirit* (see chap. 1, n. 82), pp. 373–83, quotation from p. 382.
63. Rosemary Radford Ruether, "Misogynism and Virginal Feminism in the Fathers of the Church" in Ruether, *Religion and Sexism*, pp. 150–83.
64. Eleanor McLaughlin, "Equality of Souls, Inequality of Sexes: Woman in Medieval Theology" in Ruether, *Religion and Sexism*, pp. 213–66, quotation from p. 244.
65. Daly, *The Church and the Second Sex*, p. 50.
66. I am indebted to Carla Maria Henning, "Canon Law and the Battle of the Sexes," in Ruether, *Religion and Sexism*, pp. 267–91, for the substance of my summary of canon law. The quotation from Brodersen appears on p. 273.
67. McKenzie, *Source*, p. 204.
68. Henning, "Canon Law," p. 286.
69. See notes 42, 45 and 50.
70. Casey Miller and Kate Swift, *Words and Women: New Language in New Times* (New York: Doubleday Anchor, 1977), p. 19.
71. Ruether, "Sexism and God-Talk" in *Women and Men: The Consequences of Power,*

ed. Dana Hiller and Robin Sheets (Cincinnati: Office of Women's Studies of the Univ. of Cincinnati, 1977), p. 409.

72. Krister Stendahl, "Enrichment or Threat? When the Eves Come Marching In," in *Sexist Religion and Women in the Church: No More Silence*, ed. Alice L. Hageman (New York: Association Press, 1974), pp. 117–23, quotation from p. 120.

73. "Cleaning up Sexist Language" (Chicago: 8th Day Center for Justice pamphlet, 1980), p. 35.

74. Margaret Farley, "Moral Imperatives for the Ordination of Women," in *Women and Catholic Priesthood: An Expanded Vision*, ed. Ann Marie Gardiner (New York: Paulist Press, 1976), pp. 35–51, quotation from p. 44.

75. The antagonisms unleashed in the Chicago archdiocese in 1983 give supporting evidence for the point: such demonstrations against the archbishop over a church matter would have been unheard of twenty years ago. See also *Why Can't a Woman Be More Like a Man?* (n. 48): "However if the Church does increasingly speak of the dignity of women being equal to that of men (as it does) then it does not explain how this is consistent with its own practices of discrimination against women both in relatively small and in important matters (girl servers at Mass to women priests). In the absence of any convincing justification of this inconsistency, cynicism is bound to be the result, whether one agrees with the theological rhetoric or not. Indeed, whatever our individual stance on the question of women priests, we should all be concerned about the Church appearing to want to have things both ways" (p. 26).

76. *Task Force Report on the Role of Women in the Church of Southeast Wisconsin* (Milwaukee: *Catholic Herald*, supplement, 9 December 1982). Archbishop Weakland wrote the preface to the report, saying that listening was the goal of the task force and that the "process, the journey [begun by the task force] must be one of reconciliation."

77. *Why Can't a Woman Be More Like a Man?* See also the pastoral letter of the British bishops, *The Easter People* (1980), in which the bishops say, "Traditional and unquestioned attitudes towards women and your role may have to be changed. We ourselves and our clergy may well have to be persuaded gently of our insensitivity and our assumptions of male dominance" (para. 178).

78. *Task Force Report*, p. 11A.

79. Ibid., p. 9A. See also, *Why Can't Woman Be More Like a Man?* "Observations about the clergy formed an important part of the participants' perceived relationship with the Church, mainly because the Church was seen as being represented, if not personified, by the clergy. A strong feeling of rejection was experienced by many. Women were treated as servants, fit to make the tea and clean churches but not fit to participate in the ministry or decision-making process even at parish level. The Church was defined as 'the best men's club in the world.'" (p. 10).

80. *Task Force Report*, p. 10A.

81. Mary O'Connell, "Pastors: Parishes Still Follow the Leader," *U. S. Catholic*, vol. 47 (April 1982), pp. 17–24. See also, Robert J. McClory, et al., "Forum: Ministry Special," *National Catholic Reporter* vol. 18 (22 October 1982), pp. 7–24.

82. I am indebted to Mary Cove, formerly director of the Christian Leadership Center, Marian College, Indianapolis, for these statistics and for sharing with me so generously her ideas about parish life. She was also one of the resource people for a seminar funded by the Lilly Endowment, Roman Catholic Women in the Parish, held in Indianapolis in 1982.

83. Rosenberg and Sullivan, *Women and Ministry* (see n. 1).
84. Doris Gottemoeller and Rita Hofbauer, ed., *Women and Ministry: Present Experience and Future Hopes*, Proceedings of the Symposium based on *Women and Ministry* (Washington, D.C.: Leadership Council of Women Religious, 1981).
85. Joseph Fichter, *Priest and People* (New York: Sheed & Ward, 1965), says, "Responsibility and decision-making rest directly in the hands of the priest, while the laity remain in an ancillary position. This implies that the 'new emergence' of the laity will alter both the image of the priest and the organizational structure of the parish" (p. 200).
86. In private conversation and as part of a talk delivered at the Cultural Perspectives of American Catholicism Conference held at Loyola University, Chicago, September 15, 1984.
87. "A supposed dichotomy between individual and society is one of the premises perpetuated by mechanisms of oppression. It entails a hierarchy of values which at one and the same time sustains and hides from public recognition the isolation of individual people from one another and the fragmentation of their experiences. What is generally accepted as trivial and as truly relevant, what is called 'merely subjective' and 'objective,' and finally, what is understood by the terms 'rational' and 'irrational'— all these distinctions belong to the hierarchy of power" (Hart, "Toward a Theory" [see n. 15], p. 31. See also *Why Can't a Woman Be More Like a Man?* (p. 9): "It was clear that whilst the participants did not align themselves to the extreme camp of the women's liberation movement, they were acutely aware of the developing professional roles of women in modern, industrial society. They expected their Church to be able to accommodate these changes."
88. The phrase is Elisabeth Schüssler Fiorenza's, worked out first at the Women Moving Church Conference (1982). See "The Intersection of Feminism and the Church," in *Women Moving Church*, ed. Diann Neu and Maria Riley (Washington, D.C.: Center of Concern, 1982), p. 25. In a more developed form it can be found in *In Memory of Her: A Feminist Theological Reconstruction of Christian Origins* (New York: Crossroad, 1983), pp. 343–51.
89. Neu and Riley, *Women Moving Church*, p. 3. See also *Why Can't a Woman Be More Like a Man?* (p. 5): "Women . . . have found themselves in the role of second, or even third class citizens in a rigidly hierarchical institution." Also, p. 6: "Many women [move] out of the Church altogether because the Church does not seem to be 'where the action is.'"
90. Sidney Callahan, *The Illusion of Eve* (New York: Sheed & Ward, 1965), p. 214.
91. Mary Bader Papa, *Christian Feminism: Completing the Subtotal Woman* (Chicago: Fides/Claretian, 1981), p. 186.
92. Cunneen, *Sex: Female, Religion: Catholic* (see n. 49), p. 158.
93. Kaye Ashe, *Today's Woman, Tomorrow's Church* (Chicago: Thomas More Press, 1983), p. 183.
94. Joan Ohanneson, *Woman: Survivor in the Church* (Minneapolis: Winston Press, 1980), pp. 2, 187.
95. Mary Daly, *Beyond God the Father* (Boston: Beacon Press, 1973). In some ways Daly's whole method is defined by her insistence on naming her own experience, defining and inventing her own words, and otherwise making it clear that women will not and cannot be defined and categorized by men.
96. Ohanneson, *Woman*, p. 137.
97. Papa, *Christian Feminism*, p. 62.
98. This is certainly not a new question. See Marie Maugeret, "Christian Feminism

in France," *The Crucible*, vol. 1 (June 1905), pp. 32–36: "It was not more admitted by Catholics that one could be Catholic and '*feministe*' than it was admitted among *feministes* that one could be *feministe* and Catholic. For the one as for the other, the terms '*feministe*' and Catholic were irreconcilable: it was necessary to choose between the two" (p. 34.)

CHAPTER 3: INSIDE OUTSIDERS

Epigraphs: "Decree on the Appropriate Renewal of Religious Life" para. 2, in *The Documents of Vatican II*, ed. Walter M. Abbot (New York: America Press, 1966), p. 468; Maryellen Muckenhirn, quoted in Marcelle Bernstein, *The Nuns* (Philadelphia: J. B. Lippincott, 1976), p. 271; Anita Caspary, quoted in ibid., p. 154.

1. At the end of Goethe's *Faust*, we meet woman as archetype:
   Das Ewig-Weibliche   The eternal feminine
   Zieht uns hinan.   Beckons us upward.
   An archetype, like a Platonic idea, is above criticism, endowed with absolute truth. "Thus, as against the dispersed, contingent, and multiple existences of actual women, mythical thought opposes the Eternal Feminine, unique and changeless. If the definition provided for this concept is contradicted by the behavior of flesh-and-blood women, it is the latter who are wrong: we are told not that Femininity is a false entity, but that the women concerned are not feminine" (de Beauvoir, *Second Sex* [see chap. 1, n. 12], p. 286).
2. Janice Raymond, "Nuns and Women's Liberation," *Andover-Newton Quarterly*, vol. 12 (Mar. 1972), pp. 201–12, quotation from p. 202.
3. Rosemary Radford Ruether, "Ruether Reflects on History: Nun–Lay-woman," *Probe*, vol. 12 (July/Aug. 1984), p. 2.
4. Ibid. See also Joan Morris, *The Lady Was a Bishop* (New York: Macmillan, 1973).
5. The approval of constitutions has opened several disturbing controversies and has led some sisters to consider the consequences of official disapproval. See Joan Turner Beifuss, "Nuns Debate 'Noncanonical' Status," *National Catholic Reporter*, vol. 20 (2 Mar. 1984), pp. 12, 18. See also related articles in the same issue: Anita Caspary, "Are Sisters Being Asked to Fit Preconciliar Mold After 20 Years' Renewal?" and Richard J. Hill, "Is 'Opting Out' a No-win Situation?" As serious as the debate over the product—the actual approval or disapproval of constitutions written by the sisters themselves—is the Vatican abrogation of process. The Carmelites, who have been working for more than twenty years on their constitutions, have recently seen their entire process destroyed by Vatican decree. "Pope orders Vatican to write constitution for Carmelites," said the National Catholic Religious News Service headline (30 Jan. 1985). The story explained that even though 80 percent of the world's Carmelite nuns have approved of their present process, it was to be discontinued in favor of an officially mandated, pre–Vatican II model. Besides being a grave injustice, an action that ignored twenty years of good faith and experience, the Vatican move was menacing: sisters were told in advance that they would have to accept the new constitutions or "find other forms of consecrated life."
6. After arguing that the careers open to those in convents were "greater than any other[s] ever thrown open to women in the course of modern European history," Lina Eckenstein went on to say that when convents were closed down in the sixteenth century, "women lost the last chance that remained to them of activity

outside the home circle. The subjection of women to a round of domestic duties became more complete when nunneries were dissolved, and marriage for generations afterwards was women's only recognized vocation." *Women under Monasticism* (Cambridge: Cambridge Univ. Press, 1896), p. 478.

7. Sara Maitland, *A Map of the New Country: Women and Christianity* (London: Routledge & Kegan Paul, 1983), p. 50.

8. M. Angelica Seng, OSF, "The Sister in the New City," in *The Changing Sister* ed. Sister M. Charles Borromeo Muckenhirn (Notre Dame, Ind.: Fides Press, 1965), pp. 229–62, quotation from p. 253.

9. Virginia Woolf, *Three Guineas* (New York: Harcourt Brace Jovanovich, 1966; orig., 1938), pp. 78–82, p. 106.

10. Carolyn Heilbrun *Reinventing Womanhood* (New York: W. W. Norton, 1979), p. 68. Heilbrun's work is exceptionally clear and persuasive, arguing that womanhood must be reinvented so that women will no longer be inhibited from a full formation of a self. Paulo Freire, *Pedagogy of the Oppressed* (New York: Continuum, 1982) makes many of the same points about the inability of oppressed peoples to admit their oppression: their identification with the oppressors leads them to what Freire calls a "culture of silence."

11. Dorothy Sölle, *Suffering*, (Philadelphia: Fortress Press, 1973), p. 73.

12. Heilbrun, *Reinventing Womanhood*, p. 66.

13. Ibid., p. 39.

14. Woolf, *Three Guineas*, pp. 106–18.

15. Schüssler Fiorenza, *In Memory of Her* (see chap. 2, n. 88). Her argument was worked out in a shorter version in "'You Are Not to Be Called Father'" (see chap. 2, n. 61), pp. 301–19.

16. Mark 9:29 has Jesus explain to his disciples that some devils can be driven out only by prayer and fasting. Some early hermits took this text as a mandate to lead penitential lives of prayer and fasting in order to confront and defeat some of the demons that trouble the world. This text, in addition to Mark 8:34 (commanding disciples to take up the cross to follow Jesus) and Matthew 5:48 (which commands disciples to "be perfect") form part of the scriptural basis for monastic life.

17. *The Shepherd of Hermas*, similitudes 5.3.3, in *The Apostolic Fathers*, vol. 2, trans. Kirsopp Lake, (London: William Heinemann, 1934), p. 159.

18. Rosemary Radford Ruether, pointing to the debilitating effects of splitting reality into two parts, argues that the transcendent or authoritative spheres are always male: the various dualisms of ancient philosophical systems — soul/body, spirit/matter, head/body, masculine/feminine, *logos/eros* — grant "male" concepts or words superior status, suggesting "that women can represent only the subjected side of the dualism" ("Sexism and God Talk" [see chap. 2, n. 71], pp. 409–25, quotation from p. 416).

19. In various ways this compliment has been handed to strong women: both Teresa of Avila and Catherine of Siena were backhanded with it. Jerome, the translator of the Bible who spent much time advising women, says this: "As long as woman is for birth and children, she is different from man as body is from soul. But when she wishes to serve Christ more than the world, then she will cease to be a woman and will be called a man." *Commentarius in Epistolam ad Ephesios*, p. xvi, *Patrologia Latina*, ed. J. P. Minge (Paris: Garnier Fratres, 1887), vol. 26, col. 567.

20. Marcelle Bernstein, *The Nuns* (Philadelphia: J. B. Lippincott, 1976), p. 235.

21. Sister Bertrande Meyers, *Sisters for the 21st Century* (New York: Sheed & Ward, 1965), p. 27.

22. Ibid., p. 28.
23. Sister Bertrande Meyers, *The Education of Sisters* (New York: Sheed & Ward, 1941).
24. Meyers, *Sisters for the 21st Century,* p. 33.
25. Ibid., p. 36.
26. Madeleva Wolff, "The Education of Our Young Religious Teachers," *National Catholic Educational Association Proceedings and Addresses,* 1949.
27. Meyers, *Sisters for the 21st Century,* p. 45.
28. *Letter of His Holiness John Paul II to the Bishops of the United States,* 3 Apr. 1983, and *Essential Elements in the Church's Teaching on Religious Life as Applied to Institutes Dedicated to Works of the Apostolate,* 31 May 1983, by the Sacred Congregation for Religious and for Secular Institute (Chicago: Institute on Religious Life, 1983). In 1983 the pope appointed the archbishop of San Francisco, John R. Quinn, to direct the efforts of the American bishops to be in dialogue with and render pastoral service to American sisters. The commission was also to study the decline in vocations. Knowledgeable sources, however, insist that the commission's real purpose is to investigate religious orders in the United States, with special attention to women. Furthermore, by 1986, most American orders of sisters will have submitted their new constitutions to Rome for approval: those that do not conform to new (stricter) guidelines will be rejected. "The Vatican's Congregation for the Religious and the American sisters are at total odds," Archbishop Rembert Weakland was quoted as saying in *Newsweek* (19 Mar. 1984), p. 98. Because so many American sisters have been college presidents, high-level hospital administrators and generally successful women, the directives from the Vatican, treating them as children, are even more humiliating.
29. Marie Augusta Neal, "The Relation between Religious Belief and Structural Change in Religious Orders: Developing an Effective Measuring Instrument," *Review of Religious Research,* vol. 12 (Fall 1970), pp. 2–16, and "The Relation between Religious Belief and Structural Change in Religious Orders: Some Evidence," *Review of Religious Research,* vol. 12 (Spring 1971), pp. 153–64.
30. Marie Augusta Neal, "A Theoretical Analysis of Renewal in Religious Orders in the U.S.A.," *Social Compass,* vol. 18 (1971), pp. 7–25, quotations from pp. 11, 12.
31. LCWR includes members from 90 percent of active women's religious orders in the United States. Those not represented by LCWR are not easy to place. Some of them belong to the Consortium Perfectae Caritatis, a conservative union of religious women. In September 1970, the report of CMSW about the future disturbed approximately fifty conservative women superiors, who then met secretly with Thomas Dubay (the conservative priest leader of the "traditionalist movement"), seven bishops, and the apostolic delegate. After this meeting, they withdrew from CMSW and formed their own organization. Other sisters not in LCWR can be found in the Institute for Religious Life, an organization of laypersons, bishops, and religious superiors, highly conservative in orientation and background and funded by conservative laypeople.
32. In 1967 the Sacred Congregation for Religious (SCR) became SCRIS, Sacra Congregatio pro Religiosis et Institutis Saecularibus. See *Annuario Pontificio,* 1983, p. 1533. In Spring 1985 they dropped "Sacra" to become, simply CRIS. All Roman congregations dropped the word sacred from their titles.
33. Sisters Uniting attempts to provide a forum for nine sister groups across the nation: Association of Contemplative Sisters, Las Hermanas (Hispanic sisters), National Coalition of American Nuns, National Sisters Vocation Conference, Religious Formation Conference (successor of SFC), Sisters for Christian Community (a noncanonical con-

gregation), National Assembly of Religious Women, National Black Sisters Conference, and the now-defunct National Sisters Communication Conference.

34. Quoted from masthead of their newsletter, *Center Focus.*

35. The full text of Kane's remarks were quoted in Teresa Carpenter, "Courage and Pain: Women Who Love God and Defy Their Churches," *Redbook,* vol. 155 (Apr. 1980), pp. 19, 149–56, quotation from p. 151. Many of those who found Kane's remarks "radical" or otherwise impolite have likely not read the text, which is exceedingly polite, couched in traditional religious language, and gentle.

36. Published by Mother Sixtina of the Sisters of St. Francis of the Martyr, St. George, Alton, Illinois, the apology appeared in the *Washington Post*, (Friday, 12 October 1979).

37. Andrew Greeley, quoted in *Newsweek* (19 Mar. 1984), p. 97. It is hard to obtain accurate figures in a period of flux. "The membership in religious communities is already diminishing more speedily than statisticians seem able to track . . . the Catholic and secular press consistently use the rounded figure of 121,000 remaining sisters . . . yet, even as we write this, December 16, 1983, NCR arrived with still another indication that sisters may be an endangered species. The number is now 96,000, a decrease of 47 percent in 15 years" (Lillanna Audrey Kopp, "Memos from His Holiness, Big Brother," *National Catholic Reporter,* vol. 20 [13 Jan. 1984], pp. 9, 16–17, quotation from p. 17). These figures, which appeared in the *National Catholic Reporter* and were quoted from that source by Kopp, are probably not accurate. LCWR sent a correction to NCR after the article appeared. In the latest survey data, Marie Augusta Neal insists that sisters today number 130,000. See her *Catholic Sisters in Transition: From the 1960s to the 1980s* (Wilmington, Del.: Michael Glazier, 1984).

38. Though SFC was not feminist in its origins or intentions, many of the feminist sisters in the contemporary church began there and developed alliances, and later became presidents or executive directors of LCWR: e.g., Mary Daniel Turner, Elizabeth Carroll, Margaret Brennan.

39. The 1960s witnessed an unprecedented number of sisters leaving "religious life" for "life in the world." At the same time, the energy of the council inspired a number of books about sisters that, whether or not they had much impact on the laity, were surely read in convents and were probably responsible for developing a new consciousness among sisters. Among the most important of the period are Meyers, *Sisters for the 21st Century* (see n. 21); Muckenhirn, *Changing Sister* (see n. 8); Suenens, *Nun in the World* (see chap. 1, n. 60); and Sister M. Charles Borromeo, ed., *The New Nuns* (New York: New American Library, 1967).

40. "While the Church is bound to give witness to justice, she recognizes that anyone who ventures to speak to people about justice must first be just in their eyes. Hence we must undertake an examination of the modes of acting and of the possessions and life style found within the Church herself." This quotation and others about women having "their own share of responsibility" in the church and all members having "some share in the drawing up of decisions" can be found in "Justice in the World," the document from the Synod of Bishops, Second General Assembly, 30 Nov. 1971. The document can be found in *The Gospel of Peace and Justice: Catholic Social Teaching Since Pope John,* ed. Joseph Gremillion (Maryknoll, N.Y.: Orbis Books, 1976), pp. 513–29.

41. American Sisters have been featured in *Ms.* (Sept. 1983), in a four-part series in the *Washington Post* (Dec. 1983), in *The Boston Phoenix* (Oct. 1982), and in the *Chicago Sun-Times* (Feb. 1983). Each article features sisters in "nontraditional jobs" and

attempts to explain why sisters are undertaking these roles in contemporary society. The four women killed in El Salvador in 1980 held national attention for several weeks and inspired documentary specials on PBS, congressional inquiries, and demonstrations.

42. An issue of *The Way,* vol. 15 (Jan. 1975), was devoted entirely to leadership and changing perceptions of ecclesiastical authority. See also John L. McKenzie, *Authority in the Church* (New York: Sheed & Ward, 1966).

43. Former superior of the Sisters of Loretto, Mary Luke Tobin was president of LCWR from 1963–67. Her memoirs have been published as *Hope Is an Open Door* (Nashville: Abingdon Press, 1981). Margaret Brennan, an Immaculate Heart of Mary Sister (Monroe, Michigan), is a professor of theology at St. Michael's College, Toronto. She was president of LCWR from 1972–3. Joan Chittester, president of LCWR 1976–77, is prioress of the Erie, Pennsylvania, Benedictines and an author of books on sister renewal and feminism, e.g., *Climb Along the Cutting Edge: An Analysis of Change in Religious Life* (New York: Paulist Press, 1977), and *Women, Ministry and the Church* (New York: Paulist Press, 1983). Mary Daniel Turner, executive director of LCWR 1972–78, is a Sister of Notre Dame de Namur.

44. "Reverend Alfred Mendez, CSC, of Notre Dame, coordinator of this 'largest congress of religious ever held,' is quoted in the August 22, 1952, *Record,* diocesan newspaper of Louisville, Kentucky, as explaining the purpose of this congress thus: 'Because of the greater vitality of religious life in the U. S., Rome is looking here for answers concerning religious life and the adaptation that must be made in the modern world.'" (Helen Sanders, *More Than a Renewal: Loretto Before and After Vatican II: 1952–1977* [Nerinx, Ky.: Sisters of Loretto, 1982], p. 16). In the early years of renewal, sisters were told in many different ways that they were the strength and hope of the church. Official promotion of education might be understood analogously by remembering that the British insisted on educating Indians so that the empire could have more law clerks; they apparently did not anticipate that education would lead to a movement for independence.

45. Sister M. Aloysius Schaldenbrand, "Asylums: Total Societies and Religious Life," in Borromeo, *New Nuns,* pp. 115–27, quotation from p. 115. I am relying here on Schaldenbrand's summary of Goffman's work and have, in general, paraphrased her article in describing its relevance to religious life.

46. Marie Augusta Neal, "Sociology and Community Change," in Muckenhirn, *Changing Sister* (see n. 8), pp. 9–44. See also her "Religious Communities in a Changing World," in Borromeo, *New Nuns,* pp. 142–52. Neal, a member of the Sisters of Notre Dame de Namur, has been a pioneer of social justice activity for sisters since the 1950s, which may account for her own community's knowledgeable involvement in various justice projects. Neal edited the research report of her community's "pedagogy project," a reflection and an analysis of the community's work around the world. See *The Gospel Agenda in Global Perspective* (n.p., 1981).

47. Helen Rose Fuchs Ebaugh, *Out of the Cloister: A Study of Organizational Dilemmas* (Austin, Tex.: Univ. of Texas Press, 1977), p. 125.

48. *National Catholic Reporter,* vol. 3 (Sept. 1965).

49. Bernstein, *Nuns* (see n. 20), p. 149.

50. Ibid., pp. 150, 151.

51. Ibid., p. 152. The curious status of nuns as "laywomen" is clear in this quotation. On the one hand, the Second Vatican Council and Roman authorities insist that nuns *are* laywomen; i.e., they have no privileged status within the church. Yet,

whenever the authorities want to punish or intimidate sisters they threaten to *reduce* them to the status of laywomen.

52. Lillanna Kopp, *Sudden Spring: 6th Stage Sisters* (Waldport, Oreg.: Sunspot Publications, 1983). This is a sociological analysis of trends of change in Catholic sisterhoods and gives the background for and experience of SFCC.

53. Kopp was very active during renewal, giving lectures and writing articles, mostly about systems. See her "Bureaucratic Dysfunction in American Convents," in Borromeo, *New Nuns* (see n. 39), pp. 184–200. Kopp, perhaps to rankle as well as to inform, often cites unlikely allies to make her points. The quotation about hierarchy, expressing her own opinion exactly, is attributed to Robert Townsend, executive of American Express International and chief executive of Avis Corporation. In Kopp, *Sudden Spring,* p. 51.

54. Telephone interview with Kopp (29 Oct. 1984). I asked her if there was any chance of the group admitting married people or nonvowed women into the community in the future, and she said that this year's assembly had *begun* to talk about making the vows optional, a conversation that, she said, might well lead to admission of married couples and others.

55. Attributed to Cassian Yuhaus, director of CARA, and cited in Kopp, *Sudden Spring,* p. 3. Emerging Communities (180–200 new groups, mostly small and noncanonical) were those described as exploring, risking, creating, etc; Diminishing Congregations (4–10 traditional groups in each major city) were those said to be resisting change, languishing, amalgamating, and dying; and Renewing Congregations (many of the traditional groups) were those described as adapting, reorganizing, integrating, diversifying.

56. For more detailed information on the BVMs, see their *Constitutions* (Dubuque, Iowa: Sisters of Charity of the Blessed Virgin Mary, 1982). An indication of how quickly they were able to mobilize can be found in *Proceedings of the Institute on Problems That Unite Us* (1966); the institute, held at Mundelein College, Chicago, July 31–Aug. 20, 1965, included an impressive array of speakers and resolutions. A contemporary look at the BVMs can be found in *Women of Promise* (Dubuque, Iowa: Sisters of Charity BVM, 1980).

57. The two best published sources for the Sisters of Loretto are Sanders, *More than a Renewal* (see n. 44); and Tobin *Hope is an Open Door* (see n. 43).

58. Tobin, *Hope is an Open Door* p. 67. For a discussion of the reasons for the lawsuit, see pp. 42–44.

59. A contemporary picture of Maryknoll sisters can be found in *Women in Mission: Maryknoll Sisters Today* (Maryknoll, N.Y.: Maryknoll Sisters of St. Dominic, 1977). The deaths of the four American women in El Salvador was the subject of at least two television documentaries, "Choices of the Heart" and "Roses in December." An excellent article is Stephen T. DeMott, "'Our own blood spilled in El Salvador': The Families of Four Slain Churchwomen Carry on Their Fight for Justice," *Maryknoll Magazine,* vol. 77 (Dec. 1983); pp. 36–57. For an account of the lives of these Maryknoll sisters in their own words see Judith M. Noone, *The Same Fate as the Poor* (Maryknoll, New York: Maryknoll Sisters, 1984).

60. A packet of seven papers by noted theologicans, including moral theologians like Charles Curran and Richard McCormick, can be obtained from the Washington Theological Union, Silver Spring, Maryland. Madonna Kolbenschlag, "The Case of Sister Mansour," *Commonweal,* vol. 110 (17 June 1983), pp. 359–64, is an excellent summary of the issues. The editorial by Thomas E. Clarke in *America,* vol. 149 (1 Jan. 1983), p. 20, saw the proceedings as "degrading."

61. Agnes Mary Mansour, as quoted in *Commonweal* (see n. 60), p. 363.
62. Richard McCormick, "Notes on Moral Theology: 1983," *Theological Studies,* vol. 45 (Mar. 1984), pp. 119–22. See also Mary Kay Blakely, "The Nun's Revolt: Sister Agnes Mary Mansour: Her Vow to the People," *Ms.* (Sept. 1983), pp. 55 f., 102f. For an excellent explanation of how a Catholic in public office might personally oppose abortion but allow non-Catholic constituents to be prochoice, see Joseph F. Donceel, "Catholic Politicians and Abortion," *America,* vol. 151 (2 Feb. 1985), pp. 81–83.
63. Kenneth Woodward, et al., "Vows of Defiance," *Newsweek* (19 Mar. 1984), pp. 97–100.
64. David R. Carling, Jr., "Facing the Canons: Two Sisters Seek Office," *Commonweal,* vol. 111 (27 Jan. 1984), p. 38.
65. "Will Religious on the Left Please Step Down?" *National Catholic Reporter* vol. 19 (16 Sept. 1983), p. 23.
66. Kolbenschlag, "Case of Sister Mansour," p. 361.
67. Clare Dunn was a sister of St. Joseph of Carondolet, California Province.
68. In 1978 the RSMs began a study of the ethical aspects of tubal ligation and gave it a general recommendation in cases where the good of the patient deemed it essential. In 1980, in a letter to their hospitals, the General Administrative Team of the order tried to draw hospital administrators into the dialogue. The letter was *not* a mandate for a procedure but an invitation to talk about one. The letter was sent anonymously to Rome and to the NCCB, which precipitated a meeting between five bishops and six RSMs (both groups accompanied by theological consultants). Two preliminary meetings (Sept. and Dec. 1981) were exploratory, a substantive meeting was scheduled for March 1982. Early in 1982 the RSMs were informed that the meeting had been cancelled and that a "Committee of Verification" had been appointed by Rome to verify two questions: (*a*) do the RSMs accept the magisterium's teaching on tubal ligation? and (*b*) will they withdraw their November letter to their hospitals? The sisters responded that they accepted the teaching but disagreed with it and that they would withdraw the letter; they intended to urge continued study and consultation. The apostolic delegate told them their agreements were accepted and the case closed. In August 1982, however, a letter to the RSMs from Cardinal Pironio (SCRIS) told them that their response was *not* satisfactory; in November Pironio wrote to Teresa Kane requiring *"obsequium religiosum,"* a directing of the mind and will toward acceptance of magisterial teaching. The sisters agreed to take no public stand and to continue studying the matter. SCRIS then instructed the sisters that they must promise to "study with a view to accepting" the teaching. What makes this case particularly interesting is the lack of discussion of the substantive issue; indeed, as McCormick has pointed out, when it was scheduled for discussion Rome wrote to say that there was nothing to discuss. Furthermore, Rome appears to assume in this instance that dissent, by itself, constitutes a hardening of the mind and will and that the only ones required to examine their position are the sisters. Finally, Rome's reaction can be interpreted as an abuse of authority and power. I am indebted for this summary to Richard A. McCormick, "Notes on Moral Theology" (see n. 62), pp. 110–14, and would also point to a feminist analysis of the problem by Margaret Farley, "Power and Powerlessness: A Case in Point," CTSA Annual Publication 37 (1982), pp. 116–19.
69. Betty Barrett, quoted in Carol Krucoff, "The Subtle Revolution: A New Sense of Service," *Washington Post* (Wed., 21 Dec. 1983).

70. Kopp, *Sudden Spring* (see n. 52), p. 36.
71. Quoted in Bernstein, *Nuns* (see n. 20), p 22. See also Peter Hebblethwaite, "'Homogenized' Habit Sign of Consecration, Sign of Convention," *National Catholic Reporter,* vol. 19 (29 July 1983), p. 9.
72. Ewens, *Role of the Nun* (see chap. 1, n. 89), pp. 14–31.
73. Although these words were written to describe housewives, not contemplative nuns, the words fit the traditional religious vocation. See Claudia von Werlhof, "The Proletarian Is Dead; Long Live the Housewife?" in *Household and World Economy* ed. Joan Smith, Immanuel Wallerstein, and Hans-Dieter Evers, (Beverly Hills, Calif.: Sage Publications, 1984) pp. 131–47. My translation was provided by Mechthild Hart from the original German essay.
74. *Ecclesiae Sanctae,* issued *motu proprio* (6 Aug. 1966) implementing four decrees of Vatican II, including *Perfectae Caritatis* (Washington, D.C.: National Catholic Welfare Conference, 1966).
75. "Recently, notices have appeared in the press of attendance of contemplative religious at symposia, workshops and similar gatherings which may have serious effects on their contemplative vocation.

    "In the name of the members of the Pontifical Commission, Archbishop Leo C. Byrne, Bishop Edward J. Herrmann and myself, may I respectfully request that our contemplative religious abstain from attendance at such gatherings while the question of their renewal and adaptation is under study" (Letter from Cardinal-Designate Archbishop John J. Carberry, 18 Apr. 1969). In November 1968, SCRIS named Carberry to head a pontifical commission of bishops to examine the general issue of renewal of cloistered communities. The commission was "to learn from cloistered communities of religious women their views concerning renewal in religious life, with the understanding, however, that the ideals of the contemplative life will be preserved and encouraged" (letter from Carberry to all contemplative houses [19 Nov. 1968]). The tone of the letter was cordial, but the probable purpose of the commission was to keep contemplative sisters from "renewing" beyond boundaries that male superiors would set for them. The sisters' plans to hold meetings in Woodstock, therefore, offended and puzzled those on the commission whose idea of contemplative sisters was limited to a model of gratefully obedient children waiting for "father's permission" for any move.
76. *Venite Seorsum* ("Instruction on the Contemplative Life and the Enclosure of Nuns") was issued by SCRIS 15 Aug. 1969. A digest of the document can be found in *Sisters Today,* vol. 41 (Nov. 1969), along with a report of the Woodstock meeting and further reflections by contemplatives on the issues of enclosure and participation in their own government. See also John C. Haughey, "A Future for Contemplatives?" *America,* vol. 121 (4 Oct. 1969), pp. 261–64.
77. The letter (31 Aug. 1969) was a protest against the norms imposed by *Venite Seorsum,* not necessarily against its theology. In the letter the sisters compared some of their own reflections — fruit of the Woodstock meetings — with the directives of the SCRIS document and said that the SCRIS document had caused them "concern and apprehension." They were particularly distressed that "this restrictive 'Instruction' could be promulgated before our views had been presented to the Sacred Congregation or to our American Bishops." They protested the violations of collegiality and sought the support of the American bishops as well. The response was depressing. Cardinal Antoniutti, Prefect of the Sacred Congregation, wrote to Carberry (2 Jan. 1970) to say that *Venite Seorsum* was prepared at the command of the pope and that these norms now constitute the law in force

for the cloister of nuns. In response to criticism of the directive, Antoniutti said, "Some monasteries — actually a few — have expressed opposition to the cloister in the sense of the Instruction. After mature consideration of all the circumstances and by determination of the Holy Father, monasteries of this type may develop another kind of religious life, leaving their traditional canonical form of papal cloister." In other words, those who wish to experiment will be forced to leave or to develop a new kind of life.

78. Teresa of Avila, *The Life of the Holy Mother Teresa of Jesus,* trans. E. Allison Peers (London: Sheed & Ward, 1946), vol. 1, p. 61.
79. Nancy Miller, sister in the Baltimore Carmelite monastery, as quoted by Carol Krucoff, "In the Quiet of the Cloister: Prayers Make a Difference," *Washington Post* (Mon., 19 Dec. 1983).
80. See note 28.
81. Mark Day, "U.S. Religious Women Advise Vatican: 'Don't Push Garb Issue,'" *National Catholic Reporter,* vol. 19 (29 July 1983), p. 1.
82. Robert L. Johnston, "Women Religious Meet, Reaffirm Orders' Ways," *National Catholic Reporter,* vol. 19 (26 Aug. 1983), p. 1.
83. Kopp, "Memos from His Holiness, Big Brother" (see n. 37), p. 17.
84. Muckenhirn, in Borromeo, *New Nuns* (see n. 39), p. 5.
85. Abigail McCarthy, "The Nuns' (Old) Story: Encountering Obstacles Is Nothing New," *Commonweal,* vol. 110 (18 Nov. 1983), pp. 616–67, quotation, p. 617.

CHAPTER 4: ORDINATION, COLLECTIVE POWER, AND SISTERHOOD

Epigraphs: Denise Levertov, "Didactic Poem," in *The Sorrow Dance* (New York: New Directions, 1963), p. 81; Rosemary Radford Ruether, *Sexism and God-Talk* (Boston: Beacon Press, 1983), p. 11.

1. "Commentary of the Declaration of the Sacred Congregation for the Doctrine of the Faith on the Question of Admission of Women to the Ministerial Priesthood," in *Women Priests: A Catholic Commentary on the Vatican Declaration* ed. Leonard Swidler and Arlene Swidler, (New York: Paulist Press, 1977), pp. 319–37, quotation from p. 319.
2. Arlene Swidler, "Ecumenism and the Lack Thereof," in *Women Priests,* pp. 65–69.
3. In 1971 and 1973 the Anglican bishop of Hong Kong ordained three women with the agreement of his synod. In 1974 eleven Anglican women were ordained in Philadelphia, a move which later led to approval of women's ordination by the American Episcopal church. For the Anglican story and its history, see Norene Carter, "The Episcopalian Story," in Ruether and McLaughlin, *Women of Spirit* (see chap. 1, n. 87), pp. 356–72.
4. St. Joan's International Alliance, originally the Catholic Women's Suffrage Society, was founded in London in 1911; in 1959 it began working for women's rights within the church. See Rosemary Ruether, "The Roman Catholic Story," in *Women of Spirit,* pp. 373–83.
5. Haye van der Meer, *Women Priests in the Catholic Church: A Theological-Historical Investigation* (Philadelphia: Temple University Press, 1973).
6. Ida Raming, *The Exclusion of Women from the Priesthood,* (Metuchen, N.J.: Scarecrow Press, 1976).

7. *Ministeria Quaedem*, apostolic letter, *motu proprio*, laying down norms regarding the sacred orders of the diaconate (15 Aug. 1972). English translation in *The Tablet*, vol. 226 (23 Sept. 1972), pp. 917–19. See also Margaret Brennan, "It's Not What Paul Said—But What He Didn't Say," *National Catholic Reporter*, vol. 9 (8 Dec. 1972), pp. 7–8.

8. "Theological Reflections on the Ordination of Women," *Origins* (May 1972).

9. Van der Meer, *Women Priests*, p. xxvi.

10. Daly, *The Church and the Second Sex* (see chap. 1, n. 27), p. 11.

11. A "core commission" was established after the November meeting, and in January 1976 WOC was officially established.

12. United States Catholic Conference, (USCC) news statement (3 Oct. 1975), as found in Gardiner, *Women and Catholic Priesthood* (see chap. 2, n. 80), pp. 193–97. See the commentary in *Commonweal*, vol. 103 (16 Jan. 1976), pp. 42–44.

13. Elizabeth Carroll, "The Proper Place for Women in the Church," in Gardiner, *Women and Catholic Priesthood*, pp. 13–24, quotation from p. 21.

14. Rosemary Radford Ruether, "Ordination: What is the Problem?" in Gardiner, *Women and Catholic Priesthood*, pp. 30–34, quotation from p. 33.

15. Margaret Farley, "Moral Imperatives for the Ordination of Women," in Gardiner, *Women and Catholic Priesthood*, pp. 35–51, quotations from pp. 36, 45.

16. Ruether, "Ordination," p. 31.

17. Farley, "Moral Imperatives," p. 46.

18. Ibid., p. 47.

19. Anne Carr, "The Church in Process: Engendering the Future," in Gardiner, *Women and Catholic Priesthood*, pp. 66–88, quotation from p. 79.

20. The declaration can be found in Swidler and Swidler, *Women Priests* (see n. 1), pp. 37–49.

21. For an analysis of the variation between these two documents, see John R. Donahue, "A Tale of Two Documents," in Swidler and Swidler, *Women Priests*, pp. 25–34.

22. Leonard Swidler, in Swidler and Swidler, *Women Priests*, p. 3

23. For a discussion of this principle as articulated by Karl Rahner, see Swidler and Swidler, *Women Priests*, p. 4.

24. "Women and the Priestly Ministry: The New Testament Evidence" *Catholic Biblical Quarterly*, vol. 41 (1979), pp. 608–13.

25. Maureen Dwyer, ed. *New Woman, New Church, New Priestly Ministry* (Rochester, N.Y.: Women's Ordination Conference, 1980).

26. Edward J. Kilmartin, "Apostolic Office: Sacrament of Christ," *Theological Studies*, vol. 36 (1975), pp. 243–64, quotation from p. 261.

27. Ibid., pp. 262, 263.

28. Anne Carr, "Questions for the Future," in Dwyer, *New Woman, New Church*, pp. 83–92.

29. Richard McBrien, "Institutional and Ministerial Implications of the New Ecclesiology," in Dwyer, *New Woman, New Church*, pp. 93–95, quotation from p. 93.

30. Margaret Brennan, "What Kind of Ecclesiology Will We Need in the Future?" in Dwyer, *New Woman, New Church*, pp. 96–100, quotation from p. 99.

31. Carolyn Heilbrun, "A Response to Writing and Sexual Difference," *Critical Inquiry*, vol. 8 (Summer 1982), pp. 805–11, quotation from p. 806.

32. Elisabeth Schüssler Fiorenza, "Sexism and Conversion," *Network*, vol. 9 (1981), pp. 15–22.

33. See, e.g., Vincent J. Donovan, *Christianity Rediscovered: An Epistle from the Masai* (Notre Dame, Ind.: Fides/Claretian, 1978), which is a journal of his radical approach

to missionary work. Beginning with the assumption that Christianity is a value, he has no preconceived notions about anything traditionally associated with Christianity. His method is to move from village to village preaching the basic tenets of Christianity and leaving each village with the responsibility for nourishing its own church. The experience of various Maryknoll missionaries in Africa and Latin America also testifies to new approaches to traditional ecclesiology being stimulated by missionary work.

34. See, e.g., Tissa Balasuriya, *The Eucharist and Human Liberation* (Maryknoll, N.Y.: Orbis Books, 1979), who argues that the Eucharist has been "in captivity" and used to oppress men and women. The political dimensions of the Eucharist, he believes, call for an entirely new world order.

35. Women were originally called together to coordinate their energies in supporting American Catholic efforts during World War I. After the war, this group was established as the National Council of Catholic Women, a division of the National Catholic Welfare Conference. Most of my information about NCCW comes from my research at their headquarters in Washington, D.C., from published documents about the organization, and from the excellent work of Esther MacCarthy, "Catholic Women and War: The National Council of Catholic Women, 1919–1946," *Peace and Change*, vol. 5 (Spring 1978), pp. 23–32.

36. Since the Grail archives were not available while I was doing my research, I have relied on Alden V. Brown, "The Grail Movement in the United States, 1940–1972" (see chap. 1, n. 45). I have also consulted Grail members, especially Janet Kalven.

37. Information from NCCW archives.

38. "Equal Rights Amendment Found Wanting" (Washington, D.C.: NCCW, n.d.).

39. "Women in the Church: A Position Paper."

40. Winifred E. Coleman, "NCCW's Past *Can* Be Prologue," *Catholic Woman* (May/June 1981), p. 1.

41. "Justice for Women: A Position Paper."

42. Founding Documents of NCCW in the NCCW archives, p. 18.

43. MacCarthy, "Catholic Women and War," p. 28.

44. "Justice for Women," p. 2.

45. "Women in the Church."

46. Ibid.

47. Thomas C. Fox and David John, "U.S. Catholic Women Call for Disarmament," *National Catholic Reporter*, vol. 17 (16 Oct. 1981), p. 1.

48. MacCarthy, "Catholic Women and War."

49. Winkie LeFils, as quoted in Fox and John, "U.S. Catholic Women," p. 24.

50. Pius XI to Cardinal Bertram of Breslau, 12 Nov. 1928. Quoted in Luigi Civardi, *A Manual of Catholic Action* (New York: Sheed & Ward, 1935), p. 3.

51. Brown, "Grail Movement" (see chap. 1, n. 45), p. iv. For an analysis of the politics of Catholic Action and the struggle between papal power and the autonomy of the laity, see Jean Guy Vaillancourt, *Papal Power, A Study of Vatican Control over Lay Elites* (Berkeley, Calif.: Univ. of California Press, 1980).

52. John Ryan, an American Catholic social reformer (1868–1945) was the author of the bishops' program for social reconstruction (written in 1919). Many of the suggestions it offered were also part of President Franklin D. Roosevelt's New Deal, program and the friendship between Ryan and Roosevelt was acknowledged in Ryan's biography, which was subtitled *The Right Reverend New Dealer*.

53. Founded by Dorothy Day and Peter Maurin in 1934, the Catholic Worker move-

ment was the fountainhead of Catholic radicalism in the United States. See Piehl, *Breaking Bread* (see chap. 1, n. 46).

54. "The *liturgical movement* worked to bridge the gap between altar and people by emphasizing the liturgy as an act of communal worship in and through Christ, the head of the Church, and by recovering the Thomistic principle, taught at the Council of Trent, that the sacraments are both signs and causes of grace. As *signs* of grace, they must be intelligible" (Richard McBrien, *Catholicism* [Minneapolis: Winston Press, 1980], p. 646). Centered at St. John's Benedictine Abbey in Collegeville, Minnesota, the liturgical movement and its publication, *Oratre Fratres* (later retitled *Worship* [1951]) were highly significant in the liturgical changes mandated by Vatican II. McBrien lists a number of extremely influential movements between the two world wars: the liturgical movement, the biblical movement, social action, the lay apostolate, ecumenism, the missionary movement, and theological renewal all played a part in moving the Roman Catholic church toward Vatican II. See Garry Wills, *Bare Ruined Choirs,* (New York: Doubleday, 1971), pp. 38–60.

55. Introduced into the United States in Harlem (1938) by Russian-born Baroness Catherine de Hueck, Friendship House was an attempt to involve Catholics in racial justice issues.

56. Edwin V. O'Hara, bishop of Great Falls, Montana, founded the National Catholic Rural Life Conference, which was an agricultural remedy for modern social ills. He hoped to interest Catholics in small family-owned farms as a way to participate in a special kind of Catholic life. Grail members were often active in Rural Life conferences, and their purchase of Grailville (an 183-acre farm in Loveland, Ohio), made with the help of Cincinnati archbishop McNicholas in 1944, was their way to "get back to the land" and provide a center for renewal and formation away from the distractions of the city.

57. Brown, "Grail Movement," pp. 314 f.

58. See my "Single Blessedness?" *Commonweal,* vol. 106 (26 Oct. 1979), pp. 588–91.

59. The Grail sponsored a lay missionary program and an Institute for Overseas Service that allowed participants to make either a five-year commitment or a permanent one. They also opened an International Student Center and "City Centers" in Detroit, Cincinnati, Philadelphia, Brooklyn, and Lafayette, Louisiana, that involved hundreds of young women in aposotolic work in inner-city renewal, interracial work, and community development. In the 1960s, however, most of these programs diminished or died out due to strong competition from other groups (like the Papal Volunteers). See Brown, "Grail Movement," pp. 113–221.

60. Brown, "Grail Movement," p. 46.

61. Ibid., pp. 214–16.

62. In 1966, a member of the Grail national staff wrote the publishers to ask them to discontinue Kalven's pamphlet, since "it is no longer adequate to the complexities of the question in this day and age, and no longer reflects the author's thinking on the subject" (Brown, "Grail Movement," p. 305 n).

63. Joseph T. Nolan, "Grailville's Valiant Women," *America,* vol. 78 (4 Oct. 1947), pp. 9–11.

64. Brown, "Grail Movement," p. 321.

65. "Grail Movement," a Grail pamphlet (n.p., n.d.).

66. The Cornwall Collective, *Your Daughters Shall Prophesy: Feminist Alternatives in Theological Education* (New York: Pilgrim Press, 1980), pp. 136–41.

67. Besides *Your Daughter Shall Prophesy* Grail conferences have produced these works: Linda Clark, Marian Ronan,and Eleanor Walker, *Image-Breaking, Image-Building: A Handbook for Creative Worship with Women of Christian Tradition* (New York: Pilgrim Press, 1981); and Janet Kalven and Mary I. Buckley, eds., *Womanspirit Bonding* (New York: Pilgrim Press, 1984).

68. *NAWR-GRAM* (July 1981) published by the National Assembly of Women Religious, 1307 S. Wabash, Chicago IL 60605. My compilation of NARW causes comes from their newspaper, *Probe*, from interviews with their executive director, Marjorie Tuite, and from attendance at their national meeting (Aug. 1983) in Chicago. *Probe* has been remarkably perceptive on feminist issues within the Roman Catholic church, often publishing articles that lead to wide argument and deeper insight. A case in point is the raising of the "nunwomen/laywomen" issue in the February/March 1982 issue. That debate continues and in the summer of 1984 was the focus of a national conference held at Grailville.

69. The theme of the 1984 annual meeting, held in Cleveland, was "We Cannot Live Life as Usual: Breaking with the OLD, Blessing the NEW." The theme of the 1983 meeting was "The Spirituality of Politics: A Woman's Concern." Both give some indication of the wide-ranging intent of NARW.

70. "NCAN: A Backward Glance," prepared for the 1981 NCAN Board meeting as a way of reflecting on its history. My information about NCAN comes from their newsletters and interviews with former presidents and members. One of the speakers at their foundational meeting in 1969 was Mary Daly, then being harassed by Boston College in a nationally famous tenure dispute. NCAN's first official action was a defense of Daly and a demand for a faculty review committee to review the decision on her tenure.

71. Ann Patrick Ware, "When Rebel Nuns Go Public," *Ms.,* vol. 12 (Sept. 1983), p. 103; reprinted in *NCAN News,* vol. 13 (Sept. 1983), p. 3. See also NCAN newsletters for June and September 1982 (which outline the NCAN position on the Hatch amendment and defend its rationale).

72. Ware, "When Rebel Nuns Go Public."

73. Headquartered at 1307 S. Wabash Avenue, Chicago, the Institute of Women Today is directed by Margaret Ellen Traxler, former president of NCAN. My information about them comes from interviews with Traxler and from reading their newletters and publications. See Margaret Traxler, "The Institute of Women Today," in *The Roads They Made: Women in Illinois History,* ed. Adade Mitchell Wheeler and Marlene Stein Wortman (Chicago: Charles H. Kerr, 1977), pp. 153–58. Traxler has written more than a hundred articles. See, for example, "Women in Prison," *Response* (Jan. 1980).

74. Margaret Traxler, "Sexual Abuse of Women in Prison," *The Witness,* vol. 67 (June 1984), pp. 10–11.

75. Traxler, "Institute of Women Today," p. 158. A study at the University of Nebraska (reported on National Public Radio 22 Nov. 1984) suggests the opposite: women get lighter sentences because of their sex.

76. "Prison Poets Sing of Joys, Woes," *Chicago Tribune* (1 Aug. 1982).

77. Founded in 1974 to speak for Catholics who favor reproductive rights, Catholics for a Free Choice advocates "reproductive freedom, separation of church and state, access to medically safe abortions for all women whatever their economic resources, minimization of the need for abortion through expanded programs on contraception, sex education and child care, and the right of Catholics to dissent from church teachings on sexuality and childbearing." *Conscience,* vol. 4 (Oct./Nov. 1983), a special issue of their journal prepared for Womanchurch

Speaks. CFFC lobbies, advertises, and publishes pamphlets on Catholic pluralism on abortion as well as addressing other issues pertinent to sexuality. Their
journal, *Conscience,* is published bimonthly.

78. Focusing on homosexual ministry, New Ways was founded in 1977 by School
Sister of Notre Dame Jeannine Gramick and Salvatorian Father Robert Nugent,
both of whom have now been ordered out of that ministry by the Vatican. Their
newspaper, *Bondings,* focuses on lesbian and gay issues and publicizes various disputes about homosexuality within the church. See also Jeannine Gramick, ed.,
Homosexuality and the Catholic Church (Chicago: Thomas More Press, 1983); and
Robert Nugent, ed., *A Challenge to Love* (New York: Crossroad, 1983), both of
which address political and personal issues of gay and lesbian Catholics in the
church.

79. Founded in 1983, CCL is an educational and support group for Catholic lesbians.
It sponsors workshops and conferences for lesbians and also participates in workshops on sexual orientation. The CCL newsletter, *Images,* is published every three
months to give Catholic lesbians — nuns and laywomen — a forum for questions
and for exchange of information and support.

80. The National Black Sisters Conference is itself a testimony to the double marginalization of black women. Operating with no office and no staff, very limited
financial resources, and volunteer help, Black Sisters have to worry about their
own viability as an organization as well as their purpose and the practicalities
of trying to be prophetic in a racist society when they have very little money for
travel, publicity, workshops, and so on. They do have an annual meeting and participate in the National Office for Black Catholics Conference.

81. A consciously ecumenical group with a broad range of interests, WATER was
founded in 1982 by Mary E. Hunt and Diann Neu to enable women to share skills
and resources as religious feminists. WATER sponsors lectures and workshops
and an annual gathering called Connecting Conversations. Founded in 1975, CCW
is "an organization whose purpose is to call women of the Archdiocese of Chicago
to full participation in the mission of the church." They sponsor retreats and liturgies, publish a newsletter, *CCW Update,* bimonthly, coordinate efforts to promote women's ordination, and otherwise organize and activate Catholic women
in the Chicago area.

82. As the American bishops met in Chicago (at the Palmer House) in May 1977,
two Dominican sisters and one laywoman, all activists (Delores Brooks, Donna
Quinn, and Rosalie Rinehart), called as many organizations as they could think
of to come to the bishops' meeting and then to begin to form some sort of network for communication and support. Rinehart and Quinn, long-time activists
on women's issues, had both been part of the core commission for the Women's
Ordination Conference.

83. Neu and Riley, *Women Moving Church* (see chap. 2, n. 88), p. 2. This 28-page tab-
loid report of the conference contains specific information about the process, participants, and content of the meeting. It was at this meeting that Elisabeth Schüssler
Fiorenza articulated "gathering together the ecclesia of women who in the angry power of the Spirit are sent forth to feed, heal and liberate their people who
are women"; see "Gather Together in My Name: Toward a Christian Feminist
Spirituality," ibid., pp. 11, 25.

84. Some sponsoring groups, members of the coalition, withdrew from the Womanchurch meeting before the conference began. Although it is impossible to pin-
point a reason, the presence of Catholic lesbians and Catholics for a Free Choice

might have had something to do with it. In any case, LCWR, NCCW, the Ladies Auxiliary of the Knights of St. Peter Clavier, Black Sisters Conference, and the Center of Concern all withdrew support before November 1983.

85. Kevin Klose, *Washington Post* (13 Nov. 1983).
86. Joan Beifuss, "Amidst Laughter, Tears and Talks, Women Set Course," *National Catholic Reporter* vol. 20 (25 Nov. 1983), p. 1.
87. Rosemary Radford Ruether, "Womanchurch Calls Men to Exodus from Patriarchy," *National Catholic Reporter,* vol. 20 (23 Mar. 1984), p. 16.
88. Kenneth Woodward et al., "The Pope Vs. the U.S. Church," *Newsweek* 102 (10 Oct. 1983), p. 77. See also Robert J. McClory, "Bishops Letter: 'Laity, Nuns out of Seminaries,'" *National Catholic Reporter,* vol. 19 (7 Oct. 1983), pp. 1, 28.
89. Judith Davis, "Personal Reflection on Women in the Parish," prepared for New Catholic Women seminar, Indianapolis (1982). This seminar, one of six funded by the Lilly Endowment, concentrated on Roman Catholic women and parish life.
90. Fritz, *Dreamers and Dealers* (see chap. 2, n. 19), p. xii.
91. Elisabeth Schüssler Fiorenza, "The Ecclesia of Women: Towards a Feminist Catholic Sisterhood," *Probe,* vol. 11 (Feb./Mar. 1982), pp. 1, 3.
92. A national conference was held at Grailville in July 1984 and drew one of the largest weekend crowds in their history. In February 1984, a group of nuns and laywomen met for a retreat in Colorado to talk about experimentation and cooperation. See Margaret Murphy, "Lay, Religious Women Propose Forging Links," *National Catholic Reporter,* vol. 20 (17 Feb. 1984), p. 8. See also the following articles by Rosemary Radford Ruether: "Women's Spirit Bonding," "Is Bonding Possible?, and "Ruether Reflects on History: Nun-Lay Woman," both in *Probe,* 12 (July/Aug. 1984), pp. 1, 2.
93. Barbara Deming, in Fritz, *Dreamers and Dealers,* p. 110.
94. Ruether argues that nuns originally had more of a clerical privilege than they do now and that the present moves on the part of the Vatican to define them as laywomen is, in fact, a way to demote them from power. See articles cited in note 92.
95. See Chapter 3 about nuns as outsiders. When feminists say that men have monopolized human experience, leaving women unable to imagine themselves as both ambitious and female, I wonder if sisters are an exception to that generalization. I wonder, in other words, if laywomen are uncomfortable with sisters because they are *not* outsiders (the notion that they have clerical privilege), or because they *are* outsiders and know it (meaning that they can do what the rest of us find so painful, become feminists and reinvent womanhood)? Do people who resent nuns do so because they transcend sex with their virginity, or because they are the one group of women in our experience who *have* been able to imagine themselves both as ambitious (e.g. college presidents) and as female?
96. Heilbrun, *Reinventing Womanhood* (see chap. 3, n. 10), p. 31.
97. Carol Gilligan, *In a Different Voice* (Cambridge: Harvard Univ. Press, 1982).
98. Miller, *Towards a New Psychology of Women* (see chap. 2, n. 34), pp. 125–33.
99. James Carroll, "On Not Skipping the Sermon," *Commonweal,* vol. 111 (2–16 Nov. 1984), pp. 603–5, quotation from p. 605.
100. Alison M. Jaggar, *Feminist Politics and Human Nature* (Totowa, N.J.: Rowman & Allanheld, 1983), p. 8.
101. Joan Ohanneson, *Woman: Survivor in the Church* (see chap. 2, n. 95), p. 77.

CHAPTER 5: ENLARGING THE DISCIPLINE

Epigraphs: Charlotte Perkins Gilman, *His Religion and Hers* (New York: Century, 1923), p. 45; Brigilia Bam, quoted in Susannah Herzel, *A Voice for Women* (Geneva: World Council of Churches, 1981), p. 65; Dorothy Sölle, *The Strength of the Weak* (Philadelphia: Westminster Press, 1984), p. 47.

1. As related in Alma Lutz, *Created Equal* (New York: John Day, 1940), pp. 11-12. See also Lois W. Banner, *Elizabeth Cady Stanton: A Radical for Woman's Rights* (Boston: Little, Brown, 1980), p. 15.
2. Mary Daly, "The Women's Movement: An Exodus Community," *Religious Education,* vol. 67 (Sept./Oct. 1972), pp. 327-33.
3. See Charlotte Perkins Gilman, *His Religion and Hers: A Study of the Faith of Our Fathers and the Work of Our Mothers* (New York: Century, 1923).
4. Ralph Keifer, "Schillebeeckx on Ministry: Herald of a New Reformation?" *Commonweal* vol. 108 (3 July 1981), pp. 401-3, quotation from p. 402.
5. Alfred North Whitehead (1861-1947), an English mathematician-turned-philosopher, spent his philosophical life at Harvard University. See *Process and Reality: An Essay in Cosmology* (New York: Social Sciences Book Store, 1941). He has had an enormous impact on theology through his students and colleagues (Charles Hartshorne, Henry Nelson Wieman, Shubert Ogden, John Cobb, Daniel Day Williams, and others). It is quite possible that "process thought" is the application of his general ideas rather than a devoted exposition of his system. My understanding of process has come partly from reading as well as from discussion with those who have a deeper understanding than I. In general, I am indebted to W. Norman Pittinger, *Process Thought and Christian Faith* (New York: Macmillan, 1968), and *The Lure of Divine Love: Human Experience and Christian Faith in a Process Perspective* (New York: Pilgrim Press, 1979); Daniel Day Williams, *The Spirit and the Forms of Love* (New York: Harper & Row, 1968); and, for a clarification of Whitehead's own writing, Donald W. Sherburne, ed., *A Key to Whitehead's Process and Reality* (Chicago: Univ. of Chicago Press, 1966). For a combination of feminism and process, see Sheila Greeve Davaney, ed., *Feminism and Process Thought* (New York: E. Mellen Press, 1981). For a recent introductory work, see Marjorie Suchocki, *God, Christ, Church: A Practical Guide to Process Theology* (New York: Crossroad, 1982). Assuming blame for my own errors of understanding, I am also indebted to James G. Hart and Jean Alice McGoff for long talks about process thought.
6. Karl Rahner (1904-1984), author of more than four thousand books and articles, has been enormously influential in both Catholic and Protestant churches. A University of Chicago poll (1978) found that "554 North American theologians from 71 different denominations named Rahner — after Paul Tillich and Thomas Aquinas — as the greatest influence on their work" (Eugene Kennedy, "Quiet Mover of the Catholic Church," *New York Times Magazine* (23 Sept. 1979), p. 22. He is, nevertheless, not immediately accessible to those not professional theologians. The best introduction to the man and his work is Leo J. O'Donovan, *A World of Grace: An Introduction to the Themes and Foundations of Karl Rahner's Theology* (New York: Seabury Press, 1980). See also Ronald Modras, "Karl Rahner at 80: Still Asking Questions," *National Catholic Reporter,* vol. 20 (9 Mar. 1984) pp. 9, 5. In an interview (1970) about Vatican II, Rahner said: "I would see as the goal toward which the Church and the Church's theology have to strive the realization

of a more living and vital unity between what I called the horizontal and the vertical dimensions, that is, between the Christian's relationship to God, and his relationship to the world . . . we have to come to see much more clearly than before that a more radical spirituality brings with it a more radical responsibility for the world." ("Karl Rahner," a special issue of *America,* vol. 123 (31 Oct. 1970), pp. 356 f.

7. McBrien, *Catholicism* (see chap. 4, n. 54), p. 219. I am indebted to McBrien for his summaries of Blondel, Maréchal, and Teilhard and for a general outline of modern Catholic theology. Blondel (1861–1949) achieved fame early with his dissertation, *"L'Action."* For him, the human will (which produces action) can never satisfy itself. A classic introduction to Blondel's thought can be found in Maurice Blondel, *The Letter on Apologetics and History and Dogma,* translated, annotated, and introduced by Alexander Dru and Illtyd Trethowan (London: Harvill Press, 1964), pp. 13–116.

8. Pierre Teilhard de Chardin (1881–1955), a French Jesuit paleontologist. Better known to Catholics as a religious, even mystical, writer, he was forbidden to publish his religious writings during his lifetime. When his work came out after his death, it caused a minor sensation. *The Phenomenon of Man* (New York: Harper & Row, 1959) and *The Divine Milieu* (New York: Harper & Row, 1961) were both quite popular. His collected essays, *The Future of Man* (New York: Harper & Row, 1964), make his position very clear: for him evolution has not stopped but has shifted its emphasis from the material to the spiritual world. For Teilhard, life is movement and the future is to be welcomed precisely because humanity will be closer to divinity. For a good assessment of his work, see Donald P. Gray, "The Phenomenon of Teilhard," *Theological Studies,* vol. 36 (1975), pp. 19–51. For a centenary anniversary evaluation of Teilhard's relevance to the contemporary situation, see Robert Faricy, "The Omega Point," *The Tablet,* vol. 235 (2 May 1981), pp. 418 f.

9. McBrien, *Catholicism,* pp. 128–32.

10. Martin Heidegger (1889–1976) was an existentialist philosopher who formulated an argument for personal existence as a unique, transcendent possibility rooted in immediate temporal relationships. From this and from Heidegger's notion of "horizon" Rahner understood that spirit is a dynamism (*eros*) toward being. See Rahner's *Spirit in the World* (New York: Herder & Herder, 1968), in which spirit is a power that reaches beyond the world, beyond our accessible reality. Rahner was constrained to show that human knowing can be spirit in the world.

11. Anne E. Carr, "Starting with the Human," and Michael J. Buckley, "Within the Holy Mystery," both in O'Donovan, *A World of Grace,* make the connection clearly. Also see the fine brief tribute to Rahner by David Tracy, "'All is Grace' A Rooted Radical," *Commonweal,* vol. 111 (20 Apr. 1984), p. 230. For an excellent essay of Rahner's, see "Experience of Self and Experience of God," in his *Theological Investigations,* vol. 13 (New York: Seabury Press, 1975), pp. 122–32.

12. Influenced by Friedrich Nietzsche, these "death of God" theologians were part of a mid-1960s movement. The best representatives are Paul van Buren, *The Secular Meaning of the Gospel* (New York: Macmillan, 1963); and Thomas Altizer, *The Gospel of Christian Atheism* (Philadelphia: Westminster Press, 1966).

13. From the latin word *saeculum* (the world), secular theologians like John A. T. Robinson, *Honest to God* (Philadelphia: Westminster Press, 1963), and Harvey Cox, *The Secular City* (New York: Macmillan, 1965), argued that the church is *in* the world, not above it, and that the mission of the church and of Christians is to the world.

14. See Jürgen Moltmann, *Theology of Hope* (New York: Harper & Row, 1967), in which he argues that the real problem for Christian theology is the future. He moved eschatological hope into the present as a challenge to change the way things are in the here and now.

15. Jürgen Moltmann, *The Crucified God* (New York: Harper & Row, 1974), p. 327.

16. In Johannes Metz, *Followers of Christ: Perspectives on Religious Life* (New York: Paulist Press, 1978). Metz argues for the prophetic and secular character of the Christian spirit. See also *The Emergent Church: The Future of Christianity in a Postbourgeois World* (New York: Crossroad, 1981), *Faith and the World of Politics* (New York: Paulist Press, 1968), and *Perspectives of a Political Theology* (New York: Herder & Herder, 1971).

17. *Praxis*, from the Greek meaning to do or to act, is essentially a Marxist term. According to Marx, praxis is more important than pure rational thought. Different from practice, praxis is intentional, having an aim or theory behind it: praxis is action plus reflection. For a discussion of its roots and applications see Jagger, *Feminist Politics and Human Nature* (see chap. 4, n. 99), pp. 54–60.

18. McBrien, *Catholicism* (see chap. 4, n. 54), p. 222.

19. Paulo Friere, *Pedagogy of the Oppressed* (New York: Continuum, 1970).

20. The documents can be found in Gremillion, *Gospel of Peace and Justice* (see chap. 3, n. 40), pp. 445–76.

21. L. John Topel, *The Way to Peace: Liberation through the Bible* (Maryknoll, N.Y.: Orbis Books, 1979), p. 150.

22. Gremillion, *Gospel of Peace and Justice,* pp. 25, 42–45, and *passim*.

23. Mary Daly, *The Church and the Second Sex, with a new, Feminist, Post-Christian Introduction by the Author* (New York: Harper Colophon, 1975), p. 11.

24. "The protest of feminism against the blind rage of sexism . . . runs like a morally biased fault throughout human history. . . . Here, as in other forms of bias . . . one is staggered by the overwhelming evidence of anguished human suffering. . . . Millions upon millions of women have been battered, dominated, raped, tortured and destroyed simply because they were women" (Matthew Lamb, *Solidarity with Victims* [New York: Crossroad, 1982], pp. 6 f.).

25. Carol P. Christ, "Why Women Need the Goddess: Phenomenological, Psychological and Political Reflections," in Carol P. Christ and Judith Plaskow, eds., *Womanspirit Rising* (New York: Harper & Row, 1979), pp. 273–87; Starhawk (Miriam Simos), *The Spiral Dance: A Rebirth of the Ancient Religion of the Great Goddess* (New York: Harper & Row, 1979).

26. Much of the introductory material in this section appeared in my "Who's Watching Big Sister?" *Cross Currents,* vol. 32 (Winter 1983/84), pp. 455–61.

27. Two fine examples of Margaret Farley are "Moral Imperatives for the Ordination of Women," in Gardiner, *Women and Catholic Priesthood* (see chap. 2, n. 74), pp. 35–51, and "An Ethic for Same-Sex Relations" in Nugent, *Challenge to Love* (see chap. 4, n. 78), pp. 93–106. For Mary Hunt, see, e.g., "Lovingly Lesbian: Toward a Feminist Theology of Friendship," in Nugent, *Challenge to Love,* pp. 135–55. For Joann Wolski Conn, see, e.g., "Women's Spirituality: Restriction and Reconstruction," *Cross Currents* vol. 30 (Fall 1980), pp. 293–308.

28. See Chapter 4, note 14. Carr was also slated to be part of the bishops' dialogue in preparation for their pastoral on women in the church but resigned after signing "A Diversity of Opinions Regarding Abortion Exists among Committed Catholics," in the (Sun. 7 Oct. 1984) *New York Times*. See Joan Turner Beifuss,

"Theologian Resigns After Signing Abortion Statement," *National Catholic Reporter,* vol. 20 (19 Oct. 1984), p. 21.

29. Anne E. Carr, *The Theological Method of Karl Rahner* (Missoula, Mont.: Scholar's Press, 1977). See also her articles, "Starting with the Human" (see n. 11), and "Theology and Experience in the Thought of Karl Rahner," *Journal of Religion,* vol. 53 (July 1973), pp. 359–76.

30. See, e.g., Anne Carr, "The Church in Process: Engendering the Future," in Gardiner *Women and Catholic Priesthood,* pp. 66–68; "Women's 'Place,' Ordination and Christian Thought," *Listening,* vol. 13 (Spring 1978), pp. 158–75; "New Questions," in Dwyer, *New Woman, New Church* (see chap. 4, n. 25), pp. 83–92.

31. Anne Carr, "The New Feminist Theology: A Review of the Literature," *Religious Studies Review,* vol. 3 (Oct. 1977), pp. 203–12, quotation from p. 205.

32. This description is a paraphrase of Carr's projected book *Christian Symbols and the Experience of Women* as it appears on her application for the Harvard Divinity School Women's Studies in Religion Program, 1982. I thank Carr for sharing it with me.

33. Anne Carr, "Is a Christian Feminist Theology Possible?" *Theological Studies,* vol. 43 (June 1982), pp. 279–97, quotation from p. 282.

34. Ibid., p. 286.

35. See, e.g., Anne Carr, "Theological Anthropology and the Experience of Women," *Chicago Studies,* vol. 19 (Summer 1980), pp. 113–28; "The God Who Is Involved," *Theology Today,* vol. 38 (Oct. 1981), pp. 314–28; and "On Feminist Spirituality," *Horizons,* vol. 9 (Spring 1982), pp. 96–103.

36. Carr, "Starting with the Human" (see n. 11).

37. Carr, "Theological Anthropology," p. 128.

38. Carr, cited, "God Who Is Involved."

39. Carr, Harvard application (see n. 32), p. 4.

40. Elisabeth Schüssler Fiorenza, *Der vergessene Partner, Grundlagen, Tatsachen und Möglichkeiten der beruflichen Mitarbeit der Frau in der Heilssorge der Kirche* (Düsseldorf: Patmos, 1964).

41. In my review of Schüssler Fiorenza's *In Memory of Her* ("Who's Watching Big Sister?" see n. 26), I misread some information on her history of involvement in women's issues and gave the mistaken impression that she did not claim them for her own until 1972. I regret the error.

42. Elisabeth Schüssler Fiorenza, "'Our Heritage is Our Power': Theological Reflections for Roman Catholic Women's Seminar," (unpublished). This paper was presented at a seminar on Roman Catholic feminist theologians in March 1983. That seminar, funded by the Lilly Endowment, was one of a series of seminars conducted for religious leaders in Indiana from 1981 to 1984.

43. Elisabeth Schüssler Fiorenza, "Feminist Theology as a Critical Theology of Liberation," *Theological Studies,* vol. 36 (1975), pp. 605–26.

44. Associated with Jürgen Habermas and others, critical theory—sometimes referred to by way of its location as the Frankfurt School—attempts to show that history and texts are not neutral but result from and participate in expressions of domination, oppression, and alienation. Scholarship, canonization of a tradition, interpretation, and so on are therefore not "value-free" or neutral but result from particular political standpoints, and clearly embody "interested" presuppositions, and lead to advocacy-supporting conclusions. That this political process may be unconscious or denied does not argue for its nonexistence.

45. Schüssler Fiorenza, "Feminist Theology," p. 616.

46. Elisabeth Schüssler Fiorenza, "Women Apostles: The Testament of Scripture," in Gardiner, *Women and Catholic Priesthood* (see chap. 2, n. 74), pp. 94–102.

47. Elisabeth Schüssler Fiorenza, "We Are Still Invisible: Theological Analysis of 'Women and Ministry'" in *Women and Ministry: Present Experience and Future Hopes,* ed. Doris Gottemoeller and Rita Hofbauer (Washington, D.C.: LCWR, 1981), pp. 29–43.

48. Schüssler Fiorenza, "Ecclesia of Women" (see chap. 4, n. 91), pp. 1, 3. Schüssler Fiorenza was also the featured speaker at the national conference on the nuns/laywomen controversy at Grailville, July 1984.

49. Elisabeth Schüssler Fiorenza, "The Apostleship of Women in Early Christianity," in Swidler and Swidler, *Women Priests* (see chap. 4, n. 1), pp. 135–40; "Women in the Early Christian Movement," in Christ and Plaskow, *Womanspirit Rising* (see n. 25), pp. 84–92; "Feminist Spirituality, Christian Identity and Catholic Vision," in Christ and Plaskow, *Womanspirit Rising,* pp. 136–48; see, e.g., "Toward a Feminist Biblical Hermeneutics: Biblical Interpretation and Liberation Theology," *The Challenge of Liberation Theology,* ed. Brian Mahan, (Maryknoll, N.Y.: Orbis Books, 1981), pp. 84–92; "'You are not to be called Father'" (see chap. 2, n. 61).

50. For example, at the second WOC conference, "To Comfort or to Challenge: Theological Reflections," in Dwyer, *New Woman, New Church* (see chap. 4, n. 25), pp. 43–60. Also see "Gather Together in My Name," in Neu and Riley, *Women Moving Church* (see chap. 2, n. 88), pp. 11, 25.

51. Elisabeth Schüssler Fiorenza, "Discipleship and Patriarchy: Early Christian Ethos and Christian Ethics in a Feminist Theological Perspective," in *The Annual of the Society of Christian Ethics: Selected Papers, 1982,* ed. L. Rasmussen (Waterloo, Ont.: CSR, 1982), pp. 131–72.

52. Ibid., pp. 158 f.

53. Schüssler Fiorenza, *In Memory of Her* (see chap. 2, n. 88), p. xii.

54. Ibid., p. 334.

55. Schüssler Fiorenza, "Toward a Feminist Biblical Hermeneutics," p. 100.

56. Rosemary Radford Ruether, "Feminist Theology and Religion," presented at Lilly Endowment Seminar, March, 1983, (see n. 42) p. 17.

57. See, e.g., Rosemary Radford Ruether "Social Sin," *Commonweal,* vol. 108 (30 Jan. 1981), pp. 46–48. See also *Disputed Questions: On Being a Christian* (Nashville: Abingdon, 1982), for an autobiographical account of her interest in various questions.

58. See, e.g., Ruether's published dissertation, *Gregory of Nazianzus* (Oxford: Clarendon Press, 1969), and her article "Misogynism and Virginal Feminism in the Fathers of the Church," in *Religion and Sexism* (see chap. 2, n. 8), pp. 150–83.

59. See, e.g., "Why I Believe in Birth Control," *Saturday Evening Post,* vol. 237 (4 Apr. 1964), pp. 12–14; "Divorce: No Longer Unthinkable," *Commonweal,* vol. 86 (14 Apr. 1967), pp. 117–19; "Pastoral Education for New Communities," *Theology Today,* vol. 26 (July 1969), pp. 187–94; "Education in Tandem: White Liberal, Black Militant," *America,* vol. 122 (30 May 1970), pp. 582–84; *The Radical Kingdom* (New York: Harper & Row, 1970); *The Church Against Itself* (New York: Herder & Herder, 1967); *Faith and Fratricide* (New York: Seabury Press, 1974); "Christian Anti-Semitism and the Dilemma of Zionism," *Christianity and Crisis,* vol. 32 (17 Apr. 1972), pp. 91–94; "Mother Earth and Megamachine," in Christ and Plaskow *Womanspirit Rising* (see n. 25), pp. 43–53; "Racing Toward Doomsday: Nuclear Armaments and American Policy," *Explor,* vol. 3 (1977), pp. 15–17; and "'Basic Communities': Renewal at the Roots," *Christianity and Crisis,* vol. 41 (21 Sept. 1981), pp. 234–37.

60. See *Disputed Questions* (see n. 57) for an account of Ruether's work in the civil rights and antiwar movements.

61. Rosemary Radford Ruether, "Feminist Theology and Religion," p. 23.

62. See, e.g., Rosemary Radford Ruether, "Schism of Consciousness," *Commonweal*, vol. 88 (31 May 1968), pp. 326–31.

63. Rosemary Radford Ruether, "Of One Humanity," *Sojourners*, vol. 13 (Jan. 1984), pp. 17–19, quotation from p. 17.

64. Rosemary Radford Ruether, "Male Chauvinist Theology and the Anger of Women," *Cross Currents*, vol. 21 (1971), pp. 173–85.

65. Ruether, *Religion and Sexism* (see chap. 2, n. 8).

66. Ruether and McLaughlin, *Women of Spirit* (see chap. 1, n. 82); Rosemary Radford Ruether and Rosemary Skinner Keller, *Women and Religion in America* (San Francisco: Harper & Row 1981, 1983, and forthcoming); this latter series is divided into colonial period, nineteenth century, and contemporary period.

67. Rosemary Radford Ruether, *New Woman, New Earth: Sexist Ideologies and Human Liberation* (New York: Seabury Press, 1975), p. xii.

68. Ibid.

69. Rosemary Radford Ruether, *To Change the World: Christology and Cultural Criticism* (New York: Crossroad, 1981), p. 11.

70. For a description of how this strategy was received by the feminist community at Harvard in the early seventies, see Ruether, *Disputed Questions*, pp. 52–54.

71. Ibid., p. 31.

72. Rosemary Radford Ruether, *Sexism and God-Talk* (Boston: Beacon Press, 1983).

73. Ruether, "Of One Humanity" (see n. 63).

74. Ibid., p. 17.

75. Ruether, *Sexism and God-Talk*, pp. 18 f.

76. Ruether, *To Change the World*, p. 17.

77. For her essay on Magdalene, see Ruether, *New Woman, New Earth*, pp. 36–59.

78. Ruether, *Sexism and God-Talk*, p. 258.

79. Ruether, "Of One Humanity," p. 17.

80. Ruether, *To Change the World*, p. 25.

81. Ruether, "Of One Humanity," p. 19.

82. Mary Daly, *Pure Lust* (Boston: Beacon Press, 1984).

83. In Mary Daly's "post-Christian introduction" to the revised edition of *The Church and the Second Sex* (see n. 23), she says that her single greatest impetus for writing that book was the Second Vatican Council. Remembering her experience in Rome in 1965, she called the council an "unintended self-satire on Catholicism," (p. 10) but was not so cynical in the immediate postconciliar era. Daly's "The Problem of Speculative Theology," *The Thomist*, vol. 29 (1965), pp. 177–216, was steeped in tradition, yet alive to possibility. "A Built-In Bias," *Commonweal*, vol. 81 (12 Jan. 1965), pp. 508–11, an attack on the concept of "the eternal feminine," was her first feminist essay. In "Dispensing with Trivia," *Commonweal*, vol. 88 (31 May 1968), pp. 322–25, she described the postconciliar Catholic "underground" and urged Catholics to dispense with trivia in order to focus on "what really matters— the striving toward a higher level of human existence and toward the hidden but living God."

84. Mary Daly, "Return to the Protestant Principle," *Commonweal*, vol. 90 (6 June 1969), pp. 338–41, written almost immediately after her tenure fight, talked about "growth in self-understanding," and "Mary Daly on the Church" *Commonweal*, vol. 91 (14 Nov. 1969), p. 215, was almost sanguine: Daly talks about "mutually

transforming confrontation" and confesses to being "naïve enough to think that in some sense I can win."

85. Mary Daly, "After the Death of God the Father," *Commonweal,* vol. 94 (12 Mar. 1971), pp. 7–11, was her last article for that journal and the last in a "Catholic" publication. Her next two articles sketched out some of the arguments for her next book. "Courage to See," *Christian Century,* vol. 88 (22 Sept. 1971), pp. 1108–11, was an embodiment of Jesus' frustrated statement about prophets despised in their own countries. "The Spiritual Revolution: Women's Liberation as Theological Re-education," *Andover-Newton Quarterly,* vol. 12 (Mar. 1972), pp. 163–76, was the lead article in an issue devoted especially to feminist questions. The feminist movement, Daly said, leads to spiritual revolution and "a qualitative new way of looking at the world."

86. Mary Daly, *Gyn/Ecology* (see chap. 2, n. 28), p. 368.

87. Mary Daly, *Beyond God the Father* (Boston: Beacon Press, 1973). These insights about oppression are indebted to Friere's pedagogy of the oppressed and so show some of Daly's relationship to liberation themes at this point in her life.

88. Carter Heyward, "Speaking and Sparking, Building and Burning," *Christianity and Crisis,* vol. 39 (2 Apr. 1979), pp. 66–72. She argues that Daly is a "subjective idealist," and though I argue with her caricature of idealism as a "contemporary manifestation of Gnostic dis-embodiment," I think her point about Daly's relative dis-ease with practical matters is well taken.

89. Mary Daly, "The Qualitative Leap Beyond Patriarchal Religion," *Quest,* vol. 1 (1975), pp. 20–40, is a more extensive version of "A Short Essay on Hearing and the Qualitative Leap of Radical Feminism," *Horizons,* vol. 2 (1975), pp. 120–24. These articles summarize her theses — most of which come from *Beyond God the Father* — in a radical fashion.

90. Daly, "Qualitative Leap," p. 22.

91. Ibid., p. 27.

92. Daly, *Gyn/Ecology,* p. 315.

93. "The knowing of this deadly intent has been necessary for our a-mazing process of exorcism. It is equally necessary for moving on the Labyrinthine Journey of Ecstasy" (ibid., p. 315).

94. Ibid., pp. 89–106. "The term *paranoia* is appropriate to describe movement beyond, outside of, the patriarchal "mind-set" (ibid., p. 316). See also pp. 125, 341, 401.

95. Daly, *Beyond God the Father,* p. 65.

96. Whether this power to engage feelings explains reviewers who compare her to Hitler and Idi Amin, however, is doubtful. The reactionary Catholic journal *Catholicism in Crisis* (Oct. 1984), pp. 33–42, published a symposium of reviews on *Pure Lust.* One reviewer felt compelled to warn readers against Daly as one would warn a populace about a genocide plot. Richard Roach, a Jesuit moral theologian at Marquette, used the occasion to build a "slippery-slope" argument for the diabolical effects of contraception. In a warning every bit as frightening as anything Daly has published, Roach said: "Contracepting Catholic couples should sit down and read Daly's book. The wife in particular should ask herself, is this what I want? Is this how I really feel about men? If not, she should go to the medicine cabinet, throw out her contraceptive pills, march off to confession, and then take her husband with her to a good class in Natural Family Planning. Maybe they should even have a child. The alternative is some form, even though attenuated, of Daly's lesbianism" (p. 42).

97. Guerrilla theater disrupts the conventional order, draws a moral or political issue

into an emotional arena, advertises important issues by making extreme statements about them, and is itself a spectacle. Daly's later work is, I think, a kind of guerrilla theater that might be compared to WITCH (the Women's International Terrorist Conspiracy from Hell), a guerrilla theater group formed on Halloween 1968 as "an all-woman Everything. It's theater, revolution, magic, terror, joy, garlic flowers, spells. It's an awareness that Witches and gypsies were the original guerrillas and resistance fighters against oppression—particularly the oppression of women—down through the ages. . . . It's a total concept of revolutionary female identity" (Robin Morgan, *Sisterhood Is Powerful* [New York: Vintage Books, 1970], pp. 603-5).

98. 1 Kings 18:17-41.
99. *Fembot* is an invented word to describe female robots, those women unable to do anything other than the commands of the fathers.
100. Heyward, "Speaking and Sparking" (see n. 88), p. 72.
101. Daly, "Qualitative Leap," (see n. 89), p. 33.
102. Midge Quant, "Mary Daly's Latest Philosophical Quest," *New Directions for Women,* vol. 13 (Sept./Oct. 1984), p. 14. Quant's review of *Pure Lust* objects to the dualism she finds in Daly.
103. Carol Anne Douglas, "Review Commentary," on *Pure Lust* in *Off Our Backs,* vol. 14 (June 1984), pp. 20-23, quotation from 22. Douglas sets Daly within a Catholic framework—remembering some of her old articles in *Commonweal* and discussing some of the Catholic aspects of *Pure Lust*—in an essentially positive review, but criticizes Daly for so easily dismissing other perspectives and arguing that there is only one feminist theory.
104. See, e.g., *Pure Lust,* p. 448, where she acknowledges her debts to the things of the earth, animals, rivers, butterflies, rabbits and trees. It is, perhaps, revealing that the cover of *Gyn/Ecology* shows a labrys (a double-bladed ax) on a menacing reddish background while *Pure Lust* is green and gold and inside features a drawing of a spiral with a butterfly flying free and upwards from an imbedded labrys. These things, I think, are more life-cycle-grounded and earth-(not world)-loving than was evident in earlier work.
105. See n. 83.
106. Daly, "Dispensing with Trivia," (see n. 83).
107. Daly, *Pure Lust,* p. 121.
108. Matilda Joslyn Gage, *Woman, Church and State* (1893). Subtitled *The Original Exposé of Male Collaboration Against the Female Sex,* it was reissued (Watertown, Mass.: Persephone Press, 1980) with an introduction by Mary Daly.
109. I am indebted to my graduate student Kathy Dallas Romy for my information about Stanton's project. See "*The Woman's Bible*: An Historical Perspective" (unpublished M.A. thesis, Dept. of Religious Studies, Indiana Univ., 1983).
110. A ground-breaking essay was that of Valerie Saiving, "The Human Situation: A Feminine View," *Journal of Religion,* vol. 40 (1960), pp. 100-12, which noted the differences between masculine and feminine experience and challenged traditional categories of sin and grace as inadequate for women. Judith Plaskow, *Sex, Sin and Grace: Women's Experiences and the Theologies of Reinhold Niebuhr and Paul Tillich* (Washington, D.C.: University Press of America, 1980), built on Saiving's insights to call for a new theology inclusive of female experience.
111. "Women Doing Theology," a special issue of *The National Catholic Reporter,* vol. 20 (13 Apr. 1983).

CHAPTER 6: AFFIRMING THE CONNECTIONS

Epigraphs: W. B. Yeats, "Lines Written in Dejection," from *The Wild Swans at Coole,* in *The Collected Poems of W. B. Yeats* (New York: Macmillan, 1959), p. 143; Hallie Inglehart, "Expanding Personal Power Through Meditation," in *The Politics of Women's Spirituality,* ed. Charlene Spretnak (New York: Doubleday, 1982), p. 296; Dorothy Sölle, *The Strength of the Weak* (Philadelphia: Westminster Press, 1984), p. 47.

1. "Dogmatic Constitution on the Church," in *The Documents of Vatican II,* ed. Walter M. Abbott (New York: America Press, 1966), p. 29.
2. Karl Rahner, "Experience of Self and Experience of God," in *Theological Investigations XIII* (New York: Seabury Press, 1972), pp. 122–32, quotation from p. 124 f.
3. I have not been able to find the source of this quotation cited by Charles Williams, *The Descent of the Dove* (Grand Rapids: Eerdmans, 1972; orig., 1939), p. viii.
4. Dionysius is the name given to the author of a collection of mystical writings dating from the sixth century. She (or he) gave the *via negativa* its classical expression by describing the process in terms of *purgation* (obliteration of bad habits and repentence for sins), *illumination* (cleansing from attachments and enlightenment regarding spiritual realities), and *union* (deeply intimate union with God and habitual practice of virtues). The *Cloud* is an English mystical treatise by an anonymous author indebted most to Dionysius.
5. Meister Eckhart, a German Dominican, was a famous preacher and spiritual director who taught at the University of Paris but is primarily remembered for his sermons. In a time when even such great theologians as Thomas Aquinas were under suspicion, Eckhart, too, was suspected of heresy and some of his work condemned. Since his condemnation led to a large part of his work being lost, and since he has been "used" to champion various movements (from romanticism to Nazi "Deutschreligion"), it is not easy to find a fair reading of him. I am indebted here to Matthew Fox, *Breakthrough: Meister Eckhart's Creation Spirituality in a New Translation* (New York: Doubleday Image, 1980).
6. See my "Dante and the Baptized Imagination," *Desert Call,* vol. 12, no. 2 (1977), pp. 12–17.
7. *God/ess* is Rosemary Radford Ruether's term for the fullness of divinity, a divine person that is undivided even though the term combines masculine and feminine words for the divine, *God* and *Goddess. Sexism and God-Talk* (see chap. 5, n. 87), p. 46.
8. Maureen Fiedler, "Political Spirituality," *Musings from Rocinante,* Quixote Center Newsletter (Jan. 1984), p. 1.
9. Dorothy Sölle, *The Strength of the Weak: Toward a Christian Feminist Identity* (Philadelphia: Westminster Press, 1984), p. 47.
10. Ibid., p. 82.
11. Building on the work of a nineteenth-century scholar, J. J. Bachofen, *Myth, Religion and Mother Right* (Princeton, N.J.: Princeton Univ. Press, 1967; orig., 1861), several feminist scholars have worked to reconstruct the history of Goddess worship and delineate her importance as the central deity for feminists in search of a religious expression that does not debilitate them. See, e.g., Carol P. Christ, "Why Women Need the Goddess," in Christ and Plaskow, *Womanspirit Rising* (see chap. 5, n. 25), pp. 273–87; Naomi Goldenberg, *The Changing of the Gods* (Boston: Beacon Press, 1979); Starhawk, *The Spiral Dance* (see chap. 5, n. 25); and Merlin Stone, *When God Was a Woman* (New York: Dial Press, 1976). A select bibliogra-

phy on the Goddess is available through the Center for the Study of New Religious Movements, Graduate Theological Union, Berkeley, California.

12. Carol P. Christ, "Symbols of Goddess and God in Feminist Theology," in *Book of the Goddess,* ed. Carl Olson (New York: Seabury, 1983), p. 231.

13. Starhawk, *The Spiral Dance,* p. 8.

14. Christ, "Symbols of Goddess," p. 234.

15. A more conservative approach to the problem of God's masculinity is the attempt to recapture and use feminine characteristics and names for the deity. See Joan Chamberlain Engelsman, *The Feminine Dimensions of the Divine* (Philadelphia: Westminster Press, 1979). Many feminist theologians who remain within the framework of historical Christianity insist on articulating the feminine dimensions of the divine and so have responded favorably to the work of Goddess feminists. See, e.g., Patricia Wilson-Kastner, "Christianity and New Feminist Religions," *Christian Century* (9 Sept. 1981), pp. 864–68; or Virginia Ramey Mollenkott, "An Evangelical Feminist Confronts the Goddess," *Christian Century* (20 Oct. 1982), pp. 1043–46.

16. Starhawk, *The Spiral Dance,* p. 8.

17. Christ and Plaskow, *Womanspirit Rising* (see chap. 5, n. 25). This useful volume of essays begins with Valerie Saiving's 1960 questioning of the appropriateness of traditional categories of sin for women and ends with Christ's *apologia* for the Goddess.

18. Elizabeth Gould Davis, *The First Sex* (London: Penguin Books, 1970), and Merlin Stone, *When God Was a Woman,* argue that matriarchal societies existed long before patriarchal ones and that they were basically peaceful, agrarian, and centered on Goddess worship. Anthropologists have challenged the matriarchy theory on the evidence. See, e.g., Joan Bamberger, "The Myth of Matriarchy: Why Men Rule in Primitive Society," in *Women, Culture and Society* ed. by Michele Zimbalist Rosaldo and Louise Lamphere (Stanford, Calif.: Stanford Univ. Press, 1974), pp. 263–80. The "debate" has, so far, ended in a standoff, each side dismissing the other for blindness to "the evidence." See "Are Goddesses and Matriarchies Merely Figments of Feminist Imagination?" in *The Politics of Women's Spirituality: Essays on the Rise of Spiritual Power within the Feminist Movement,* ed. by Charlene Spretnak (New York: Doubleday Anchor, 1982), pp. 541–63.

19. Christ, "Symbols of Goddess" (see n. 12), p. 250.

20. Ruether, *Sexism and God-Talk* (see chap. 5, n. 72), p. 46. Ruether has been critical of the Goddess movement and witchcraft on several issues. In "A Religion for Women: Sources and Strategies," *Christianity and Crisis,* vol. 39 (10 Dec. 1979), pp. 307–11, she agrees that feminists must adopt feminine images of the divine but argues that the adoption of witchcraft is uncritical and dogmatic. Ruether does not believe that feminists need to abandon biblical religion. In "Goddesses and Witches: Liberation and Countercultural Feminism," *Christian Century* (10–17 Dec. 1980), pp. 842–47, she compares Goddess feminism to a romanticized Victorian vision of male and female nature and says that Goddess feminism had the effect of excusing all women from ethical existence: "If evil is male, then women don't have to take responsibility for it. They can be the great innocents or victims of history. Their only ethical task is to purge themselves of all traces of male influence; then their naturally good selves will be revealed and will re-create the world" (p. 844).

21. Schüssler Fiorenza, *In Memory of Her* (see chap. 2, n. 88), pp. 18 f.

22. Ben L. Kaufman, "Women 'Exiles' Seek New Ways to Express 'Female Image of

God'" *National Catholic Reporter,* vol. 20 (21 Oct. 1983), p. 11. Paula O'Neill, a product of the Roman Catholic school system and former chair of her parish liturgy committee, and Debra Jaken El-Dabh, also a Roman Catholic, agreed that the ceremony was a "statement about the need to restore 'the goddess within' to the godhead which they found had become distressingly, exclusively masculine in the hands of the church.'"

23. Linda Clark, Marian Ronan, and Eleanor Walker, *Image-Breaking, Image-Building: A Handbook for Creative Worship with Women of Christian Tradition* (New York: Pilgrim Press, 1981), p. 3.

24. Held November 30 to December 2, 1984, this workshop, led by Ronan and others, is part of the process for producing a book of the same name (quotation is from the brochure advertising the workshop). Proverbs 8:22–36 virtually identifies Wisdom as a Goddess, present at the creation of the world, a preexistent divine being.

25. Christ, "Why Women Need the Goddess" (see n. 11), p. 273.

26. Spretnak, *Politics of Women's Spirituality* (see n. 18).

27. Fiedler, "Political Spirituality" (see n. 8), p. 5.

28. "Sexism and Conversion," *Network,* vol. 9 (May/June 1981), pp. 15–22. Redstockings was a radical feminist group founded in the late 1960s: see Fritz, *Dreamers and Dealers* (see chap. 2, n. 18), pp. 26–27. The "Redstockings Manifesto" can be found in Morgan, *Sisterhood Is Powerful* (see chap. 5, n. 97), pp. 598–601.

29. Ruether, *Sexism and God-Talk* (see chap 5, n. 72), p. 213.

30. "Will Religious on the Left Please Step Down?" *National Catholic Reporter* vol. 20 (16 Sept. 1983), p. 23.

31. See my "Pilgrimage — From Theory to Practice," *Desert Call,* vol. 13, no. 2 (1978), pp. 12–16, vol. 13, no. 3 (1978), pp. 18–22.

32. See special issue of *National Catholic Reporter,* vol. 17 (17 July 1981), devoted to Roman Catholic women celebrating the Eucharist. The action of these women is spiritual because it is a sharing in the most ancient celebration of the Christian church; it is political because it claims a power belonging to the community that has been corrupted by clericalism. In celebrating the Eucharist, feminists participate in a paradigm shift, locating sacramental power in the community rather than in ordained representatives. The theological basis for this perception and practice exists even though ecclesiastical rules forbid it. In developing their own eucharistic rituals, therefore, and in appropriating those celebrated by the church, feminists provide a spiritual and political alternative to the way Eucharist is at present celebrated within Roman Catholicism.

33. "In Christian hagiography, the sadomasochistic content of the paeans to male and female martyrs is startling, from the early documents like the *Passion of Saints Perpetua and Felicity* into the High Middle Ages. But the particular focus on women's torn and broken flesh reveals the psychological obsession of the religion with sexual sin, and the tortures that pile up one upon the other with pornographic repetitiousness underline the identification of the female with the perils of sexual contact. For, as they defend their virtue, female martyrs of the Christian calendar are assaulted in any number of ingenious and often sexual ways: in the *Golden Legend,* Agatha's breasts are cut off; Apollonia's teeth are torn out, then she is burned to death; Juliana is shattered on a wheel 'until the marrow spurted out,' then plunged into a lead bath; Euphemia is tormented with all sorts of refinements and then beheaded; Catherine of Alexandria is also broken on a wheel. The theme did not draw to a close in the Middle Ages, for one of the saints most recently canonized

by the Vatican fits into this pattern exactly: Maria Goretti, born in 1890, was murdered at the age of eleven by a young man from her village, whom she knew. He tried to rape her, and when she resisted, stabbed her many times with a stiletto. She was taken to a hospital, where she freely forgave him from her heart and was made a Child of Mary by her local priest. . . . Of all the ways different societies define sexual crime and deal with it, of all the ways sexual mores are instilled into that society's youth, this must rank as the strangest." (Marina Warner, *Alone of All Her Sex: The Myth and the Cult of the Virgin Mary* [New York: Alfred A. Knopf, 1976], p. 71). Whether or not Warner is right that this Catholic way of dealing with sexual mores is "the strangest," I do not know. It is instructive in this regard to read Maxine Hong-Kingston, *The Woman Warrior* (New York: Vintage Books, 1977), pp. 3–5, where the Chinese mother warns her daughter about the perils of premarital pregnancy.

34. de Beauvoir, *Second Sex* (see chap. 1, n. 12), pp. 743–53, quotes accounts of female saints who licked up patient's vomit with their tongues, filled their mouths with excrement of men sick with diarrhea, drank water—full of scabs and pus—just used to wash lepers, etc. *The Oxford Dictionary of the Christian Church,* ed. F. L. Cross (Oxford: Oxford Univ. Press, 1974) is another source for the lives of female saints. See, e.g., the entry on Saint Elizabeth of Hungary (1207–1231), who was ordered by her spiritual director, Conrad of Marburg, to give up her children and to submit to physical chastisement at his hands. Conrad was a papal inquisitor.

35. Sölle, *Strength of the Weak* (see n. 9), pp. 86–105.

36. Eleanor McLaughlin, "Women Power and the Pursuit of Holiness in Medieval Christianity," in Ruether and McLaughlin, *Women of Spirit* (see chap. 1, n. 82), pp. 100–130, quotation from p. 121.

37. Teofanes Egido, "The Historical Setting of St. Teresa's Life," in *Carmelite Studies: Spiritual Direction,* ed. by John Sullivan (Washington, D.C.: Institute of Carmelite Studies Publications, 1980), pp. 122–82.

38. Whether, in fact, Teresa's willingness to admit sisters to her convents without reference to their blood purity was a truly radical position can be debated. My friend Helen Nader, a Renaissance historian at Indiana University, says that the arguments about blood purity and conversion were common among Spanish upper classes at that time and that Teresa's position was "not unusual."

39. Egido, "Historical Setting," pp. 165, 142.

40. Her two most important treatises, *The Way of Perfection* and *The Interior Castle,* are classics of Roman Catholic spirituality. Teresa's focus on God as a lover in search of "his beloved" (the soul) and her analogy of the soul as an "interior castle" in which God dwells at the center give her work a passionate and immediate quality. Other mystics of her day received "messages" from God destined for the church, but Teresa's experiences converged in a deepening of her own inner life: for her, God is always near and one's task is to learn to become present to that nearness within oneself.

41. Egido, "Historical Setting," p. 128.

42. Ibid., p. 130. See also *The Collected Works of Teresa of Avila,* vol. 2, translated and introduced by Kieran Kavanaugh and Otilio Rodriguez (Washington, D.C.: Institute of Carmelite Studies Publications, 1980), pp. 19–28. The translators note the climate of antifeminism in which Teresa worked and wrote and argue that her "defense of women was clear and forceful." The mistrust of women by her society made it especially difficult for her to found monasteries of women dedicated to a life of prayer.

43. Catherine Romano, "A Psycho-Spiritual History of Teresa of Avila: A Woman's Perspective," in *Western Spirituality: Historical Roots, Ecumenical Routes*, ed. Matthew Fox (Sante Fe, N.Mex.: Bear, 1981), pp. 261–95, quotation from p. 261.

44. Joann Wolski Conn, "Women's Spirituality: Restriction and Reconstruction," *Cross Currents* vol. 30 (Fall, 1980), pp. 293–308, 322, quotation from p. 303.

45. Perhaps my own experience was unique and perverse, but as a freshman in a Dominican women's college in Ohio, I joined the Third Order as a "novice" and went faithfully to meetings each month. Far from hearing about Catherine's political savvy and other powerful attributes, I was regaled with her penances, mortifications, and bizarre practices. I washed out as a novice shortly before Christmas.

46. Carola Parks, "Social and Political Consciousness in the Letters of Catherine of Siena" in Fox, *Western Spirituality*, pp. 249–60, quotation from p. 253.

47. C. H. Lawrence, "St. Catherine: Loving Critic," *The Tablet* (26 Apr. 1980), pp. 392–94, quotation from p. 392.

48. Ibid., p. 394. McLaughlin, "Women Power" (see n. 36), may be one of those whom Lawrence is faulting. She says: "Catherine was a powerful and effective woman by anyone's standards. She dominated Pope Gregory and, to a lesser extent, Urban VI" (p. 117).

49. Alice Walker, *In Search of Our Mothers' Gardens* (New York: Harcourt Brace Jovanovich, 1984), p. xi.

50. *The Revelations of Divine Love of Julian of Norwich*, trans. and intro. by James Walsh (London: Burns & Oates, 1961), p. 88. For a psychological reading of Julian with important community ramifications see the brilliantly suggestive work of Elisabeth Jameson Koenig, "The Book of Showing of Julian of Norwich: A Test-Case for Paul Ricoeur's Theories of Metaphor and Imagination" (Ph.D. diss., Columbia University, 1984). Koenig explores the links between imagination and self-understanding in "Imagination and the Face of God in Julian of Norwich," *New Catholic World* vol. 225 (Nov./Dec. 1982), pp. 260–63.

51. See, e.g., Phyllis Trible, *God and the Rhetoric of Sexuality* (Philadelphia: Fortress Press, 1976); also Elaine Pagels, *The Gnostic Gospels* (New York: Random House, 1979), pp. 48–69.

52. Caroline Walker Bynum, *Jesus as Mother: Studies in the Spirituality of the High Middle Ages* (Berkeley and Los Angeles, Calif.: Univ. of California Press, 1982), pp. 11–69. This is an extraordinarily useful, beautifully written book. I am indebted to Bynum for my organizing insights in this section.

53. Ibid., p. 139. In 1984 the Cathedral of St. John the Divine in New York City removed a four-foot-high bronze statue of a female Jesus when it became the center of a bitter controversy. It had been part of a Holy Week display on "Feminine Spirituality" and was defended by the dean of the cathedral, but the bishop called it "theologically and historically indefensible." Titled *Christa* by the sculptor, Edwina Sandys, it apparently offended those who otherwise would have been able to defend symbols of Jesus with different skin colors and ethnic characteristics because it "totally changed the symbol." From *Her Say*, excerpted in *New Directions for Women* vol. 13 (July/Aug. 1984), p. 5.

54. Bynum, *Jesus as Mother*, pp. 170–262.

55. Barbara Hill Rigney, *Lilith's Daughters: Women and Religion in Contemporary Fiction* (Madison, Wis.: Univ. of Wisconsin Press, 1982), p. 8. For a clear and outspoken denial of the power of Mary theologically, see Kari Børresen, "Mary in Catholic Theology," in *Mary in the Churches*, vol. 168 *Concilium*, ed. Hans Küng and Jürgen

Moltmann (New York: Seabury Press, 1983), pp. 48–56. For Børresen, Mary's role as mother of the church is predicated on an androcentric and outdated anthropology; her significance as a liberation figure is eclipsed by the fact that it is Christ and not she who liberates; her value for feminists is absurd since it rests on an androcentric typology; and her ability to symbolize the feminine dimensions of the divine is a "deviation" since "if both woman *and* man are made in God's image, *God must be feminized* . . . approaching the problem by divinizing Mary, on the other hand, is heretical" (p. 55).

56. Madonna Kolbenschlag, *Kiss Sleeping Beauty Good-Bye: Breaking the Spell of Feminine Myths and Models* (New York: Doubleday, 1979), p. 201. Various attempts have been made to revise Mary in the light of contemporary needs. See e.g., Raymond E. Brown et al., *Mary in the New Testament* (Philadelphia: Fortress Press/New York: Paulist Press, 1978); Donal Flanagan, *The Theology of Mary* (Hales Corners, Wis.: Clergy Book Service, 1976); Andrew M. Greeley, *The Mary Myth: On the Femininity of God* (New York: Seabury Press, 1977); and Rosemary Radford Ruether, *Mary—The Feminine Face of the Church* (Philadelphia: Westminster Press, 1977). For an analysis of the role and function of Mary in Orthodox Christianity see Nikos Nissiotis, "Mary in Orthodox Theology," in Küng and Moltmann, *Mary in the Churches,* pp. 25–39; and for a similar article about Mary in Protestantism see Gottfried Maron, "Mary in Protestant Theology" (ibid., pp. 40–47).

57. Warner, *Alone of All Her Sex* (see n. 33). See also John L. McKenzie, "The Mother of Jesus in the New Testament," in Küng and Moltmann, *Mary in the Churches,* pp. 3–11: "One asks whether [Mary] will meet or can ever be hoped to meet the needs of modern devotion—whether the beautiful, sinless gentlewoman who achieved the impossible fulfillment of uniting virginity and motherhood is not as much of a dodo as Saints Philomena, Christopher and Valentine. *If devotion to Mary is to revive, it must take an entirely new form*" (p. 10).

58. Note, e.g., that when Pope John Paul II visited the shrine of the Lady of Fatima in Portugal (1982) he said that the revelations at Fatima contain "the call of the gospel itself," a statement that calls for critical analysis and rejection, since the main message of Fatima was that Catholics ought to "say the rosary." Peter Hebblethwaite, covering the visit, later noted, "There could hardly be a clearer expression of the links among Fatima, nostalgia, snobbery and political reaction." See "Fatima's 'Disturbing Remedy' for World," *National Catholic Reporter,* vol. 18 (28 May 1982), p. 7, and his article "Pope's Visit to Fatima Casts 'New' Church Role for Mary," in the same issue, p. 11. At the same time, Mary is being reclaimed by Catholic women committed to Vatican II; see, e.g., Kathleen Burke, "Mary's Role Reclaimed by Vatican II Women," *National Catholic Reporter,* vol. 19 (29 July 1983), p. 4, which reports a Mary conference at Mundelein College (Chicago) in which Mary was interpreted as the first disciple, a prophet, the mother of the church, a model for human behavior, a wisdom figure, a comforter, the mirror of justice and queen of peace, titles traditionally used by Catholics now being nontraditionally claimed as expressions of female power. These papers exist in published form. See *Mary According to Women,* ed. Carol Frances Jegen (Kansas City, Mo: Leaven Press, 1985).

59. Ruether, *New Woman, New Earth* (see chap. 5, n. 67), p. 50.

60. Sölle, *Strength of the Weak* (see n. 9), pp. 42–48. Sölle calls Mary a "sympathizer" and uses her as a model for those who would undermine the power of the ruling classes, quotation from p. 46.

61. Mary Gordon, "Coming to Terms with Mary" *Commonweal,* vol. 109 (15 Jan. 1982), pp. 11–14, quotation from p. 11.
62. John Chrysostom, quoted in Gordon, "Coming to Terms with Mary," p. 12.
63. Gordon, "Coming to Terms with Mary," p. 12.
64. H. D., *Trilogy* (New York: New Directions, 1973; orig. 1944–46). H[ilda] D[oolittle] 1886–1961, was a modernist poet whose *Trilogy,* three long poems written under the devastating impact of World War II, is a masterpiece of interlaced Christian and pagan imagery. Though H. D. was reared as a Moravian, clearly knew the Bible very well, and fills *Trilogy* with quotations and images from the Gospel of John and the Book of Revelation, the poem is not primarily religious: her interests are in creativity, ancient Goddesses, divine images, and poetry itself. H. D.'s suggestion about there being "Mary's a-plenty" reflects a practice not always good for women. "This trend," says Elisabeth Moltmann-Wendel, speaking of the lumping together of various New Testament Marys, "had the sorry consequence that church fathers, popes and bishops, and following them, artists and writers, could throw all the Marys into the stock pot and take out again and present an appropriate selection from them in accordance with their needs" (*The Women Around Jesus* [New York: Crossroad, 1982], p. 65). I agree with Moltmann-Wendel that unfortunate results have come from conflating text traditions, but I believe the technique (not unlike psychosynthesis) could be used, symbolically, in a powerful and imaginative way for women and is therefore a legitimate interpretive move in search of a more appropriate Mary symbol.
65. Carlo Caretto, *Letters for the Desert* (Maryknoll, N.Y.: Orbis Books, 1972), p. 135.
66. Eckhart's God, like nature, abhors a vacuum and can leave nothing empty. When we empty the self, therefore, we give birth to God in ourselves. Put another way, when we let go of our own plans, we allow God to emerge within us. For Eckhart this is not a *via negativa* for the sake of nothingness, but "the reason for emptiness is fullness" (Fox, *Breakthrough* [see n. 5], pp. 166–293, quotation from p. 197).
67. See, e.g., Catharina Halkes, "Mary and Women," in Küng and Moltmann, *Mary in the Churches,* pp. 66–73; and Ruether, *Sexism and God-Talk* (see chap. 5, n. 72), pp. 152–58.
68. Edward Schillebeeckx, *Mary Mother of the Redemption* (New York: Sheed & Ward, 1964), p. 119. Schillebeeckx's interpretation is helpful when placing Mary in an ecumenical perspective. For this task, see also Kari Børresen "Mary in Catholic Theology" (see n. 56), who suggests that future trends in Mariology will have to follow the leads laid down by Vatican II, i.e., a return to Christology in which only Christ manifests the divine (not Mary) and in which Mary has no ecclesiological attributes.
69. Rosemary Radford Ruether, "Liberation Mariology," *The Witness,* vol. 62 (Oct. 1979), pp. 15–18, quotation from p. 18. Reprinted in an extended version, "She's a Sign of God's Liberating Power," *The Other Side,* vol. 104 (May 1980), pp. 17–21. For Moltmann-Wendel, *Women Around Jesus,* a more radical exegesis of Mary is possible today because the "Bible is no longer the book that stabilizes government and confirms the existing order. It has fallen into the hands of the powerless, and the question is what it has to say to them and what 'power' it gives them" (p. 7).
70. Gordon, "Coming to Terms with Mary," p. 13.
71. Barbara Thomas, quoted by Kenneth Woodward, "What Mary Means Now," *Newsweek,* vol. 93 (1 Jan. 1979), pp. 52–53, quotation from p. 53.
72. John W. Lynch, *A Woman Wrapped in Silence* (New York: Macmillan, 1956), pp. 4 f.

73. As a spokeswoman for the *anawim,* see Brown et al., *Mary in the New Testament* (see n. 57). Mary has also been used by missionaries to appeal to the contemporary *anawim,* the marginalized in impoverished countries. The Mexican-American Cultural Center, for example, in attempting to phrase the gospel in terms of the poor, has pictured Mary as a poor unwed mother. For an analysis of the impact of Our Lady of Guadaloupe on Mexican Catholicism, see Virgil Elizondo, "Mary and the Poor: A Model of Evangelizing Ecumenism," in Küng and Moltmann, *Mary in the Church,* pp. 59–65.

74. R. E. Sheridan, *Mary in Maryknoll Today* (Maryknoll, N.Y.: Maryknoll Fathers pamphlet, 1978), p. 14. Sheridan makes several points about Mary in the missionary situation: she hears, accepts, the word of God and acts on it, steps into the unknown, and "in these days of liberation . . . Mary was far ahead of her time . . . [the] *Magnificat* serves as a blueprint for radical social action" (p. 7).

75. Scripture scholars and theologians know that "there is no historical basis for the beliefs in the Immaculate Conception or assumption of Mary," McKenzie, "Mother of Jesus" (see n. 58), p. 4, but both doctrines are still invoked in the Catholic church, sometimes with the suggestion that as elevations of the woman, Mary, they are good for women in general. Mary Daly, *Pure Lust* (see chap. 5, n. 82), has recently pointed out the dangers of both doctrines for women. In the assumption, Daly says, "as Mary went up, women went down without realizing it" (p. 128), and the Immaculate Conception is for her a symbol for the erasure of the self: in the Immaculate Conception Mary is robbed of her own power to name herself or experience herself as autonomous even before she is born. As a doctrine, Daly argues, the Immaculate Conception has functioned to deceive women, since it is no more than crippling tokenism, preventing radicalism in women. Tokenism, Daly says, gives women the illusory sense of progress and obliterates the memory of oppression, so that tokens function to betray both themselves and women in general. A feminist theology of Mary, therefore, must, at the very least, "set Mary free from the image that has been made of her and from the projections attached to her by a male and priestly hierarchy," Catharina Halkes, "Mary and Women," p. 66. The connections between Mary and the Goddess, I believe, must be exploited by feminist theologians, though this position is strongly opposed by Børresen, "Mary in Catholic Theology" (see n. 56).

76. Elisabeth Moltmann-Wendel, *Women Around Jesus,* p. 10. Also, see n. 65 for Moltmann-Wendel's resistance to textual conflation. At the same time, she does encourage the use of theological imagination in "reading the Bible as a book of liberation" (p. 9).

77. Elizabeth Cady Stanton, *The Woman's Bible, Part II* (Seattle: Coalition Task Force on Women and Religion, reprint, 1974; orig., 1898), p. 143.

78. Edward J. Mally, "The Gospel According to Mark," in *The Jerome Biblical Commentary,* ed. Raymond E. Brown, Joseph A. Fitzmeyer, and Roland E. Murphy (Englewood Cliffs, N.J.: Prentice-Hall, 1968), 2:60.

79. H. D., *Trilogy* (see n. 65), p. 135.

80. Moltmann-Wendel, *Women Around Jesus,* p. 25.

81. Ibid., p. 70.

82. Sölle, *Strength of the Weak* (see n. 9), p. 46.

83. Denise Levertov, *The Sorrow Dance* (New York: New Directions, 1967), p. 12.

Index

Fetterley, Judith, 5
Fichter, Joseph, 63
Fiedler, Maureen, 187
Foner, Philip, 21
*For Colored Girls Who Have Considered
Suicide When the Rainbow is Enuf*
(Shange), 186
Formation and sisters, 82
Friedan, Betty, 45, 48
Friendship, theology of, 156
Friere, Paulo, 152–153
Frontier women, 25–30

Gadamer, Hans-Georg, 157
Gage, Matilda Joslyn, 177
Geertz, Clifford, 183
Generic male words, 58–59
Gibbons, Cardinal, 20, 221–222
Gideon, story of, 203
Gillespie, Mother Angela, 31
Gilligan, Carol, 141
Gilman, Charlotte Perkins, 145
Glenmary Sisters, 92–94
God: authority of, 87–88; death of,
151; dualism and, 169; and Julian of
Norwich, 197–198; in liturgy, 58;
and Mary, 203; old God, 147–148;
renaming of, 172; for Teresa of
Avila, 193
God/ess, 169, 181, 185
Goddess, 155, 182–186
Goffman, 90–91
Gordon, Linda, 43
Gordon, Mary, 202, 206
The Grail movement, 42, 119,
122–127; historical theories about,
220; lay missionary program, 243;
workshops, 185–186
Greek Orthodox women, xiv
Greeley, Andrew, 86, 89
Grimké, Angelina, 6
Grimké, Sarah, 6
Guardini, Romano, 123
Guerrilla theater, 253–254
Gyn/Ecology (Daly), 173–174, 175, 184
Gynocentric writing, 174

Habermas, Jürgen, 157
Habits, wearing of, 106
Hagiography, 191
Haines, Helen, 17
Hannah, canticle of, 204

Hardey, Mother Mary Aloysia, 27
Hartley, Olga, 37
Hatch Amendment. *See* Abortion
H.D., 203, 210
Hefta, mystics at, 199–200
Heidegger, Martin, 150, 194, 248
Heilbrun, Carolyn, 75, 117, 140–141
Heinzleman, Gertrude, 111
Hennesey, James, 1, 14, 24
Heyward, Carter, 172
High school teachers, 79
*Historiography of the American Catholic
Church 1785–1943* (Cadden), 13
"Historiography of Women's Religious
Communities in the Nineteenth
Century" (Misner), 14
*The History of the Catholic Church in the
United States* (Shea), 12
History, women in, 4–10
Homosexual ministry, x, 131, 245
Horaria, 82
Horizon of Being, 150
Humiliata, Mother Mary, 93
Hunt, Mary, 115, 156
Hymns, 59–60

The Illusion of Eve (Callahan), 66
Image-Breaking, Image-Building, 185
Immaculate Conception, 170, 262
Immaculate Heart of Mary Sisters
(IHM), 93–94
Immigrants, women as, 38
Inferiority stereotype, 39–42, 52
Inglehard, Hallie, 180
In Memory of Her (Schüssler Fiorenza),
162
Institute of Women Today, 130–131
International Women's Year, Mexico
City, 85
Irwin, Inez Hayes, 32
Isabella Association, 12
Isis ceremony, 185

Jaggar, Alison, M., 143
Janeway, Elizabeth, 40, 42, 51
Jerome, Saint, 56
Jesus: commands of, 78; Grail
movement and, 123–124; lost in the
Temple, 205–206; motherhood of,
198–199; resurrection of, 208–209;
Schüssler Fiorenza on, 164; and
women, 54–55